ROUTLEDGE LIBRARY EDITIONS: LINGUISTICS

Volume 51

WEAKENING PROCESSES IN THE HISTORY OF SPANISH CONSONANTS

WEAKENING PROCESSES IN THE HISTORY OF SPANISH CONSONANTS

RAY HARRIS-NORTHALL

LONDON AND NEW YORK

First published in 1990

This edition first published in 2014
by Routledge
4 Park Square, Milton Park, Abingdon, Oxon OX14 4RN
605 Third Avenue, New York, NY 10017

First issued in paperback 2016

Routledge is an imprint of the Taylor & Francis Group, an informa business

© 1990 Ray Harris-Northall

All rights reserved. No part of this book may be reprinted or reproduced or utilised in any form or by any electronic, mechanical, or other means, now known or hereafter invented, including photocopying and recording, or in any information storage or retrieval system, without permission in writing from the publishers.

Trademark notice: Product or corporate names may be trademarks or registered trademarks, and are used only for identification and explanation without intent to infringe.

British Library Cataloguing in Publication Data
A catalogue record for this book is available from the British Library

ISBN 13: 978-0-415-64438-9 (Set)
ISBN 13: 978-1-138-98700-5 (pbk)
ISBN 13: 978-0-415-72740-2 (hbk)

Publisher's Note
The publisher has gone to great lengths to ensure the quality of this reprint but points out that some imperfections in the original copies may be apparent.

Disclaimer
The publisher has made every effort to trace copyright holders and would welcome correspondence from those they have been unable to trace.

Weakening Processes in the History of Spanish Consonants

Ray Harris-Northall

Routledge
London and New York

First published 1990
by Routledge
11 New Fetter Lane, London EC4P 4EE
29 West 35th Street, New York, NY 10001

© Ray Harris-Northall 1990

Disc conversion by Columns of Reading

All rights reserved. No part of this book may be reprinted or
reproduced or utilized in any form or by any electronic, mechanical,
or other means, now known or hereafter invented, including
photocopying and recording, or in any information storage or retrieval
system, without permission in writing from the publishers.

British Library Cataloguing in Publication Data

Data available on request
ISBN 0-415-00742-9

Library of Congress Cataloging in Publication Data

Data applied for

Contents

Acknowledgements vi
Abbreviations vii

1 Introduction 1

2 Weakening in Intervocalic Position 6

3 Weakening in Absolute Final Position 37

4 Syllable-Final Consonants 56

5 The Consequences of Syncope 93

6 Conclusion 116

References 135
Subject Index 145
Index of Forms 148

Acknowledgements

This book is a revised and considerably updated version of my doctoral thesis, presented at the University of Birmingham in 1985. Many people assisted, both directly and indirectly, in the preparation of the thesis, and have continued offering their inestimable help in the subsequent revisions it has undergone.

My principal debt of gratitude, I am happy to recognize, is owed to Suzanne Romaine, who supervised the thesis and gave encouragement at all times during its development, as well as detailed and practical help whenever it was needed. For providing initial guidance, my thanks are due to Peter Ricketts; and for his indefatigable energy, unflagging support and, at times, astonishing belief in what I was doing, to Roger Wright.

It also gives me great satisfaction to express my appreciation to Patricia Shaw and Emilio Alarcos Llorach of the University of Oviedo for their help and indulgence, and to many other colleagues and friends for their unfailing, and often unwitting, help.

Finally, special thanks to Routledge for their patience and assistance in the preparation of this book.

The blame for any inaccuracies, inconsistencies or incongruities in what follows is, however, to be placed fairly and squarely on the shoulders of the author, whose obstinacy in matters of dogma has sometimes led him not to follow the advice so freely and generously given by those mentioned.

Abbreviations

ad.	adjustment
ant	anterior
Ar.	Arabic
arch.	archaic
As.	Asturian
assim.	assimilation
attr.	attraction
bk	back
C	consonant
Cast.	Castilian
Class.	Classical
cons	consonantal
cont	continuant
cor	coronal
Ct.	Catalan
dem.	demonstrative
Dn.	Danish
Fr.	French
G.	German
Gl.	Galician
hi	high
imp.	imperative
It.	Italian
lab	labial
lat	lateral
Med.Sp.	Medieval Spanish
M.Sp.	Modern Spanish
Mz.	Mozarabic
n.	noun
nas	nasal
obst	obstruent
Oc.	Occitan

O.It.	Old Italian
orth.	orthographic
O.Sp.	Old Spanish
part.	particle
pl.	plural
pres.	present
pret.	preterite
Pt.	Portuguese
Rm.	Rumanian
SD	structural description
sg.	singular
Sl.	Slavic
son	sonorant
Sp.	Spanish
strd	strident
subj.	subjunctive
syll	syllabic
tnse	tense
v.	verb
V	vowel
vce	voice
vib	vibrant
voc.	vocalic
vwl	vowel

For my Mother and Father

Chapter one

Introduction

After the publication of Chomsky and Halle (1968), the maximum exponent of what has come to be known as the 'standard' generative theory of phonology, there was an outburst of activity among phonologists anxious to test, demonstrate or constrain the possibilities of such a powerful apparatus. Inevitably, perhaps, there was an immediate attempt to apply Chomsky and Halle's model to historical linguistics, resulting in the publication of various studies, including King's (1969) monograph, which was then taken, perhaps prematurely, to be the basic text in the field.

The assumptions underlying synchronic generative theory have had wide-reaching effects in the generativists' view of historical developments. Thus, the requirement that linguistics should only concern itself with the investigation of an abstract, homogeneous set of data (or, as Chomsky would paradoxically have it, a 'homogeneous speech-community' (Chomsky 1965:3)) means the reduction of information on historical developments to a sort of one-track progression from time T_1 to T_2 allowing of no consideration of variation, digression, incomplete change, false starts, or any other of the phenomena we need to recognize in historical linguistics.[1]

This viewpoint was actively encouraged by several factors. First, the standard generative theory deals in categorical, static rules which cannot cope with variation phenomena and are limited to the expression of the results, and only the results, of changes that have been completed. Variation, in any case, is a performance phenomenon for generative linguists, and, as such, is excluded from their studies. Second, the insistence on discarding any performance data, since sound change exclusively involves a change in Chomskyan 'competence' (King 1969:84), means that historical linguistics can only be seen as the constant substitution of one grammar (that is, 'state') by another; it is difficult to see how investigation into the history of a language can be carried out within such a static, isolated model.[2] Third, the formalism of the synchronic theory was largely taken over by historical phonologists, and with it, the formal requirements of simplicity by feature-counting, rule-collapsing and so on, which, as we aim to show, are simply not relevant in many cases in historical processes. Fourth, as a logical next step from the interpretation of sound change as rule change, all historical processes were seen as non-gradual, largely as an extrapolation of the fact that some are difficult to envisage as gradual (King 1969:109–13). (In fact, even some of those seen by King as impossible to realize gradually, can actually be interpreted as having precisely this type of realization; see Lass (1978).)

It was relatively easy, of course, to transplant the array of formalisms in use in synchronic analysis onto historical analysis, because in many cases historical analysis had already been undertaken in the search for synchronic underlying forms;[3] where the history of a language was insufficiently documented, the procedure followed to arrive at an underlying representation had often closely resembled what historical linguists traditionally called reconstruction. There was therefore a virtually wholesale translation of the formal repertoire of the standard theory into diachronic terms.

It should be made clear that we do not mean to suggest that the application of generative concepts to historical linguistics has been totally infructuous; the more perceptive linguists working in this framework have produced valuable insights into some aspects of change: Kiparsky's work, for example, stands out in this respect (Kiparsky 1982 is a useful selection), thanks, perhaps, to a healthy lack of that dogmatism shown by other writers of the school. Nor do we wish to suggest that all historical linguists working in the generative paradigm maintain the extreme views of King (1969); many of them clearly do not, and King himself moved away from them in later work (King 1974). But nevertheless it remains true that the standard model of generative phonology is still used in historical analysis and all data (carefully selected) confined in its straitjacket (see, for instance, the comments on Eastlack (1977) in note 5), to the point that, in Lass's words, it seems 'many generative phonologists . . . have adopted Procrustes as a culture hero' (Lass 1978:280, note 24).

Synchronic generative theory, meanwhile, has not been without its detractors: debates on abstractness, rule ordering, naturalness, psychological reality, and a host of other (inter-related) phenomena (see Goyvaerts 1981a) filled the specialized journals during the 1970s and have given rise to myriad new varieties of phonological theory: natural generative phonology, natural phonology, upside-down phonology and atomic phonology being among the most widely known (see Dinnsen (1979) for an interesting, but inconclusive, taste of the variety available), not to mention variationist and developmentalist studies (among others), whose premises are, of course, quite different. However, we are not, with this study, attempting to make a contribution to analyses with a purely synchronic aim – if, indeed, such constructs can exist. It is merely our intention to point out the impossibility of applying the standard generative theory to historical developments.

Spanish presents a number of advantages for this type of study. Principally, it is a language with a long documented history of more than a thousand years; we naturally have an abundance of Latin documentation too. It is also a language whose contemporary varieties are numerous, thanks to socio-historical factors, thus providing us with more advanced or backward lects for the study of change as it progressed (or progresses), as it was truncated or as it began; in the historical perspective we are also fortunate in the sense that the languages most closely related to Spanish are equally well documented. Finally, the history of Spanish phonology, or at least, aspects of it, have been studied from many angles during this century; broadly speaking, we find the neogrammarian tradition represented in Menéndez Pidal (1958), structuralism in Alarcos Llorach (1971) and Martinet (1970:257–325), and generative studies are numerous: Harris (1969),[4] Otero (1971, 1976), Hartman (1974) and Eastlack (1976) being the most significant. Recently a wide-ranging study based on criteria of relative chronology has been published by Pensado Ruiz (1984).

All the generative studies suffer in greater or lesser measure from the same evils. Leaving aside for the moment Harris's study, which is written from a different viewpoint and is in any case considerably broader than the others, the rest are forced into making sweeping generalizations and creating rules which are completely unnatural in the sense that the processes they represent bear no resemblance to what we know happens in natural languages; that is to say, they break away from substantive evidence in order to satisfy the conceptual requirements of the theory, as we shall see.[5]

To some extent, this is due to a delusion produced by the theory itself: since a great deal of synchronic analysis in fact relies in generative phonology upon techniques (such as reconstruction) appropriate to historical inquiry, the same type of formal structure has unquestioningly been applied to historical developments, which therefore emerge with a veneer of similarity to synchronic rules. The validity of such formulations is then considered in the same light as that of synchronic rules, without taking into account the basic question of the dynamic nature of change, and the fact that what interests generativists in a synchronic grammar is a sequence of rules (which satisfy certain metatheoretical requirements we have already mentioned) and which will generate the correct output and only the correct output for a particular state of the language in question, thereby providing an insight into language in general; while historical linguistics should presumably be interested not simply in the output of rules (that is, the results of change), but also, or primarily, in how change begins, how it is implemented, spread, and completed or truncated, as the case may be.[6] Only investigation into these phenomena will help us to understand the dynamics of language, and it is this investigation which we believe is severely impeded by the implantation of the standard generative theory in the study of language history.

An indication should be made here of certain terminological usage within this study. First, the term 'Latin' is used to denote, in general, the language of the Empire. Like Wright (1982, especially pp. 52–4; 1983), we can find no positive benefit in the use of a term such as 'Vulgar Latin', but rather a clear disadvantage in the misleading idea it conjures up of the existence of a sharply defined Classical/Vulgar dualism (see also Lloyd 1979). For the same reasons, the establishment of a quasi-uniform 'Proto-Romance' system (as, for example, in Hall 1976) seems equally futile; as Malkiel rightly points out, 'once we decide to credit Latin with a wealth of socio-educational and provincial dialects, any need for postulating Proto-Romance except as a construct disappears at once' (1978:486). Surely it would be totally unnatural to suggest that Latin did not enjoy the variation evident in other languages. We have therefore limited any further qualification to cases in which an etymon considered differs notably from the standard Latin dictionary-form, providing the latter and labelling it as 'Classical'.

Second, the modern dialect under principal consideration is the variety of Spanish known as Castilian, that is, roughly, the variety spoken in the area of Old Castile and recognized as 'standard' in the Peninsula.[7] Following common usage, it is normally referred to here as 'Spanish', or as 'Castilian' if there is any possibility of ambiguity. Other varieties of Spanish are named as required.

The term 'Medieval Spanish' refers to the Castilian standard of the thirteenth century, based on the varieties spoken around Burgos and Toledo, and used in the work carried out under the patronage of Alfonso X 'El Sabio' (reigned 1252 to 1284). 'Old Spanish' refers to forms found in Spanish up to (and usually including) the time of this thirteenth-century standardization.

Notes

1. For a study of sound change in progress showing these features, see Labov, Yaeger and Steiner (1972).
2. For comments on the static model of linguistics, as against the dynamic (that is, developmentalist) one, see Bailey (1982). Most linguists long ago realized that the study of a particular dialect in isolation could only produce, at best, a distortion of reality. Schiffman comments that 'Scholars who work on languages of the I[ndian] L[inguistic] A[rea] are constantly aware (or face serious consequences, if they are not) of the fact . . . that there is simply no way to talk about such things as the "ideal speaker/hearer", or categorical rules, or any of the other theoretical constructs that assume the isolation or isolability of a language from language use and social conditioning' (1982:186).
3. Cases are too numerous to warrant any individual citation; perhaps the most famous instance is Chomsky and Halle's (1968) synchronic recapitulation of the Great Vowel Shift in English. And more recently, Lightner has claimed that 'to do synchronic analysis of NE [i.e., Modern English – RHN] . . . we have to return to 3000 BC' (Lightner 1981:96). Diachronic data were also frequently used as external evidence in support of synchronic analyses too. See Botha (1973:136–64).
4. Harris's study is primarily synchronic, but, bearing in mind our comments above, it is interesting from the historical viewpoint too.
5. A recent extension of this is the interest in writing computer programmes to simulate historical derivation by rule (see Eastlack 1977). It is hardly surprising that such a programme 'provides . . . rather conclusive [sic] evidence in support of the theory of language change propounded in King's (1969) discussion' (Eastlack 1977:84), when it is based exclusively on the same premises as King's book; that is to say, that sound change is systematic, regular and categorical rule change.
6. As Eckert (1980:208) says, 'The purpose of a categorical treatment is to "generate" the correct modern forms from a protocorpus. Here . . . simplicity is the primary basis for judging rules, so that categorical historical rules cut the phonetic inventory into the largest chunks that can yield the correct results.'
7. Like most 'standards', this variety is really an amalgam of the speech of several linguistic areas.

Chapter two

Weakening in Intervocalic Position

The consonantal process in the history of Spanish which has been most often cited in the generative literature[1] is that of what is often referred to as the weakening of the intervocalic obstruents, schematically represented as:

pp → p → b → β
tt → t → d → ð
kk → k → g → ɣ

This schema is to be understood in the following way: Latin possessed, in intervocalic (word-internal) position, voiceless and voiced single and geminate stops with bilabial, dental and velar points of articulation. The voiced geminates were rarely found, and on the basis of their infrequency are usually considered as of marginal interest, if they are considered at all; they were reduced to single consonants and later spirantized (for examples and further comments, see below, pages 13–14, and Martinet (1982:9–10)). For this reason, they are not included in the traditional schema reproduced above. The other three types of segments – voiceless geminates and voiced and voiceless single stops – underwent a shift which in structuralist terms involved a chain movement (see Martinet (1970:257–96, 1982); Alarcos Llorach (1971:243)); that is, the voiceless geminates simplified (pp → p), the single voiceless stops voiced (p → b), and the voiced stops spirantized (b → β). The changes brought about are illustrated below:[2]

I.	CIPPU	→	cepo	**branch, snare**[3]
	CUPPA	→	copa	**glass, cup**
	GUTTA	→	gota	**drop**
	MITTERE	→	meter	**to put**
	BUCCA	→	boca	**mouth**
	SICCU	→	seco	**dry**

II.	LUPU	→	lobo	wolf
	CEPULLA	→	cebolla	onion
	PRATU	→	prado	field, meadow
	VITA	→	vida	life
	SECURU	→	seguro	safe, sure
	SECARE	→	segar	to reap
III.	CABALLU	→	ca[β]allo	horse
	BIBERE	→	be[β]er	to drink
	SUDARE	→	su[ð]ar	to sweat
	NIDU	→	ni[ð]o	nest
	PLAGA	→	lla[ɣ]a	wound, sore
	AUGUSTU	→	a[ɣ]osto	August

These examples show the first consonant shift in Old Spanish, bearing in mind that the intervocalic consonants in group II were realized, not as fricatives as in Modern Spanish, but as the stops [b], [d], and [g]. These forms have subsequently undergone a regular second shift in the same direction, thus yielding the modern pronunciations:[4]

IIA.	LUPU	→	lobo	→	lo[β]o
	CEPULLA	→	cebolla	→	ce[β]olla
	PRATU	→	prado	→	pra[ð]o
	VITA	→	vida	→	vi[ð]a
	SECURU	→	seguro	→	se[ɣ]uro
	SECARE	→	segar	→	se[ɣ]ar

So far, we have seen a pattern of sound changes whose apparent regularity would delight any neogrammarian, and indeed, it is this pattern that is traditionally presented in the manuals, with greater or lesser qualification. But if we look a little more carefully, we find that the pattern is not completely 'regular'.

We can for the moment leave aside the forms in group I: this reduction of geminates was exceptionless, and common to all Western Romance. The voicing process illustrated in group II is also a feature of Western Romance in general, with few exceptions,[5] and the subsequent spirantization is a regular phonetic process of Spanish: no stops are permitted on the surface in intervocalic position, even in loanwords, such as **baby** [béjβi], **vedette** [beðét], **groggy** [gróɣi].

The forms cited in group III are somewhat misleading, however, because they do not tell the whole story. The second consonant shift also affected forms of this type, eliminating the intervocalic fricative. Thus, as well as the forms given above, we have:

IIIA.
RADICE	→	raíz	root
COMEDERE	→	comer	to eat
FOEDU	→	feo	ugly
CREDO	→	creo	believe (1st sg. pres.)
CADERE	→	caer	to fall
CRUDELE	→	cruel	cruel
VIDET	→	ve	sees (3rd sg. pres.)
LAUDARE	→	loar	to praise
AUDIRE	→	oír	to hear
LIMPIDU	→	limpio	clean
DIGITU	→	dedo	finger
FRIGIDU	→	frío	cold
LEGALE	→	leal	loyal
MAGISTRU	→	maestro	(school)teacher
RUGITU	→	ruido	noise
SAGITTA	→	saeta	arrow
VAGINA	→	vaina	sheath, pod
COGITARE	→	cuidar	to look after
SARTAGINE	→	sartén	frying pan
REGINA	→	reina	queen
LEGIT	→	lee	reads (3rd sg. pres.)

All these cases indicate a development of the type CREDO → *cre[ð]o → creo, LEGIT → *le[ɣ]e → lee, etc., which would clearly show the participation of these forms in the second consonant shift, that is, [ð] → ø and [ɣ] → ø. Note also that of the examples given in group III, Old Spanish also shows **nio** from NIDU and **suar** from SUDARE.

Latin intervocalic –B–, on the other hand, did not generally participate in the second shift;[6] thus we still have **ca[β]allo**, **be[β]er**, **ha[β]er** (< HABERE) in Modern Spanish. In other words, the first shift, as regards single intervocalic stops, had the following effect:

p → b   b → β
t → d   d → ð
k → g   g → ɣ

while the second shift, acting on these outputs, gave:

b → β β   no change
d → ð ð → ø or no change
g → ɣ ɣ → ø or no change

First of all, let us consider why the labial fricative took no part in the second shift. According to Foley (1977, chapter 3), the reason is simply that the labials are phonologically the 'strongest' stops in Romance, that is, the most resistant to change. In Danish, Foley claims (1977:25), a similar situation exists: **kage → ka[ɣ]e, bide → bi[ð]e**, while **købe** remains unchanged; that is, both intervocalic –g– and –d– spirantize, while –b– does not. And in North German, only –g– spirantizes: **sagen → sa[ɣ]en**, while **baden** and **beben** do not change. This, with similar evidence from other languages, suggests that velar segments are weaker than dentals and labials, in the sense that they are more likely to undergo weakening processes. What is more, if the dental or labial segments have weakened, the velars will have done so too; that is, the weakening of relatively stronger segments is dependent on that of relatively weaker ones. These strength hierarchies, Foley insists, are phonological and not phonetic: each segment has a phonological value, but the value may not correspond to the same phonetic segment universally. Thus, while dentals are weaker than labials in Spanish (and in Romance in general), labials are weaker than dentals in the history of Germanic (Foley 1977:48–52; Lass 1971:22–3; Escure 1977:62, note 11).

In our opinion, this last explanation weakens Foley's claims considerably. If Foley wishes to work on a level notably more abstract than the phonetic one in order to explain historical change, this is fully justified if it produces empirically viable results. When we find, however, that supposedly 'universal' hierarchies must be interpreted for one language group in one way and for another in the opposite way, it looks rather as if these interpretations are more ad hoc than Foley would wish to admit (see also Cravens 1984).

What is more, it is simply not true that the same pattern applies to all of Romance: in Rumanian, intervocalic –D– and –G– were generally maintained, while –B– was lost:

	LIGARE	→	Rm. lega	**to tie**
	CRUDA	→	Rm. crudă	**raw**
	SUDORE	→	Rm. sudoare	**sweat**
while	SCRIBO	→	Rm. scriu	**write (1st sg. pres.)**
	CABALLU	→	Rm. cal	**horse**[7]

Thus, while it may be true that Foley's claims are valid for Spanish (and we shall find more evidence that they are), it is rather doubtful whether they refer to a pan–Romance phenomenon, and much less to a universal one.

As regards the second Spanish consonant shift, the elision of [ɣ] is extremely widespread, though there are clear exceptions. Generalizations made on the basis of its situation in the word are fruitless; Canfield and Davis (1975:74) claim that in 'Iberia and southern Gaul: in posttonic position /g/ remained' but 'it often fell before the accent', which is immediately disproved by examples such as SARTAGINE → **sartén** and DIGITU → **dedo** on the one hand, and AUGUSTU → **agosto** and LEGUMEN (or *LEGUMINE) → **legumbre** 'vegetable' on the other. What seems to be true, however, is that [ɣ] is maintained before a back vowel, as in **legumbre**, **agosto** and **llaga**, as well as ROGARE → **rogar** 'to beg', NEGARE → **negar** 'to refuse', though the low vowel offered less resistance: LEGALE → **leal**, REGALE → **real** 'royal', FUMIGARE → **humear** 'to give off smoke', RUMIGARE → **rumiar** 'to ruminate', LITIGARE → **lidiar** 'to fight (bulls)', as well as NAVIGARE → **navegar/navear** 'to sail'. This resistance of the high back vowels and the variability of [a] points to the likelihood of the loss of –G– having begun before high front vowels, a possibility we shall return to later.[8]

The case of the Latin intervocalic –D– is considerably more complex in Castilian.[9] The Iberian Peninsula as a whole presents the following picture: the Catalan and Portuguese varieties on the east and west respectively show loss of –D–, as may be seen below:

CRUDELE →	Pt. cruel, Ct. cruel	**cruel**
CRUDU →	Pt. cru, Ct. cru	**raw**
GRADU →	Pt. grau, Ct. grau	**degree**
NODU →	Pt. nó, Ct. nou	**knot**
SUDARE →	Pt. suar, Ct. suar	**to sweat**

(cf. Modern Spanish **cruel**, but **crudo, grado, nudo, sudar**).

Aragonese dialects, on the other hand, show a fairly consistent preservation of the –D–, more so in medieval times before the political and social imposition of Castilian forms (see Malkiel 1960a:286–8, 1984:76, note 12; Lapesa 1981:202; Alvar 1953: 176–7).

This leaves Castilian sandwiched, as it were, between dialects where loss of –D– was the norm, and others where it was maintained, giving rise to the complex pattern we find. We therefore have both the series of forms in group IIIA, where the

–D– has been lost, and also forms such as **grado, nudo, vado** 'ford' (< VADU). More interestingly, we find that Modern Spanish **crudo, nido** 'nest' (< NIDU), **desnudo** 'naked' (based on NUDU) and **sudor** 'sweat' (< SUDORE) also appear (with greater or lesser frequency) in medieval sources as **crúo, nío, desnúo** and **suor** (Malkiel 1986:162), while at the same time modern **feo** and **frío** also turn up as **hedo** and **frido** (the latter also in placenames such as **Fontefrida**), and in Berceo **rodié** (infinitive **roer** < RODERE) appears (Corominas and Pascual 1980–: s.v. roer).[10]

Such a situation is intolerable for any regularist hypothesis without some sort of qualifying explanation. One solution that might suggest itself – that of dialect borrowing – is meaningless if we regard Castilian as having taken one of the two possible courses (i.e., either loss or preservation of –D–) and then borrowed wholesale from its eastern or western neighbours. On this scale, it would be foolish to claim that the result reflected in the majority of tokens represents that chosen by Castilian, and then write off such a large number of potential counterexamples as 'borrowings', as if they were in some way exceptional.

In other words, it is simply not possible to look upon Castilian in this case as one homogeneous, variationless dialect. That variation existed in the medieval dialect is clear from the doublets given above; how, then, are we to express the loss of –D– in generative terms? Was the rule ever part of the 'ideal speaker-listener's' grammar or not? It cannot have been an optional rule, since some forms (as far as we know) were clearly exempted from it, while others always underwent it. The only (and highly unsatisfactory) solution would be to fall back on lists of exceptions, with no indication of why they should exist.

What we are in fact confronted with is a classical wave pattern of spread, as discussed at length in Bailey (1973:65–109). If we leave aside for a moment the question of Catalan (which here has more to do with Romance developments north of the Pyrenees than in the Peninsula), we can see how, according to the wave theory, the loss of –D– began in the west, where it has virtually reached completion, and spread eastwards, being introduced as a variable rule in Old Castilian (itself no more than a convenient name for what was probably a quite heterogeneous group of dialects), where it never became categorical, and only reaching Aragonese and other eastern varieties much later, thanks to the process of Castilianization.[11] It appears, incidentally, that the voicing of intervocalic voiceless stops also spread in the same direction, which has given rise to questions of the possible influence of Celtic substrate (Martinet 1970:257–96; Malkiel 1960a:289; Jungemann 1955:132–52; for a summary of arguments and an attempt at chronology based on loanwords, see Pensado Ruiz 1984:193–204).

Now let us look at a further problem. If we were to express the first consonant shift in generative terms, it would involve the following diachronic rules:

1. $\begin{bmatrix} -\text{son} \\ -\text{long} \\ +\text{vce} \end{bmatrix} \rightarrow [+\text{cont}] \, / \, V\_\_\_V$

   (b → β, d → ð, g → ɣ)

2. $\begin{bmatrix} -\text{son} \\ -\text{long} \end{bmatrix} \rightarrow [+\text{vce}] \, / \, V\_\_\_V$

   (p → b, t → d, k → g)

3. $[-\text{son}] \rightarrow [-\text{long}] \, / \, V\_\_\_V^{12}$

   (pp → p, tt → t, kk → k)

and the second shift, rules 4 and 5:

4. $\begin{bmatrix} -\text{son} \\ +\text{vce} \end{bmatrix} \rightarrow [+\text{cont}] \, / \, V\_\_\_V$

   (b → β, d → ð, g → ɣ)

5. $\begin{bmatrix} -\text{son} \\ +\text{cont} \\ -\text{strd} \\ -\text{lab} \end{bmatrix} \rightarrow \emptyset \, / \, V\_\_\_V$

   (ð, ɣ → ø)

Rule 5, as we have seen, must be constrained in its application to the velar segment, and is only applied to the dental segment variably. It is therefore questionable whether it could even be written as one rule. It will, however, serve our purposes for the moment as it is, and we shall return to the problem later.

Let us start by concentrating our attention on the first shift. These three rules clearly reflect the action of a single process – the weakening of intervocalic consonants usually known as Western Romance lenition. Foley (1970:87–8) claims that the 'transformational analysis . . . fails to reveal any relationship among the subparts of this shift, even though there is in evidence a "weakening" '. By 'weakening' we understand a diachronic process which leads segments towards their complete effacement; Venneman's definition, quoted in Hyman (1975:165) is that 'a segment X is said to be weaker than a segment Y if Y goes through an X stage on its way to zero'.[13] As we have seen, the process in question here in the history of Spanish has led in many cases to the elision of [ð] and [ɣ], the two segments furthest advanced in the process.

In order to show the unity of the process, the only way open to us in standard generative formalism would be to collapse the rules into one. In fact, it is not difficult to collapse rules 1–3; Walsh (1979) postulates similar rules to account for the same phenomena, which he suggests could all be collapsed into rule 6:

6. $\begin{bmatrix} + \text{obst} \\ \alpha \text{ long} \\ \beta \text{ tnse} \end{bmatrix} \rightarrow \begin{bmatrix} \alpha \text{ tnse} \\ -\beta \text{ cont} \\ - \text{long} \end{bmatrix} / V\_\_\_V$[14]

Rule 6, within an early generative framework which included a feature-counting simplicity metric, would indeed have been looked upon favourably, but from a natural point of view, one has to question its formulation. The juggling of Greek-letter variables with three different features is suspiciously arbitrary and certainly has no phonetic basis. We are using 'natural' here in the sense of, for example, Hooper (1976) and not of Chomsky and Halle (1968). For them, 'naturalness' is related to feature-counting and is therefore equivalent to simplicity in formalism. This characterization has been shown to have very little to do with 'natural' in the sense of what are typical situations in natural languages (see, for example, Chen (1973b)[15]); indeed, it has often been pointed out that there seems to be no metatheoretical reason why this type of simplicity and naturalness should be associated in this way, since the result is often anything but 'simple'.

What is more, rule 6 does not faithfully reflect the shift in question: voiced geminates would not, as expected, merely simplify, but also become voiceless and spirantize. Let us consider some examples:

ABBATE	→	abad	**abbot**
ABBATTUERE	→	abatir	**to knock down**
ADDUCERE	→	aducir	**to bring forward, adduce**
*IN(N)ADDERE	→	(O.Sp.) eñadir	**to add**

Now the effect of rule 6 would be to convert voiced geminates, which are [+long, +vce], into [−vce, −long, +cont], that is,

–BB– → [ɸ], –DD– → [θ], and –GG– → [x]. As mentioned above, the question of the voiced geminates is essentially a marginal one, given their highly infrequent occurrence; but there is no evidence whatsoever of spirantization (except later, by the second shift) or loss of voice in the few existing cases. Moreover, the development of geminate voiced stops to single voiceless fricatives would not seem to be a natural one in any sense: this is merely one of the problems arising from telescoping a series of natural processes into a 'simpler' schema, following the exigencies of generative orthodoxy.

Walsh himself recognizes the problem (in his note 6), but claims, astonishingly, that 'this fact which seems to falsify the analysis presented here actually provides strong support for it', and goes on to discuss how the geminate voiced consonants came to be associated with the underlying /p t k/ segments, but still leaves us in the dark about how we are to correct the rule. With regard to the geminate segments, Walsh points out in the same note that 'These segments were . . . quite rare; so rare in fact that the standard treatments of the series of changes under discussion regularly neglect to mention them.' This is quite true, but the reason for this neglect may well lie in the difficulty of making these segments fit into any elegant summary of the changes: precisely the difficulty Walsh encounters.

One must agree with Foley then, that a transformational analysis of these processes does not do them justice or provide a satisfying insight into their relationship. What Foley (1977:34) suggests is the establishment of a strength hierarchy expressed on two parameters: one (α) indicating the relationship we have already mentioned among velars, dentals, and labials (which Foley attributes to Romance in general, but which should probably be restricted to Hispano– or perhaps Western Romance); and the other (β) reflecting the relative strength of geminate voiceless stops, single voiceless stops, voiced stops, and fricatives, as observed in the lenition of intervocalic consonants in Western Romance:

```
        4 ↑  kk  tt  pp
     3     k   t   p
  β  2     g   d   b
     1     ɣ   ð   β
           ─────────────→
           1   2   3
               α
```

Each phonological element will be assigned a value by these parameters; for example, $d=\alpha 2\beta 2$. In this way, the first Spanish consonant shift could be expressed as:

kk	→ k, $\alpha 1\beta 4$	→	$\alpha 1\beta 3$
k	→ g, $\alpha 1\beta 3$	→	$\alpha 1\beta 2$
g	→ ɣ, $\alpha 1\beta 2$	→	$\alpha 1\beta 1$
tt	→ t, $\alpha 2\beta 4$	→	$\alpha 2\beta 3$, etc.

In other words, the entire shift may be characterized as a loss of one unit of strength on the β scale, or

β strength n → β strength n−1

within what Foley (1977:29–30) claims is a universal rule of lenition, expressed as

[+voice, αn] → [+cont] / V___V

with the universal condition $1 \leq n \leq m$, that is, that strength n varies between the constant 1 and the variable m, to be determined for each language. In the cases mentioned above, m will be 1 for North German (only g → ɣ, d, and b remain), 2 for Danish (where g → ɣ, d → ð, and b remains), and 3 for Spanish (g → ɣ, d → ð, and b → β). The fact that in the second consonant shift ɣ and ð are elided while β remains unchanged is accounted for by Foley's inertial development principle (1977, chapter 7), one part of which states that weaker elements will further weaken first and more extensively; Spanish β is α3, while ð is α2 and ɣ is α1.

Foley's suggested schema elegantly sums up the Spanish consonant shifts. However, we have already questioned its claimed 'universality', and we should also look at other material not usually taken into consideration in this context.

In the first place, other intervocalic consonants than stops appeared in Latin: for example, the voiceless fricatives −F− and −S−. The consonant represented by −V− was originally realized as [w], but would seem to have become the fricative [β] at some time during or soon after the first century AD (Sturtevant 1940:142; Alarcos Llorach 1971:231–2), thus becoming confused with original intervocalic −B−, which by rule 1 also spirantized to [β]. Returning to [f] and [s] then, we find that in intervocalic position they underwent a similar process to that which affected the stops:

PROFECTU	→	provecho	**benefit**
TRIFINIU	→	Treviño	**(placename)**

(FICUS) BIFERA	→ (O.Sp.)bevra → (M.Sp.)breva	**(type of) fig**
COPHINU	→ cuévano	**pannier**
CASA	→ casa	**house**
ROSA	→ rosa	**rose**
CAUSA	→ cosa	**thing**
AUSARE	→ osar	**to dare**

Thus, [f] must have voiced, later confusing its result with the already existing [β] from original –B– and –V– in intervocalic position. (Modern Spanish orthography uses both –b– and –v– to represent the bilabial fricative [β], as well as the bilabial stop [b], which in autonomous phonological terms, are allophones of the same phoneme in complementary distribution. Whether /b/ or /β/ is taken to be underlying (or, indeed, /d/ or /ð/, /g/ or /ɣ/) in a generative framework still seems to be an open question; see note 34 below and cf. Harris (1969:37–40); Bjarkman (1978); and Lozano (1979).)

The development of [s] is not so obvious, because of subsequent processes, but the facts are that in the examples above, and others where the Latin form had intervocalic –S–, this segment voiced, as we should expect, giving in Old Spanish [z], while in forms with geminate –SS– in Latin, such as

PASSU	→ paso	**step**
SPISSU	→ espeso	**thick**
MASSA	→ masa	**dough**
CRASSU	→ graso	**fatty, greasy**

the geminate was simplified but not voiced, again as expected. These forms were regularly transcribed in Old Spanish with –ss–, in order to distinguish them from forms with [z], represented by –s– (Martinet 1970:299; Menéndez Pidal 1958:131, 134–5). This distinction (both phonetic and orthographic) has subsequently been lost by the devoicing of all Spanish sibilants (in the case of [z] → [s], virtually complete in all the Peninsula by the end of the sixteenth century (Alonso 1969:26)), though this does not affect the discussion.

The intervocalic voiceless fricatives, then, also took part in the first Spanish consonant shift, in so far as they reduced when geminate and voiced when single. This means that rules 2 and 3 are, in fact, rather more general than is usually recognized.[16] As formulated above, they will actually apply to the fricatives too, since the feature [continuant] is not specified in these rules.

The other fact which is not normally taken into account in

generative-based comments on the consonant shift is that in the Latin of the Empire (that is, what we take to be the ancestor of the Romance languages, containing both pan-Romance traits and regional variation; see Introduction, page 4 above) there is evidence that certain processes had already taken place which extended the range of intervocalic consonants at the phonetic level. These changes involved the formation of glides from the unstressed vowels [i], [e] (which had closed and merged with [i] in this context), and [u] when in the proximity of another vowel. Thus in FILIA, PUTEU, POSUI, the second vowel lost its syllabic quality. Formally, this may be represented as:

7. $\begin{bmatrix} -\text{cons} \\ +\text{hi} \\ -\text{stress} \end{bmatrix} \rightarrow [-\text{syll}] \ / \ [+\text{syll}]$

The glide resulting from the front vowel exerted a strong palatalizing influence on preceding consonants. Evidence of the palatalization (affrication) of [tj], which seems to have been the first group affected, dates back at least to the second century AD (Alarcos Llorach 1971:233, Lapesa 1981:79, Menéndez Pidal 1958:94),[17] and it is therefore clearly of interest to us to consider here the development of these consonants in intervocalic position in order to determine to what extent they fit into the pattern which has been established for the other obstruents.

Again, this situation is somewhat complicated by subsequent developments between the periods of Medieval and Modern Spanish, in the sense that the devoicing of fricatives and affricates has obscured the original results of these palatalizations. For this reason, the following examples show in the left-hand column the Latin forms and in the adjacent column the Medieval Spanish reflexes (Medieval Spanish orthography used –z– to indicate the voiced affricate [d^z] and –ç– the voiceless affricate [t^s]):

PIGRITIA	→	pereza	**laziness**
TITIONE	→	tizón	**brand (of wood)**
TRISTITIA	→	tristeza	**sadness**
PUTEU	→	pozo	**well (n.)**
ACUTIARE	→	aguzar	**to sharpen**
RATIONE	→	razón	**reason**
SATIONE	→	sazón	**maturity**
MALITIA	→	maleza	**undergrowth**
RADIARE	→	rayar[18]	**to scratch**
PODIU	→	poyo	**stone bench**

HODIE	→ hoy	**today**
FASTIDIU	→ hastío	**weariness**
PERFIDIA	→ porfía	**obstinacy**
SEDEAT	→ sea	**be (3rd sg. pres. subj.)**
VIDEO	→ veo	**see (1st sg. pres.)**
RIDEO	→ río	**laugh (1st sg. pres.)**
ERICIU	→ erizo	**hedgehog**
*CORTICEA	→ corteza	**(tree) bark**
ACIARIU	→ azero	**steel**
LAQ(U)EU	→ lazo	**bow**
FAGEA	→ haya	**beech**
CORRIGIA	→ correa	**strap**
FUGIO	→ huyo	**flee (1st sg. pres.)**
NAVIGIU	→ navío	**ship**

Reflexes of the few forms with geminate consonants are:

MATTIANA	→ ma(n)çana	**apple**
BRACCHIU	→ braço	**arm**

Unlike [t d] and [k g] the labials [p b] do not seem to have undergone palatalization. The group [–pj–] underwent metathesis (→ [–jp–]), the glide having a raising effect on the preceding vowel, while leaving [–p–] in a syllable-initial position following a glide, and hence unchanged (see note 16 and pages 62–3):

SAPIAT	→ *[sájpa]	→ *[séjpa]	→ sepa	**know**
				(3rd sg. pres. subj.)
CAPIAT	→ *[kájpa]	→ *[kéjpa]	→ quepa	**fit**
				(3rd sg. pres. subj.)

The great paucity of examples of [–bj–] resists a truly definitive analysis: we have the reflexes of HABEAM, HABEAS, etc., which have given **haya, hayas** 'have (pres. subj.)', thus suggesting at first glance a development similar to that of the groups [–dj–] and [–gj–]; and the same development as that of RUBEU → **royo** 'reddish' and FOVEA → **hoya** 'pit, hole' (Menéndez Pidal 1958:147). We shall return to this question in due course.

The first part of the process evident in the above examples was clearly a palatalization of the [−labial] stops before the palatal glide (and in some cases, the front vowels; further details below). Given the Latin orthographic system, it is not perhaps surprising that indications of palatalization are few in inscriptions. There can be, however, no doubt that the process at least began within the Latin period, since almost all the Romance languages (the exceptional case of Sardinian fits in with a general pattern of great conservatism) reflect palatalization processes which unquestionably have a common origin. The expression of this assimilation in formal terms is perfectly straightforward for the velar segments, which were palatalized before a front glide or front vowel (for further examples, see below, page 37):

$$8. \begin{bmatrix} -\text{son} \\ +\text{bk} \end{bmatrix} \rightarrow \begin{bmatrix} +\text{hi} \\ -\text{bk} \end{bmatrix} / \underline{} \begin{bmatrix} -\text{cons} \\ -\text{bk} \end{bmatrix}$$

while the inclusion of [t d] in the change leads us inevitably into a more complex formulation. The [+coronal] segments underwent palatalization to a lesser extent, in the sense that they were affected only by a following glide (i.e., the most palatal segment) but not by high vowels. However, the logical extension of rule 8, which would be:

$$9. \begin{bmatrix} -\text{son} \\ -\text{lab} \\ <+\text{cor}> \end{bmatrix} \rightarrow \begin{bmatrix} +\text{hi} \\ -\text{bk} \end{bmatrix} / \underline{} \begin{bmatrix} -\text{cons} \\ -\text{bk} \\ <-\text{syll}> \end{bmatrix}$$

would also include the element [s], which did not in fact take part in the palatalization, despite the implicational schema devised by Chen (1973a:181).[19] A more correct formulation of the SD therefore seems to be:

$$10. \begin{bmatrix} -\text{son} \\ -\text{cont} \\ -\text{lab} \\ <+\text{cor}> \end{bmatrix} \rightarrow \begin{bmatrix} +\text{hi} \\ -\text{bk} \end{bmatrix} / \underline{} \begin{bmatrix} -\text{cons} \\ -\text{bk} \\ <-\text{syll}> \end{bmatrix}[20]$$

This rule immediately presents an interesting problem for the standard generative interpretation of historical developments. In rule 8 we have the formal expression of the palatalization of two velar segments, [k] and [g]; any extension of this palatalization would presumably mean a generalization, and therefore a simplification in the rule itself (cf. King 1969: 58–63 and on page 65: 'the transmission of a grammar, whether through time or geographic space, is in general accompanied by equal or increased simplicity, and not by complication (reduction in generality)'). This, as we have seen, is not the case; partly because of the necessary exclusion of [s], which means that [−continuant] has to be inserted in rule 10 (it is absent from rule 8, since Latin had no [+continuant, +back] segments); but also because [t d] only palatalize before the glide, unlike [k g], which are also affected by the front vowels. (Another question, incidentally, is the total lack of any natural relationship between [+coronal] and [−syllabic]: they are obliged to function together in angled brackets only as a means of forcing into one rule what would otherwise be inexpressible as such in generative terms.)

We suggest, however, that this extension is a perfectly natural one. One of the premises of this study is precisely that many sound changes spread along phonetic parameters from one segment to another. It is not easy in this case to see where palatalization began, but we consider it justified to assume that the glide palatalized preceding segments earlier than the front vowels did (see note 17). All the available inscriptional evidence points to [tj] as the first palatalized segment, though we may assume that [kj] did not lag behind, judging from the fact that in the Romance languages the palatalization of both segments is common to all but Sardinian.

The relationship between all those segments finally affected by palatalization could be illustrated in the following way, where the arrow indicates the direction of the advance of palatalization:

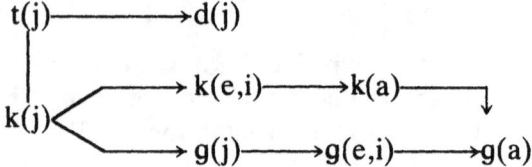

Note how the final segments, [k,g + a], underwent palatalization in the least extensive area of Romania: certain northern French and Rhaeto-Romance dialects. The diagram shows how the whole process can be broken down so that each step involves only one distinctive characteristic, either in the segment itself or in the following palatalizing context. As we should expect, the palatalization of the first elements is the most thorough, appearing in almost all the Romance languages, while the last segments to undergo it do so in the smallest area.

Returning for a moment to rule 10, we find another problem as regards its implementation. The formulation of this rule forces us to assume the effect of palatalization to have been earlier than that of spirantization (rule 1), since rule 1 would bleed rule 10 of a large proportion of its potential input and produce incorrect results. (Rule 7 will of course also be ordered before rule 10 in order to derive the glides in the determinant of the latter rule.) But if palatalization is to be expressed as a unitary process, as generativists would presumably require, such an ordering would be manifestly absurd in the case of Northern French, where [k g] followed by [a] did not palatalize until the seventh or eighth century (Straka 1956:259; Ewert 1966:71)! In saying this, of course, we are making the assumption that historical rule ordering should respect chronology, a point not usually taken up by generativists (perhaps not surprisingly, given the widespread belief that historical rules are of little interest except in so far as they concern synchronic analysis: see pages 116–17 below) but clearly, if implicitly, accepted by historical phonologists working in the tradition of Chomsky and Halle (1968) (see, for example, Otero 1971, 1976; Eastlack 1976).

The processes of weakening discussed earlier in this chapter, and that of palatalization, are doubtlessly closely interwoven in the first stages, since certain segments (intervocalic [k g] when the following vowel was front) were in principle subject to both. In the case of [k], results clearly show that palatalization was earlier than, and therefore fed, voicing (for examples, see page 18 above); whereas in the case of [g] we have a rather different situation. This segment, itself [+voice, +high], seems to have been weakened to the point of elision in intervocalic position when the following vowel was –I– already in the Imperial period. An inscription from Pompeii shows FRIDUM for FRIGIDUM (Spanish **frío** 'cold'; see also chapter 5, pages 95–6), and others show ROITUS for ROGITUS, and similar elisions of –G– (Martinet 1970:286, Menéndez Pidal 1958:94).

11. $\begin{bmatrix} -\text{son} \\ +\text{vce} \\ +\text{hi} \end{bmatrix} \rightarrow \emptyset\ /\ [+\text{syll}] \underline{\quad} \begin{bmatrix} +\text{syll} \\ -\text{bk} \\ +\text{hi} \\ -\text{mid} \end{bmatrix}$

(g → ø / V___i)

(The feature [−mid] is necessary in order to exclude the high-mid Latin vowel [e].[21]) The generalization of this rule to the mid vowel undoubtedly took place, as may be seen from the developments REGE → **rey** 'king', GREGE → **grey** 'flock', FRIGERE → **freír** 'to fry', COLLIGERE → *co[ï]ere → **coger** 'to take', but this is a later extension of the rule, judging from the lack of evidence for elision before [e] in Latin, and the assumption that elision of a [+high] segment will take place first before a fully high vowel like [i] and only later before mid vowels like [e] (see comments on Foley (1977) below).

Here again, the generativists tend to telescope this weakening into one rule: Otero (1971:308) groups the loss of [–g–] in VAGINA (Sp. **vaina** 'sheath') with that of LEGERE (Sp. **leer** 'to read') and GREGE in the same rule, chronologically placed between the beginning of the eighth and the beginning of the tenth centuries. The chronology for the loss of [-g-] (or its palatal reflex) in LEGERE and GREGE seems rather late, and it is clearly absurd for the loss of [-g-] before [-i-], judging from the Latin evidence. Otero may have wished to collapse the two rules merely to indicate their belonging to a single process but since the order of rules as expressed on pages 294–318 (Otero 1971) is *grosso modo* chronological (despite his caveat on page 292), such an appeal to generative orthodoxy does little to clarify the situation. Eastlack (1976:116, rule 31) follows Otero, here as almost everywhere else, and Lathrop (1980:87) also considers the elision a unitary process. Menéndez Pidal (1958:132–3) makes it clear that the loss of [-g-] before [-i-] is a Latin phenomenon, though he again suggests that the loss before [-e-] took place at the same time.

Apart from the elision of [-g-], there are a few other segments which take no further part in the palatalization process, due to developments which divert them from their course: the sequences [-d^{j}j-] and [-g^{j}j-], produced by the palatalization rule (10), assimilate to [-jj-]:[22]

12. $\begin{bmatrix} +\text{vce} \\ +\text{hi} \\ -\text{bk} \end{bmatrix} \rightarrow [+\text{son}] / V \underline{\qquad} \begin{bmatrix} -\text{syll} \\ +\text{son} \\ +\text{hi} \\ -\text{bk} \end{bmatrix}$

the geminate in the output later being simplified to [-j-] by the application of the last of the weakening rules, number 3. The order of the rules we have seen so far is therefore 7, 10, 11, 12, 1, 2, 3.

However, between the application of rule 12 and that of rule 1, which is considerably later, the surviving palatalized consonants underwent assibilation. There are various versions of the stages involved in this assibilation, ranging from the simplistic (Otero 1971:302–6) to the tortuous (Foley 1977:90–106); but see, for example, Alonso (1976:83–7) for a summary of the view taken by most Romance linguists.

It is not our intention here to take a stand regarding the precise phonetic values of these intermediate steps, which are not important in the context of this study, nor do we believe they can be argued for definitively, given the impossibility of gaining corroborative evidence. We shall therefore state rule 13 informally, as:

Weakening in Intervocalic Position

13. $\begin{Bmatrix} k^j \\ t^j \end{Bmatrix} \rightarrow t^s$

Before going any further, let us consider some derivations:

Rules	PUTEU	PODIU	ERICIU	CORRIGIA
7	pútju	pódju	eríkju	korrígja
10	pút^{j}u	pód^{j}ju	erík^{j}ju	korríg^{j}ja
11	___	___	___	___
12		pójju		korríjja
Vwl ad.[23]	pót^{j}jo	pójjo	erík^{j}jo	korréjja
13	pót^{s}o		erít^{s}o	
1				
2	pód^{z}o		eríd^{z}o	
3		pójo		korréja
O.Sp.	[pód^{z}o	pójo	eríd^{z}o	korréa]
Orth.	**pozo**	**poyo**	**erizo**	**correa**
Gloss	'well'	'bench'	'hedgehog'	'strap'

Rules	MATTIANA	SAGITTA	FACERE
7	mattjána	___	___
10	matt^{j}jána	sag^{j}ítta	fák^{j}ere
11	___	saítta	___
12	___	___	___
Vwl ad.	___	saétta	___
13	matt^{s}ána	___	fát^{s}ere
1	___	___	___
2	___	___	fad^{z}ére[24]
3	___	saéta	___
O.Sp.	[ma(n)t^{s}ána	saéta	fad^{z}ér]
Orth.	**ma(n)çana**	**saeta**	**fazer**
Gloss	'apple'	'arrow'	'to do, make'

As may be seen from these derivations, the only adjustments necessary to convert the output of these rules into the Medieval Spanish forms are minor: the final [–e] of [fad^{z}ére] is lost by a relatively late vowel apocope rule (see below, pages 45–6); the [–tt^s–] of [matt^{s}ána] is reduced to [–t^s–] by a regular assimilation process (see below, page 69); and the [–j–] of [korréja] is elided by another later rule:[25]

14. $\begin{bmatrix} -\text{syll} \\ -\text{cons} \\ -\text{bk} \end{bmatrix} \rightarrow \emptyset\ /\ \begin{bmatrix} -\text{cons} \\ -\text{bk} \end{bmatrix}\ \underline{\quad}\ V$

This rule will have the same effect on the derivations of NAVIGIU (Sp. **navío** 'ship'), VIDEO (Sp. **veo** 'see (1st sg. pres.)'), FASTIDIU (Sp. **hastío** 'weariness'), RIDEO (Sp. **río** 'laugh (1st sg. pres.)'), etc., as on that of CORRIGIA (see also the derivation of FRICTU → **frito** 'fried' on pages 74–5 below).

These rules are therefore for the moment satisfactory in showing the results of a series of changes between the Latin and Medieval Spanish periods, in the way in which historical phonologists working within the standard generative theory did in the 1970s. But we see several major problems: one within the theory itself, as the expression of the rules is not 'correct' in a theory which requires maximal formal simplicity in capturing 'significant generalizations' (i.e., the weakening processes cannot be collapsed convincingly – certainly Walsh's ideas cannot be upheld) and which only deals in categorical rules, when changes are not always categorical; and another concerning metatheory: what purpose do historical rules serve? These rules tell us the results of certain changes, but give no clue to how the changes came about; in fact they actively destroy evidence concerning the implementation of change.[26] These are all important issues which we shall come back to; but for the moment let us go on discussing the palatalization rules and see how far the discussion takes us.

We have seen how the dental and velar segments palatalized; now let us take a look at the labial groups [–pj–] and [–bj–]. As we have already mentioned above, the former group underwent metathesis, thus being eliminated from consideration as regards palatalization.[27] Of the latter group we have the following examples (considering –B– and –V– together):

LABIU	→	labio	**lip**
PLUVIA	→	lluvia	**rain**
*RABIA (Class. RABIES)	→	rabia	**rage**
CAVEA	→	gavia	**ditch, cell**
RUBEU	→	rubio	**blond, fair**
RUBEU	→	royo	**reddish, unripe**
FOVEA	→	hoya	**pit, hole**
HABEAT	→	haya	**have (3rd sg. pres. subj.)**

Many comments on the development of this group in Spanish seem to have been influenced by the fact that palatalization indisputably took place in French: *RABIA → **rage** 'rage', CAVEA → **cage** 'cage', and even SAPIAT → **sache** 'know (3rd sg. pres. subj.)', and SIMIA → **singe** 'monkey'; Otero (1971:302-3) gives a rule for the palatalization of the labials in Spanish, while as well as the three final items listed above, he cites French **cage** and **sache**.[28] Eastlack (1976:107) not only includes the segment [b] in the palatalization process, but also finds he has to make a specific subrule (the first part of rule 16A) to deal with it. As well as this, he unaccountably separates the palatalization of [b] from what he labels as the '(sporadic) palatalization' of [β].

On the basis of the French result, and the more clear-cut development in Portuguese, where the glide metathesized (cf. Pt. **raiva, gaiva, ruivo, noivo** alongside Sp. **rabia, gavia, rubio** and **novio** 'fiancé, bridegroom' < *NOVIU), the double Spanish development seems to have puzzled etymologists and historical grammarians alike. Some dictionaries, for example, list **royo** as Aragonese or Leonese (see Moliner 1971), others as Aragonese and Castilian (García de Diego 1955). Menéndez Pidal (1958: 147) says of the forms in the first group above: 'parecen semicultas, siendo más populares las [formas] que reducen bi, vi > y'. However, there seems to be no justification for considering a form like **lluvia** as 'semilearned' (see Malkiel 1967:1232), though **labio** probably is a borrowing from Latin, having come to replace the earlier documented form **labro** (Corominas and Pascual 1980–, s.v. labio). As Badía Margarit (1972:151) has rightly pointed out, '¿Cómo puede ser tachada de culta la voz **lluvia**, si los cultismos flagrantes son **impluvio, pluvial, pluvioso**, si **lluvia** es una palabra que ha de ser de siempre, que es propia de los medios populares rústicos, y que, como designación genérica, carece de sinónimos en competencia?'

The correct interpretation here is undoubtedly that the reduction of the labial and glide is a change pushing itself into the Castilian area from other varieties of Spanish (probably northeastern, though there is also evidence of palatalization in Mozarabic; see Menéndez Pidal 1972:264-5 and Galmés de Fuentes 1983:107, 285), but never managing to force its way to completion. Corominas and Pascual (1980–, s.v. rubio) label it as a specifically Aragonese tendency, but add that examples can be found in placenames in La Rioja, Burgos and Soria, outside Aragonese territory. In this sense, compare the placenames **Segovia** and **Segoyuela** (this latter in the province of Salamanca), which obviously share a common root. We should have learnt decades ago from dialect geographers that as change spreads, it little respects neatly drawn dialect boundaries.

The paradigm of **haya** is probably not to be explained in the same way: it could be an analogical formation based on **vaya** 'go (3rd sg. pres. subj.)' (if this is directly derived from Latin *VADEAT: see Otero (1971:87) for the derivation of **vayáis**, but cf. Menéndez Pidal 1958:293), or it could be an idiosyncratic reduction due to frequency of use as an unaccented auxiliary (Corominas and Pascual 1980–, s.v. hoya). Lyons (1978) considers the further possibility that the loss of –B– was part of a more general phenomenon affecting verb forms only.

In any case, we cannot postulate for Castilian a categorical rule palatalizing the group [–bj–], at least not without subsequently characterizing a series of totally ad hoc exceptions to it. What is more, there are reasons of a natural phonetic type why we should not expect palatalization of labials in Castilian Spanish: Foley (1977:90–106) states that the preferential order for the assibilation (via palatalization) of consonants is k, t, p (and g, d, b) in a context where they precede (in order of preference) j, i, e, a (see Chen 1973a for similar findings). We have seen that in Spanish, the phonetic segments [k, g] undergo palatalization (and in some cases are elided) before [j, i, e]; [t, d] only undergo the same process before [j], the most active palatalizing segment. According to Foley (1977:99), the likelihood of the articulation of [t, d] being affected by the palatal glide is 1/3 (compared with 1/2 for [k, g]) while it is only 1/4 for [t, d] when followed by [i, e] or [p, b] followed by [j]. As we have seen quite clearly, [t, d] are unaffected by a following [+syllabic, –back] element, and so it is unlikely, in Foley's terms (and he seems to be right) that the labials should be palatalized.

We have up to now attempted to formulate a series of rules to account for weakening phenomena and palatalizations in the history of Spanish within the framework of orthodox generative theory, and found insurmountable problems in the use of categorical rules (and therefore the belief underlying it, that is, that phonological change is simply rule change) and in the requirements of formal simplicity which belie chronology and, more importantly for generativists, are misleadingly specious in their reflection of 'true' generalizations. Some of the rules we have formulated clearly refer to similar processes and should therefore, according to generative theory, be collapsed to bring out the generalizations involved. We have already seen how Walsh's (1979) weakening rule is merely an artifice which deprives the processes involved of any phonetic transparency. Now let us consider a further example.

Rule 11 (repeated below) represents the elision of [g] before [i]; rule 5 (also repeated below), the elision of [ð] and [ɣ] intervocalically, chronologically later:

11. $\begin{bmatrix} -\text{son} \\ +\text{vce} \\ +\text{hi} \end{bmatrix} \rightarrow \emptyset \;/\; [+\text{syll}] \underline{\hspace{1cm}} \begin{bmatrix} +\text{syll} \\ -\text{bk} \\ +\text{hi} \\ -\text{mid} \end{bmatrix}$

5. $\begin{bmatrix} -\text{son} \\ +\text{cont} \\ -\text{strd} \\ -\text{lab} \end{bmatrix} \rightarrow \emptyset \;/\; V \underline{\hspace{1cm}} V$

Evidently, the context of rule 11 is 'properly included' in that of rule 5; and, bearing in mind that the spirantization rule (1) intervenes, it looks very much as if rule 5 is merely an expansion and generalization of rule 11, and as such, should be collapsed with it, from an orthodox generative viewpoint. A sample derivation, however, will serve to show that the question is not so simple as that. Early Spanish (or in some cases Western Romance in general – for a full treatment see chapter 5 below) had a process of vowel syncope in which (among other things) unstressed non-low posttonics disappeared. Hence:

	MANICA	→	manga	**sleeve**
	SEMITA	→	senda	**path**
	PORTATICU	→	(O.Sp.) portadgo →	
			(M.Sp.) portazgo	**toll**
	LEPORE	→	liebre	**hare**
	BIFERA	→	(O.Sp.) bevra →	
			(M.Sp.) breva	**(type of) fig**
	NEBULA	→	niebla	**fog**
but	SABANA	→	sábana	**sheet**
	ORPHANU	→	huérfano	**orphan**

The syncope rule (or at least part of it), however formulated, must apply after rule 2 in order to permit the voicing of [k] to [g] and [t] to [d] in the first three examples (cf. IUNCU → **junco** 'reed', DENTE → **diente** 'tooth', where voicing was blocked by the preceding consonant). On the other hand, syncope must precede rule 5, as will be appreciated from a glance at the derivations of **comer** and **hiedra** below. Let us, then, consider the derivations of four forms using the rules as we have formulated them in this chapter (rules irrelevant in this discussion are omitted):

Rules	SARTAGINE	(H)EDERA	COMEDERE	MANICA
10	sartágʲine	——	——	——
11	sartáine	——	——	——
13	——	——	——	——
Vowel ad.	sartáene[29]	——	——	máneka
1	——	éðera	komeðére	——
2	——	——	——	mánega
Diphthzatn	——	jéðera	——	——
Syncope	——	jéðra	——	mánga
5	——	——	komeére	——
Vwl rules[30]	sartén	——	komér	——
Spanish	[sartén	jéðra	komér	máŋga]
Orthog.	**sartén**	**hiedra**	**comer**	**manga**
Gloss	'frying pan'	'ivy'	'to eat'	'sleeve'

This derivation produces, apart from some minor phonetic details, the correct reflexes in Spanish. As we have said, we cannot collapse rule 5 with rule 11 because it must follow the syncope rule; but on the other hand, we cannot suppress rule 11 and hope that rule 5 (the more general of the two) will stand in for it; the result would be the following:

Rules	SARTAGINE	(H)EDERA	COMEDERE	MANICA
10	sartágʲine	——	——	——
Palatalztn	sartájine	——	——	——
Vowel ad.	sartájene	——	——	máneka
1	——	éðera	komeðére	——
2	——	——	——	mánega
Diphthzatn	——	jéðera	——	——
Syncope	sartájne	jéðra	——	mánga
5	——	——	komeére	——
Vwl rules	——	——	komér	——

Palatalization thus intervenes and would produce a form ***sarta[ǰ/ž]ne** (with an affricate or a fricative) in the same way that the voiceless velar developed in DURACINU → **durazno** '(type of) peach', RICINU → **rezno** 'bott fly' (Menéndez Pidal

1958:160), LUPICINU → **lobezno** 'wolf cub', REBUCINARE → **rebuznar** 'to bray'.[31]

This is in a sense what Foley (for example, 1977, chapter 5) refers to as interrupted rule schemata. It is clear that in the history of Spanish the Latin segments [g] and [d] have been weakened and often elided in intervocalic position. This does not mean, however, that we can formulate a rule with just that effect within the generative framework: we have encountered problems reflecting the variability of the result, and the phonetic explicability of the rule (indeed, its correct functioning) depends crucially on the schema being 'interrupted' in Foley's terminology (or on 'interdigitation' in Newton's; see Newton 1971, 1972) by a series of processes including palatalization and syncope. The collapsing of diachronic rules following criteria of simplicity and generality in their formalized SDs will lead not only to loss of naturalness in the expression of the rules as regards their transparency, but in fact in many cases simply will not produce the correct results.

Classical generative phonology is thus unable to express 'weakening' as a phenomenon: individual processes may be definable as traditional rules, but these rules have little intrinsic association with each other, and when the little association they have is exploited and they are collapsed, we are left with an (albeit ingenious) schema which may in a mechanical fashion produce the correct output (or indeed, may not), but destroys all the transparency and explicability of a basically clear phonetic change. What is more, the requirement that formally similar rules be collapsed leaves no possibility in a diachronic grammar of allowing other processes to interweave with individual parts of a schema (or even subrules), a possibility whose existence must be recognized.

It seems, then, that such diachronic changes are better accounted for by reference to the parameter(s) of a strength hierarchy. Strength hierarchies, however, do not have an absolute value across the board in any language: the phonological strength of a segment depends not only on its intrinsic properties, but also on its relationship with other, surrounding segments (see comments on different types of hierarchies, including an environmental one, in Escure 1977). Syllable, word and morpheme all seem to be relevant units in the appreciation of what processes affect what segments and to what extent.

Thus we have seen how the first Spanish consonant shift voiced intervocalic (word-internal) voiceless stops: their intervocalic position presupposes that they are syllable-initial, but we cannot generalize the context to 'syllable-initial', for word-initial voiceless stops underwent no change:

PILU	→	pelo	**hair**
PANE	→	pan	**bread**
TERRA	→	tierra	**land**
TENERU	→	tierno	**tender**
CAMPU	→	campo	**field**
COGNATU	→	cuñado	**brother-in-law**

despite the fact that these consonants would often have been intervocalic within the phrase: **la tierra** 'the land', **mi cuñado** 'my brother-in-law', **tiene pelo** 'it has hair'.[32] In fact, to describe the environment of the rule as intervocalic is trivial and to a certain extent inaccurate. Consider the following examples, where the consonants in question were followed by one of the liquids in Latin:

CAPRA	→	cabra	**goat**
APRICARE	→	abrigar	**to shelter**
PATRE	→	padre	**father**
VITREU	→	vidrio	**glass**
MACRU	→	magro	**lean (adj.)**
SOCRA	→	suegra	**mother-in-law**
AFRICU	→	ábrego	**south-west wind**
DUPLARE	→	doblar	**to double, fold**

In these examples, we see reflexes of both the first and second consonant shifts: Modern Spanish has [káβra], [páðre], [máɣro], etc., hence the changes involved are:

$$p \rightarrow b \rightarrow \beta$$
$$t \rightarrow d \rightarrow ð$$
$$k \rightarrow g \rightarrow ɣ$$

But even if we take the liquids to be [+vocalic], the contexts of rules 1 to 5 are still unsatisfactory, since the change does not occur when the order of the elements is reversed:

TURPE	→	torpe	**clumsy**
FORTE	→	fuerte	**strong**
PORTA	→	puerta	**door**
PORCU	→	puerco	**pig**
ARCU	→	arco	**arch**
PERFIDIA	→	porfía	**obstinacy**
VULPECULA	→	vulpeja	**vixen**
SULCU	→	sulco/surco	**furrow**

The whole point is, of course, that the group obstruent plus liquid was a permissible syllable-initial cluster in Latin, and has remained so in Spanish, and the stops underwent lenition in syllable-initial, but not word-initial, position after a vowel. Thus the correct context could only be expressed in terms of syllable structure:

15. V$___
where there is no # between V and $.[33]

Naturally, the same facts apply to all of the stops and fricatives; thus in initial position none of the voiced stops or fricatives undergo lenition either:[34]

BONU	→	bueno	**good**
BASIU	→	beso	**kiss**
DARE	→	dar	**to give**
DICERE	→	decir	**to say**
GUTTA	→	gota	**drop**
GAUDIU	→	gozo	**pleasure**
FOCU	→	fuego	**fire**
FACERE	→	(O.Sp.) fazer	**to do, make**
SECARE	→	segar	**to reap**
SICCU	→	seco	**dry**

Moreover, in the context V$___r, we find further traces of the consonant shifts, not normally described as such, but nevertheless clearly a part of the same process:

*COLOBRA	→	cule[β]ra	**snake**		
CATHEDRA	→	cade[ð]ra[35]	→	cadeira	→
				cadera	**hip**
INTEGRU	→	*ente[ɣ]ro	→	enteiro	→
				entero	**whole**
PIGRITIA	→	*pe[ɣ]reza	→	*peireza	→
				pereza	**laziness**

(The forms **cadeira** and **enteiro** are still found in Portuguese and Galician: the reduction of [-ej-] to [-e-] is a relatively late rule in Castilian; see Otero (1971:312, rule P49) and Menéndez Pidal (1958:178).)

With few examples, it is dangerous to draw firm conclusions, but it does seem clear that we have further corroboration of the claim that labials in Spanish are stronger than dentals and velars: note in the above examples that [ɣ] and [ð] are weakened to a glide and finally disappear, while [β] remains.[36]

Clearly, there is a crucial distinction to be made between word-internal syllable-initial position and absolute initial position, and we would suggest that this too can be expressed as a strength relationship. Lenition took place in the internal position, but not in absolute initial position. If Foley (1977:107) is correct when he claims that, according to the inertial development principle, weakening processes take place 'first and most extensively and preferentially in weak environments', this means that internal syllable-initial is a weaker position than absolute initial, since lenition, as we have seen, must be considered a weakening process.

The abandonment of categorical generative rules in the description of historical developments in favour of strength hierarchies and the correct expression of the phonetic and phonological behaviour of the elements involved therefore provides us with a much clearer understanding of the relationships between segments and their environment and the way sound changes advance spacially and temporally, even though this understanding may not have predictive power. In subsequent chapters, we shall go on to see how the phonetic relationship between segments shows how change spreads and some ways in which it is implemented. It will also enable us to make a distinction between those changes which are in some sense 'complete': that is, those which leave behind no residue in a given dialect (such as the palatalization we have discussed in this chapter), and which are probably implemented by a series of shifts in articulation, generally imperceptible to the speaker; and those which spread from segment to segment, or even lexeme to lexeme, typically leave behind lexical residue, and are fulfilled only after periods of variation, essentially sociolinguistic, within the community.

Notes

1. See, among others, Chen (1974a); Cravens (1984); Escure (1977); Foley (1970, 1971, 1972, 1975, 1977); Goyvaerts (1975:195–200); Hyman (1975:166–7); Lozano (1979); Posner (1974); Walsh (1979). Not all of these authors tackle the problem of this process from a generative viewpoint, of course: indeed, it was precisely the difficulties involved in handling such processes generatively that prompted many to choose this example. It is, however, justified to say that interest in these phenomena (once favourite data for structuralist analyses) was rekindled by the two sides of the generativist controversy.
2. We are ignoring changes in the vowel system, which lie outside the scope of this study; see note 23. The vast majority of Spanish nouns

and adjectives (including non-popular derivations) are reflexes of the Latin form in the accusative case. The final −M, typical of this inflexion (and of certain verb forms) is not indicated in the forms cited in this study normally, since its loss was so general and early in the pronunciation of Latin that it had no effect whatsoever upon any Romance development. The only exception is the −M of certain monosyllables, which we shall deal with elsewhere (see chapter 3, note 9). Cf. the note on 'Vulgar Latin' in the Introduction. For further examples and a discussion on theoretical approaches to these changes, see Pensado Ruiz (1984:21–223).
3. The glosses given are an indication of the meaning of the Modern Spanish form, unless otherwise stated.
4. There is considerable evidence that weakening is still an ongoing change in some varieties of Spanish today; see for example Lapesa (1981:506–7).
5. The notable exception is the speech of the Pyrenean valleys of Aragón and Béarn; see Jungemann (1955:227–43) and Elcock (1960:50–1). Some varieties of Old Spanish (possibly including Mozarabic) were much later in voicing the intervocalic stops than others; see Galmés de Fuentes (1983:91–100, 175–8, 201–2, 236–9) and Pensado Ruiz (1984:193–202). As we should expect, the picture in the Italian Peninsula is a complex one. For the possibility of voicing there as a process spread by lexical diffusion, see Wanner and Cravens (1980).
6. There are a few cases where it is lost: SABUCU → **saúco** 'elder tree', presumably because of the following non-low back vowel; cf. RIVU → **río** 'river', VACIVU → **vacío** 'empty'; in the imperfect endings –EBA– and –IBA–, and the perfect paradigm in −AVI, etc. These losses were probably very early; cp. pages 24–6 and see Elcock (1960:133–6). Hartman's (1974:149–50) rule is elegant in formulation but unconvincing because of the number of exceptions it leaves unexplained.
7. This loss cannot be attributed to Slavic (i.e., non-Romance) influence, since it is precisely in later Slavic borrowings that –b– is maintained: Sl. **ljubiti** → Rm. **iubi** 'to love' (see Canfield and Davis 1975:73–4).
8. In the same line, Cohen's (1971:318) comment that 'Latin g . . . generally remains in Portuguese' is simply inaccurate. It is true that Pt. **legume** and **negar** correspond to Sp. **legumbre** and **negar**, but then we also find Pt. **ruído, lê, rainha** parallel with Sp. **ruido, lee, reina**. For the unexpected preservation of Latin –G– in Sp. **mugir** (< MUGIRE) 'to low, moo' and **rugir** (< RUGIRE) 'to roar', see Malkiel (1976:29, 34; 1986, especially pages 167–8).
9. We can do little more than present a brief summary here: for a masterly treatment of this question, specifically with regard to paradigmatic resistance to loss, see Malkiel (1960a).
10. It is true that these medieval sources may have origins outside the Castilian-speaking area – specifically in León, where loss of –D– was

more widespread; but this merely confirms the view of the loss as spreading from the west, showing how Castilian was caught in the midst of opposing tendencies of loss and preservation.

11. This loss of intervocalic [-ð-] (< Latin -D-) should be distinguished from the later (and still ongoing) loss of 'secondary' [-ð-] (i.e., derived from Latin -T-), lost on a major scale in second person plural verb forms such as AMATIS → **amades** → **amáis** 'love (2nd pl. pres.)' from the fourteenth century on, and in Modern Spanish variably lost in past participles (especially of the first conjugation): AMATU → **amado** → [amáo], [amáw] (see Lapesa 1981:389, 467; Navarro Tomás 1977:101–2) and increasingly in other forms, such as **prado** [práo], [práw], etc., though such pronunciations are still occasionally stigmatized in the formal standard. This undoubtedly reflects a further step in the chain shift, and is thus probably to be associated with the loss of secondary [-ɣ-] (as in some pronunciations of **agua** (< AQUA) [áɣwa], [áwa]). See Whitley (1978, especially page 388).

12. Note that since the structural description of rule 3 is unspecified for voice, it would also, correctly, include any cases of voiced geminates; see pages 13–14.

13. For discussion of weakening as a process, see for example Lass (1984:177–81), Hock (1986:80–7), and Bauer (1988).

14. The fact that Walsh uses different features in some cases, for example [tense] rather than [voice], does not affect the discussion in any way. For the impossibility of collapsing intervocalic stop deletion into one rule in French, see Newton (1972).

15. For a more recent view of 'naturalness', see Bailey (1982).

16. In fact, voicing was more extensive in the case of [s] than in that of the stops, since [s] voiced after a glide: CAUSA → **cosa** [kóza] in Old Spanish, while the stops sometimes did not: CAUTU → **coto**, PAUCU → **poco** (see below, pages 62–3). The rules would need slight modification on this point. See Hartman (1974:151).

17. Evidence of this kind is patchy and often unreliable, but the general outline agrees with findings in other languages. See Foley (1977:90–106, particularly 93–4). Palatalization itself is perhaps difficult to view intuitively as a weakening process, though it could be considered as such if affricates (as well as fricatives) could be shown to be weaker than stops, as Lass (1984:178) and others have suggested they in fact are. On the other hand, palatalization occurred in Romance in contexts – word-initial, for instance – not normally associated with weakening processes; see below, page 37.

18. Here again, for clarity of exposition, we are following the tradition of the manuals in giving what appears to be a 'regular' result. The real situation is by no means so straightforward: intervocalic -DI- had reflexes in Medieval Spanish with [t^s] (**baço** 'spleen' < BADIU) and perhaps with a palatal fricative (**rebujo** 'tangle, wrapping' < ?REPUDIU) as well as [j]. See Malkiel (1973:239–42) and Pensado Ruiz (1984:466–70).

19. For example, CASEU → **queso** 'cheese', BASIU → **beso** 'kiss', suggesting metathesis of the palatal glide and the [s], rather than a palatalization of [sj]; see pages 75–7 for derivations.
20. The formulation of this rule is made accepting the convention that the second subrule, in which the material in angled brackets is eliminated, applies exclusively to those segments which are not [+coronal]. For details, see Sommerstein (1977:140).
21. We are using the vowel features proposed in Wang (1968) rather than Chomsky and Halle (1968). The vocalic changes which took place in Latin (see note 23) seem more amenable to analysis within a four-height system than a three-height one.
22. Note that the rule involves only assimilation, and not total coalescence, as Alarcos Llorach (1971:234) points out quite clearly. Otero (1971:301–2) links this phenomenon with a consonantal gemination in the vicinity of the palatal glide, but it seems both unnecessary and unwise to postulate such a wide application of this unstable rule, whose environment has never been made completely explicit (see also Hartman 1974:143, rule 31). Eastlack (1976) makes no mention of a possible gemination, however brought about. The idea that the result was a geminate is supported by the reflexes of these forms in Italian: PODIU → **poggio** 'hillock', HODIE → **oggi** 'today', CORRIGIA → **correggia** 'strap', all with a geminate affricate arising from subsequent affrication of the output of rule 12. Cf. also Tekavčić (1972:151): 'Il resultato della palatalizzazione davanti a /y/ [i.e., the palatal glide −RHN] è, in posizione intervocalica, sempre lungo; quello della palatalizzazione davanti a /e/, /i/ è anche breve.'
23. The rules applying to vowels in all these developments will not be discussed here in any detail, since they fall outside the limits of this study. Briefly, the quantitative distinction apparent in Latin vowels was lost, and a qualitative one appeared, i.e., [±long] → [±tense], except for [aː] and [a], where all distinction was lost. Subsequently, in all the Western Romance area, short I and U lowered and were confused with close [e] and [o] respectively. The stressed vowel of PODIU was raised by the following palatal glide to a close [ó], and did not therefore produce the diphthong [wé]; see Menéndez Pidal (1958:63).
24. The relative chronology of the shift in accent from FACERE to [fad'ér(e)] is not important here within the derivation.
25. This is similar to Harris's (1969:83) synchronic rule. But see Harris (1980) for a more detailed analysis of the problems this rule creates in a synchronic analysis, and suggestions for alterations to it.
26. Vincent (1978) also points out the need to distinguish 'process' from 'result'.
27. The few cases of [−pj−] in Modern Spanish are rather suspect. The form **apio** < APIU 'celery', judging from the lateness of its first documentation (1423, according to Corominas and Pascual 1980–) might not be completely autochthonous, though the Pt. **aipo** shows

the expected metathesis. Corominas and Pascual (1980–, s.v. pobre) suggest there may have been a gemination of the –P–.
28. The pernicious results of using data in this 'universal' manner, and of supposing French to be in some way 'more advanced', or marking a path which other Romance languages will follow, are criticized by Wright (1983).
29. Here the diphthong may have been maintained as [áj] for dissimilatory purposes. Other stages in the development of forms in –AGINE have been proposed, such as syncope of the short vowel before the loss of –G– (see the discussion in Pensado Ruiz 1984:391–410, 472), but the development outlined here seems the most satisfactory (Corominas and Pascual 1980–, s.v. andén), bearing in mind the different development of the group –GN– (see below, pages 78–81).
30. Including apocope (see below, pages 45–6) and the coalescence of certain vowels.
31. In Old Spanish, the –g– of such forms as **rugir, gente, vigilar**, represented an affricate or a fricative; see Macpherson (1975:128).
32. There are in fact a few forms in which the voiceless initial consonant has voiced: **gato** 'cat' < CATTU. Such sporadic examples are comprehensible within the terms expressed here.
33. We are using the symbol $ for syllable-division and # for word-division.
34. This is not strictly accurate, since initial b–, d–, g– are normally spirantized in Modern Spanish when preceded by a vowel in allegro speech (see Harris 1969:38); thus **hombre bueno** [ómbre βwéno] 'good man', **quiero dárselo** [kjéro ðárselo] 'I want to give it to him', **una gota** [úna ɣóta] 'a drop', etc. This is an important phenomenon to be taken into account with regard to the question of whether the underlying segments in a synchronic grammar should be /b d g/ or /β ð ɣ/. See above, page 16.
35. This is presumably represented by **kadedras** (Menéndez Pidal 1972:245).
36. Note also LIBERARE → **librar** 'to free' and ROBORE → (O.Sp.) **robre** → (M.Sp.) **roble** 'oak', though these examples may not be considered as valid as those above, since the [–br–] cluster arose later, as a result of syncope, thus making their chronology slightly, though possibly trivially, different. See chapter 5.

Chapter three

Weakening in Absolute Final Position

In the last chapter we dealt at length with the question of weakening processes affecting consonants in intervocalic position, particularly with reference to stops; though we also saw how these processes affected fricatives and affricates too. It became clear how the stops were related to each other as regards their phonological 'strength' (that is, their comparative resistance to weakening), and we adduced further evidence in support of the claim that in Spanish, decreasing strength in stops is manifested by the scale: labial, dental, velar, in that order.

On the other hand, another of the processes we mentioned, palatalization, was by no means limited in the same way as intervocalic lenition. We saw how it occurred in the same positions as lenition; compare, however, the result in absolute initial position:

CERA	→	cera (O.Sp. [tˢéra], M.Sp. [θéra])	**wax**
CIPPU	→	cepo (O.Sp. [tˢépo], M.Sp. [θépo])	**snare**
GERMANU	→	hermano (O.Sp. *[jermáno],[1] M.Sp. [ermáno])	**brother**
GINGIVA	→	encía (O.Sp. *[jendᶻía],[1] M.Sp. [enθía])	**gum**

Here, it is evident that palatalization took place quite generally and hence, unfortunately, tells us very little about positional strength or the spread of the change. It is one of those changes which, as we mentioned at the end of chapter 2, are 'complete', in that they have generalized to all environments, and have left behind no residue.

In the present chapter, therefore, we shall take a look at the development, not of a particular group of consonants undergoing a specific change, but the way in which all consonants have behaved in a particular position; here, absolute (word–)final position, which is clearly the most restricted environment for consonants in Spanish.

In principle, Latin permitted a number of consonants, and even consonant clusters, in word-final position:

-t   CAPUT, AMAT, AUT
-k   HOC, SIC, DIC, NEC
-b   AB, SUB
-d   ALIQUOD, APUD, AD, SED, QUID
-s   PEDES, IOVIS, FACIS, TEMPUS, MINUS
-m   DOMINUM, IAM, CUM, QUAM
-n   CULMEN, INGUEN
-l   SOL, MEL, FEL
-r   PUER, SUPER, SEMPER, INTER

-ns MENS, MONS, DENS
-nt SUNT, ROGANT
-ks REX, SEX, IUDEX
-st EST, POST
-nk HINC, ILLINC

Of these, it is difficult to know how many were actually pronounced in Latin by the end of the Empire: evidently, –M was not (except perhaps in monosyllables; see note 9, and Sturtevant 1940:151–3; Kent 1945:58; Väänänen 1963:69; and Hartman 1974:135–6); and the voiced stop –D was certainly unstable, as inscriptional forms like APUT, QUIT, SET (all for forms with final –D) reveal even from Republican times (Menéndez Pidal 1958:166); the same may be said of –B, whose appearance was extremely limited. We may assume final –T was generally lost, except where it served as a marker of the third person singular verb form, in which case it survived as a dental fricative even in the earliest French texts (see Vidos 1977:371–2; Ewert 1966:74–5. For its survival in Spanish, see pages 40–1 below). Final –C, as the only remaining stop, presumably did not long survive in Latin speech either.

Of the rest, –S, –L, and –R were certainly pronounced in the Western Empire (though –R later underwent metathesis in Spanish, as we shall see), and probably –N was too, though nouns of the type given in the examples came into Spanish via an analogical accusative form CULMINE, *INGUINE.

As far as the final clusters are concerned, we have in fact omitted some of those actually occurring, since they are irrelevant to the discussion: clusters like –RS (SORS), –PS

(INOPS), appear only in morphological combinations (such as the nominative singular, as cited here) which have not survived in Spanish; and orthographic –BS (URBS, PLEBS), as the Latin grammarians point out, was merely a representation of [–ps] (see Niedermann 1953:129; Kent 1945:51; Sturtevant 1940:161). Of those listed above, we know that –NS (in internal, as well as final position; see Väänänen 1963:66–7; Kent 1945:58–9; Sturtevant 1940:153–4) was reduced at an early period to –S with lengthening of the preceding vowel; the nasal-plus-stop combinations lost their second element relatively early – probably around the same time that single –C and –T were lost: examples of –NT reduced to –N appear in third-century inscriptions (Menéndez Pidal 1958:281). The same loss of the stop element applies to –ST, but the history of –X ([–ks]) is somewhat different. This cluster survived a sufficiently long time for the [k] to be weakened to [j]; thus SEX → **seis** 'six' in the same way as AXE *[ájse] → *[éjse] → (O.Sp.) **exe** [éše] → (M.Sp.) **eje** 'axle, axis'.

In summary, in the development of the Spanish forms from Latin, all final stops, whether single or forming part of a cluster, were eventually lost; thus:

CAPUT	→	cabo	**end, head**
AMAT	→	ama	**loves (3rd sg. pres.)**
AUT	→	o	**or**
SIC	→	sí	**yes**
DIC	→	di	**say, speak (sg. imp.)**
NEC	→	ni	**neither, nor**
ALIQUOD	→	algo	**something**
SUNT	→	son	**are (3rd pl. pres.)**
ROGANT	→	ruegan	**ask (3rd pl. pres.)**
EST	→	es	**is (3rd sg. pres.)**
POST	→	pues	**well, then**

Final –S (with important morphological functions, such as pluralization of adjectives and nouns, as well as marking the second person of verbs) remained:

PEDES	→	pies	**feet**
IOVIS	→	jueves	**Thursday**
FACIS	→	(O.Sp.) fazes → (M.Sp.) haces **do, make (2nd sg. pres.)**	

thus also serving to 'protect' the preceding stop in the case of SEX mentioned above. As we have already said, the final –N in the examples given was not in fact final in Hispanic Latin, since these neuter nouns were given analogical accusative forms such as *INGUINE, as their Spanish reflexes (**ingle** 'groin') show. The –N made final after the loss of –T in third person plural verb forms survives, however, as did the –N of **non** < NON 'no' (alongside **no**) in Medieval Spanish.

As regards the liquids, the Modern Spanish final –r, which appears on the infinitive of every verb as well as on other forms, is largely the result of a late [–e]-apocope rule (see pages 45–6); original Latin –R was metathesized out of final position:

INTER	→	entre	**between**
SEMPER	→	siempre	**always**
SUPER	→	sobre	**on (top of)**

Final –L, on the other hand, seems to have been maintained in

MEL	→	miel	**honey**
FEL	→	hiel	**gall, bile**
SAL(E)	→	sal	**salt**

but, bearing in mind that these were originally neuter nouns in Latin,[2] it would not be surprising to discover that they also developed analogical accusative forms *MELE, *FELE, just like *INGUINE above. In fact, evidence from other Romance languages suggests this was precisely what happened: Italian maintains a final vowel (**miele, fiele**), as does Rumanian (**miere, fiere**), and it was ancestral in the French, Occitan, and Catalan forms (Fr. **miel, fiel**; Oc., Ct. **mel, fel**), where the accented vowel developed as it normally did in a free syllable, thus clearly pointing to an etymon with a final vowel. This final –e would quite regularly have been lost in Spanish by the apocope rule mentioned above.

Whether or not this was actually the case, the liquids have always shown themselves to be more resistant to erosion than other consonantal segments: not only were they left in final position by the operation of the apocope rule, but both ancestral forms (**por** 'for, by') and borrowings from Arabic (**azul** 'blue', **azúcar** 'sugar') show the final liquid maintained.[3] On the other hand, in word-final position, Old Spanish admitted no stops, only one fricative ([s]), and one nasal ([n]). It is difficult to appreciate the significance of the scribal practice of marking the third person singular present of verbs with a final consonant (usually –t, but sometimes –d or even –z) until a relatively late period (Menéndez Pidal 1958:279–80, 1972:351–3; Lapesa 1981: 208–9); Menéndez Pidal is undoubtedly right in suggesting that a final consonant was maintained in pronunciation after the Latin period, but it seems highly unlikely that the examples found in texts from as late as the twelfth century reflect anything other than scribal habit. Tenth-century manuscripts quoted by Menéndez Pidal himself (1972:351–3) indicate considerable fluctuation, with a large number of forms showing complete loss of the consonant.

The fact that the consonant was preserved later than we should expect is probably due to its importance as a morphological marker.[4] The same may apply to the preservation of final [-s] in Western Romance (though in French it has since been lost); compare the loss of [-s] in word-final position in Italian and Rumanian, and the consequent differences in morphological patterning: while nouns and adjectives in Western Romance are generally reflexes of the Latin accusative case in both singular and plural, Italian and Rumanian have reflexes of the Latin accusative singular but nominative plural.

The appearance of a final consonant in early Old Spanish verb forms, then, should not prevent us from making the generalization that Latin final stops were lost across the board, thus suggesting that they constitute the least resistant segments in word-final position in the history of Spanish. (We will later find evidence to separate the voiced from the voiceless stops on the strength hierarchy. See pages 47–8 below.)

For the moment, we shall leave the question of the fricatives open, since Latin only had one in final position ([s]), which, for whichever of the reasons mentioned above, has survived, at least in the dialect of Spanish under consideration here (standard Castilian). The relative strength of the fricatives in this position is therefore not clear, and the weakening or loss of final [-s] is an extremely complex question to which we are unable to do justice within the framework of this study, bearing in mind the enormous amount of research that has taken place over the last few years regarding the pronunciation of [-s], particularly in Spanish America.[5]

In Peninsular Spanish, final [-s] is aspirated or lost in extensive areas of Andalusia, Murcia, Castile-La Mancha, and Extremadura (Lapesa 1981:502–3), as well as in the area of Madrid, where in recent years the aspiration or loss of [-s] has become more and more noticeable, especially in the speech of the lower socio-economic groups, even though it is still usually stigmatized in the formal standard. For all these reasons, then, in the context of this study we shall limit ourselves to the observation that in some varieties of Spanish, there is a clear weakening process involving [-s], whether it is reduced to [-h], assimilated to the initial consonant of the following word, or completely lost.

The question of word-final nasals, on the other hand, is relatively clear. We should expect a close parallelism between the relationships that obtain among the stops and those that obtain among the nasals. In the preceding chapter we found considerable evidence in support of the claim that the strongest stops in Spanish (from the point of view of their resistance to intervocalic weakening) were the labials, followed by the dentals and the velars, in order of increasing weakness. The same typology may be applied to the nasals, as in Foley (1977:59).

Now, in the discussion on weakening processes in intervocalic position, we pointed out the importance of taking into account environmental factors in the interpretation of strength parameters, and the important role played by the syllable in phonological developments. The segments affected by intervocalic lenition were, we saw, in syllable-initial position within the word: a relatively strong environment, second only to word-initial position. At this point, we must once more insist on the importance of the position a segment has within the syllable in order to understand its development and correctly interpret the phonetic parameters on which it appears.[6] In the present case, we are discussing the nasals in word-final position, which is the weakest possible position. Let us consider for a moment exactly what weakening processes involve: in most cases they are assimilation phenomena effected by surrounding segments which are stronger (either inherently or because of their position in the syllable) than the segment weakened. Thus intervocalic weakening of syllable-initial consonants involved their taking on the values for various features which characterized the surrounding vowels: voiceless stops became [+voice], voiced stops [+continuant], and so on. In a strong position such as syllable-initial, it is the (inherently) weakest consonants that offer least resistance to loss, as we clearly saw. Strong consonants have more chances of survival, or at least of resisting weakening processes, in a strong environment.

On the other hand, it is the weakest consonants that are best adapted to weak environments such as word-final position, and which will resist change much better than stronger elements.[7] This seems a more satisfactory solution than claiming, as Lass (1971) does, that word boundaries should be classed as voiceless obstruents and that processes observable in final consonants reflect assimilations to the boundary features: it is difficult to see how such a claim could be convincingly imposed on the Spanish data.[8]

Therefore, as the (inherently) strongest of the nasals, it is the labial that is first to disappear in the development of Latin into Spanish, as we have already noted (see page 38 above).[9] Latin had no velar nasal in word-final position, though this sound probably appeared in syllable-final position when followed by another velar, and when represented orthographically as –G– followed by –N– (see page 71 below). Spanish to a certain extent shares this distributional pattern in that the velar nasal only occurs in syllable-final position (including, in most styles of speech, word-final position) before another velar segment. In other words, in an autonomous phonological analysis of Spanish it only occurs as an allophonic variant of /n/ whose distribution is governed by environmental factors.

We have in fact seen that [n] is the only surviving word-final nasal in Modern Castilian; and this observation is upheld by the evidence of borrowings. Recent borrowings into Spanish which end in [–m] in their original form, have this nasal adapted to [–n] according to the surface structure condition we have described, even if the orthography maintains the original spelling:

álbum [álβun]   **album**
ultimátum [ultimátun] **ultimatum**

(see Navarro Tomás 1977:88).

What is even more interesting, however, is the fact that in some areas (Asturias, for example), speakers generally pronounce final –n as a velar; that is, the ultimate weakening of the nasal segment before its loss.[10] In other regional varieties of Spanish the consonant is in fact completely lost, leaving a nasal resonance on the preceding vowel (for example, in parts of Andalusia: see Navarro Tomás (1977:39 and note 1). For discussion of American varieties of Spanish, see for example Poplack (1980b) and Terrell (1982)). The pronunciation of both a velarized nasal and a nasalized vowel rather than a following consonantal segment are further weakenings of the word-final nasal not found in standard Castilian usage, but heard in many parts of Spain.

Our hypothesis regarding the strength of nasals in word-final position would therefore seem to be confirmed: the weakening process moves in the direction labial → dental → velar (cf. the findings of Chen (1974b) and Chen and Wang (1975); on the other hand, however, see the proposal of Guitart (1982:67), who suggests that the velar nasal is not a link in the original weakening chain, but a reformation of the nasalized vowel followed by a glottal stop). The labial has been eliminated historically and is still not admitted in the modern language; the dental is ancestral and in fact the only nasal consonant admitted in word-final position (other than the assimilation process in allegretto speech referred to above[11]) in standard Castilian; while the velar is heard in regional pronunciations, where it has taken over as the only nasal consonant admitted in this position; and in the most advanced cases, it has been effaced, leaving only the trace of nasalization on the preceding vowel.

We have already dealt in part with the question of fricatives in word-final position. As we have shown above (pages 38, 39), the only Latin fricative to appear in this position was [–s], which has been maintained in Modern Spanish. Bearing in mind, however, that on the one hand, all final stops were lost, and on the other, weakening processes have eroded final nasals, and that on the parameter of relative resonance fricatives fall between these two groups, we should expect some signs of weakening to have affected Spanish [–s], despite its strong association with clearly defined morphological categories.

This is, indeed, what we do find, as we reported above (pages 41–2). What is more, aspiration and loss of [–s] is a process which is spreading more and more in contemporary Spanish, and always taking into account the fallibility of such predictions, both social and linguistic factors seem to indicate that, *ceteris paribus*, the weakening of final [–s] is destined to increase its hold on more varieties of Castilian speech in the future.[12]

Thus the standard strength hierarchy, schematized as:

stops   fricatives   nasals   liquids
                              (weaker)
———————————————→

(cf. Hooper 1976:206; Foley 1977:145; and, for a more complex arrangement, Lass 1984:177–83) is borne out by the behaviour of final consonants in the history of Spanish. The liquids have been mentioned only briefly, because as we should expect, they are maintained and show no signs of weakening pressures.[13]

There are, of course, notable differences in behaviour among the individual segments which go to make up the groups that appear on the hierarchy above. We have already commented on this aspect of the nasal segments, but we should now turn to the question in a little more detail.

The consonants we have discussed so far are not the only ones to appear in word-final position in Modern Castilian. The contemporary language in fact admits in native forms the following consonants in absolute final position:

s	**pies** 'feet',	**eres**	'are (2nd sg. pres.)',	**mes**	'month'
θ	(represented by z)	**cruz**	'cross',	**pez**	'fish'
ð	(represented by d)	**ciudad**	'city',	**libertad**	'freedom'
x	(represented by j)	**reloj**	'clock',	**boj**	'box(wood)'
n	**pan** 'bread',	**cantan**	'sing (3rd pl.pres.)'		
l	**sal** 'salt',	**azul**	'blue',	**cruel**	'cruel'
r	**comer** 'to eat',	**mar**	'sea'[14]		

(see Alarcos Llorach 1951:37, 1971:187–8).

It would, in fact, be more accurate to say that certain styles of speech admit these consonants: specifically, there are some segments on this list (such as [ð]) which would appear exclusively in largo style, and perhaps in some cases in andante (see Harris (1969:7) for definitions). We shall return to this later.

One of the reasons for the appearance of more word-final consonantal segments in Spanish than those it inherited from Latin is the rule of [–e] apocope we have already mentioned in connection with various phenomena.[15] This rule was in effect for many centuries, though its period of greatest application was the end of the twelfth, and the thirteenth centuries (Menéndez Pidal 1958:173, 1972:186–90; Otero 1971:313). With this last phrase, of course, go certain theoretical presuppositions: 'period of greatest application' indicates that the rule passed through temporal stages of being more or less operative, that is to say that it was variable. There is empirical evidence for this: Menéndez Pidal (1972:186) reports a sporadic example of apocope from the sixth century, although Corominas and Pascual (1980–, s.v. hacia) maintain that 'está fuera de dudas que todas las E finales del latín se conservaban todavía en el S. X', and even though this isolated occurrence may well have a different explanation, it is clear from Menéndez Pidal's research into the language of historical documents that the loss of final [–e] became less sporadic and more frequent and predictable until the twelfth century, when it took place in virtually every possible case (for impossible contexts and the reason why they were impossible, see Hooper (1976:107)). Documented forms of apocope when the effect of the rule was at its peak include (with their Latin etymons):[16]

(a) MENSE → mes **month**
MESSE → mies **grain**
MARE → mar **sea**
SARTAGINE → sartén **frying pan**
MERCEDE → merced **favour**
AETATE → edad **age**

		RETE	→	red	net
		CRUDELE	→	cruel	cruel
		PISCE	→	pez	fish
		CRUCE	→	cruz	cross
(b)	i	PONTE	→	puent	bridge
		COMITE	→	cuen(d)	count, earl
		PARTE	→	part	part
		FORTE	→	fuert	strong
		HOSTE	→	huest	host, army
				humilt	humble

(< **humilde**, based on **humildad** < HUMILITATE, 'humility')

(b)	ii	NOCTE	→	noch	night
		LACTE	→	lech	milk
		PRINCIPE	→	princep	prince
		NOVE	→	nuef	nine
		SEPTE	→	siet	seven
		HABUI	→	(ove →) of	had (1st sg. pret.)

(c)		DICIT	→	diz	says (3rd sg. pres.)
		DIXI	→	dix	said (1st sg. pret.)
		EXIT	→	ex	goes out
					(3rd sg. pres.)
		SALIT	→	sal	goes out
					(3rd sg. pres.)
		PONIT	→	pon	puts (3rd sg. pres.)

The forms listed in (a) are those which have survived in Modern Spanish: in other words, those in which the consonant left in final position is [s r n l] or [ð],[17] as well as medieval [d^z], modern [θ]. Those in (b) are forms in which the alternative with [−e] eventually won out, hence modern **puente, conde, parte, fuerte, hueste, humilde, noche, leche, príncipe, nueve, siete, hube**: note that the forms in (bi) end in a cluster, those in (bii) in a single consonant. Finally, (c) lists only verb forms, whose [−e] has also been restored (or merely retained: the loss was always variable) in order to maintain the morphological patterning of the verb.[18]

This seems to point clearly to a surface phonetic patterning in Medieval Spanish that was much less constrained than that of Modern Spanish (perhaps because of French influence; see Lapesa 1975, 1981: 169, 200–1), which admits in final position neither clusters (as in (bi)) nor the single consonants of the forms in (bii) – indeed, it seems Medieval Spanish had only one important constraint on final consonants: groups of obstruent plus liquid were prohibited (Hooper 1976:107).

The first important feature of the apocope rule to note is that it reinforced the statistical frequency of consonants which already existed in final position, such as [r l n s]; but it also introduced as word-final consonants until that time unknown as such: [ð z d^z]. Of these three, [z] has devoiced to [s] (in all positions) and [d^z] has become [θ] (again, unconditionally) since the medieval period, thus bringing us back to our original list, [s θ ð n l r], plus the velar [x] (resulting from medieval voiced and voiceless palatal fricatives), which appears finally in a very limited number of forms, apparently old borrowings in most cases from other Romance languages or from Arabic: **reloj** 'clock, watch', **carcaj** 'quiver, rifle-case', and a few more. We return to this below.

The second important consequence of the apocope rule is to be noted in the forms **humilt, nuef, of** (and many other examples, like **verdat** (M.Sp. **verdad** 'truth'), **ciudat** (M.Sp. **ciudad** 'city'), **Rodric** (M.Sp. **Rodrigo**) and **Lob** (M.Sp. **Lope**) (Menéndez Pidal 1958:169), probably an ultracorrected form). This alternation of the final consonant has been interpreted in various ways, the most natural of which seems to be that Medieval Spanish had a rule devoicing final consonants (Hooper 1976:106 note 8; Lapesa 1981: 208; and Pensado Ruiz 1984:208–14). Unfortunately, the orthography is unhelpful in the case of –z, which has given rise to a lengthy controversy over its phonetic value,[19] and that of –s, but it seems reasonably sure that at least in absolute final position (that is, before a pause) they represented [t^s] and [s] respectively – in other words, were devoiced.[20]

This helps us to establish a further generalization about the consonants in word-final position: voiced stops and fricatives are devoiced in Spanish in this position.[21] At first glance, this seems to contradict much of what we have said earlier, since what we expect of consonants in final position is that they should weaken (despite Lass 1971 and Anwar 1974), when in fact the strength hierarchy referred to in chapter 2 (pages 14–15 above) shows a weakening process in exactly the opposite direction: voiceless stops becoming voiced, and voiced stops spirantizing. However, several conditioning factors must be borne in mind. First, the naturalness of the process of final devoicing must be stressed: final consonants, being in a position which per se makes them weak, are extremely liable to assimilation, and loss of voice in this case is precisely that in phonetic terms: an assimilation to the lack of articulatory activity manifested in the following pause.

The similar and well-known devoicing found in German, Russian, and other languages (including one more closely related to Spanish: Catalan (see Dinnsen 1977)) demonstrates the widespread existence of the process.

Second, we must take into account that strength hierarchies have been used somewhat simplistically with regard to their interpretation: Escure (1977) has pointed out the necessity of a combined interpretation of various hierarchies.[22] We have already seen how the labial is the consonant most resistant to change in intervocalic position, while the nasal labial was the first to disappear in final position: it would be illusory to believe we could account for all the observed phenomena with reference to one hierarchy.

It appears a natural and convincing solution to recognize that the process t → d → ð is a manifestation of weakening in intervocalic position, while d → t is a manifestation of the same phenomenon in absolute final position. As a source feature, it therefore seems that [± voice] works independently of articulation features (which are essentially those identified on 'universal' hierarchies) in their phonological relationships.[23]

Whatever the case may have been in Medieval Spanish, the process has been considerably obscured by subsequent developments: the devoicing of all sibilants obliterated any possible distinction between them in final position other than the assimilatory processes of a strictly environmental nature, while the unapocopated form eventually triumphed in the cases where a cluster, stop, or a fricative other than the sibilants would have become final. This probably explains why devoicing has received very little attention in the literature: Menéndez Pidal considers it simply 'el ensordecimiento propio de los sonidos finales' (1958: 167); Otero (1971, 1976) does not mention it in his set of rules, and neither does Hartman (1974); Eastlack (1976:122) does, but without comment. In fact there is evidence to suggest that the devoicing rule is rather more important than this merely superficial interest would indicate.

Let us retrace our steps for a moment and return to the set of segments which are supposedly permissible in word-final position in Modern Castilian: [s x θ ð n l r]. Leaving aside the nasals and liquids, already discussed (see pages 40, 42–4 above), let us take a look at the four fricatives. Of these four, we have already pointed out that the velar fricative occurs in very few forms. Some dictionaries list up to twenty-odd items whose final segment is [x] (see, for example, Stahl and Scavnicky 1973); but most are obsolete or exotic elements unknown to the majority of native speakers, who recognize perhaps five or six at most, the most common, along with a few placenames, being **reloj** 'clock', **carcaj** 'quiver' (both of which are early borrowings), plus the isolated form **boj** 'boxwood' (Latin BUXU), whose development is somewhat idiosyncratic (see Corominas and Pascual 1980–, s.v. boj and doble).

The form **reloj** is almost always realized as [rreló] when used spontaneously, and recognized as having this realization even in didactic treatises (Navarro Tomás 1977:143). From a practical point of view, then, the appearance of [x] in final position in Spanish may be considered of marginal importance: it certainly indicates the necessity of assigning [x] to a different position of strength from [s].

[θ], on the other hand, appears frequently as a word-final segment: **cruz** 'cross', **pez** 'fish', **actriz** 'actress', **hoz** 'sickle', **tez** 'skin', **avestruz** 'ostrich' may serve as examples of a large number of forms. Its pronunciation in standard Castilian shows no sign of weakening, unlike that of [ð]. Navarro Tomás (1977: 103) remarks, with regard to [–ð], that:

> La **d** final absoluta, seguida de pausa, se pronuncia
> particularmente débil y relajada . . . de hecho, la articulación
> resulta casi muda . . . .
>
> En formas nominales como **virtud, verdad, juventud,
> libertad**, etc., la pronunciación vulgar, en la mayor parte de
> España, suprime la **d** final . . . . Este uso se extiende también a
> la pronunciación familiar de las personas ilustradas . . . .En
> Valladolid, Salamanca y otros lugares de Castilla, en lugar de
> la **d** final se pronuncia . . . una θ relajada.

Alarcos Llorach notes in his list of possible word-final consonants: '/d/ (realizado a veces como cero fónico); /θ/ (que en la lengua vulgar de algunas regiones se neutraliza con el fonema anterior)'[24] (1971:187). Menéndez Pidal (1958:101–2):

> En posición final absoluta, la **d** se articula ð en la
> pronunciación cuidada, especialmente en voces poco
> corrientes, como **lid, Cid, ardid**, o en los imperativos **andad,
> corred**. . . . En la pronunciación culta más corriente la –ð se
> articula muy relajada [ð], y hasta sin voz . . . .En fin, se llega
> también a la pérdida completa: **re, se, verdá**. . . . Estas
> maneras de –**d** final . . . son la pronunciación más corriente en
> Castilla la Nueva, Andalucía y América; pero en Castilla la
> Vieja y León, al lado de la pérdida . . . se pronuncia la
> fricativa sorda θ.

In summary, then, the realization of a voiced fricative [-ð] is rare; probably limited to some manifestations of largo speech style (Harris 1969:7). The normal tendency is to pronounce the voiceless [-θ] or to suppress the consonant altogether. It is not uncommon to find native speakers incorrectly rendering infrequently used words such as **ardid** in the orthography as **ardiz** (i.e., [arðíθ] for [arðíð]). It begins to look, therefore, very much as if Modern Spanish maintains the constraint on voiced obstruents in absolute final position. The suppression or devoicing of [-ð] is hardly sufficient empirical support for this statement, but further evidence is available elsewhere.

There is a series of fairly recent loanwords of frequent occurrence in Spanish which have been accepted into the standard orthography with a final stop: **club, pub, (e)snob, (música) pop, zigzag, gag, frac, coñac, vermut** may serve as examples; the most widely used of these forms typically show complete suppression of the final consonants: [koñá], [bermú], and often [klú], [eznó], but pronunciations vary very much in relation to sociolinguistic factors, and familiarity with the language of origin of the word in question. Pronunciation with a true final stop is virtually unknown in the case of the voiced segment, though the voiceless stop is regularly heard in [póp] or [frák]; for the voiced segment, a process of spirantization is seemingly obligatory: thus [klúβ], [páβ], etc; but the most popular pronunciation also involves a devoicing of the fricative: [klúɸ], [páɸ]/[púɸ], [θiɣθáx] (cf. Lozano 1979:104), [gáx].

Another indication that this is a natural process in Castilian is the fact that inexperienced Spanish speakers will repeat English forms such as **leg, dog**, etc., as [léx], [dóx]: the pronunciation of a final (voiced) stop is initially the result of a specific effort on the part of the speaker.

These shreds of evidence are perhaps too fragmentary to provide clear support for a devoicing rule in Modern Spanish, being based necessarily on a few loanwords and other marginal phenomena; moreover, the Castilianization of these loanwords varies according to frequency of use, date of borrowing and other factors. On the other hand, the data do provide some indication, however scanty, that we should not reject the possibility of a variable rule of centuries' standing in Castilian which constrains the appearance of consonantal segments in word-final position.

We have suggested that a word-final devoicing process existed in Medieval Spanish, producing forms like **nuef** < **nueve**, **Rodric** < **Rodrigo**, **cibtat** < **cibdad**(e), etc., and that a similar process may exist (perhaps variably) in the modern language, preceded by an obligatory spirantization rule for stops in this position (and generally, in fact, in syllable-final position: see chapter 4, pages 84–6 below). This spirantization process is intimately linked with the second consonant shift (see chapter 2) and therefore did not appear until after the earliest manifestations of the apocope rule, and the devoicing rule (see above, note 17).[25] This means that the order of the rules in a synchronic grammar of Modern Spanish is not that in which they appeared historically, since it seems that devoicing accompanied the application of apocope before the appearance of the second consonant shift. There is a perfectly natural explanation for this without having recourse to rule reordering: the rule of spirantization included in the second consonant shift (chapter 2, page 12 above, rule 4) applies in a much wider variety of contexts than devoicing – it affects intervocalic stops, and eventually syllable-final ones too.

Word-final stops were therefore, let us say, faced with a choice: two potential weakening processes, loss of voice (still probably optional), or spirantization, in conflict.[26] The resolution was made in favour of the more general process, thereby maintaining a general surface phonotactic constraint: spirantization of all syllable-final stops. The devoicing rule has, however, persevered in its task, albeit in a much smaller way, (optionally?) affecting fricatives, whether derived or underlying.

This interpretation of the development of word-final consonants has produced several results:

(a) A 'universal' consonant hierarchy including both point-of-articulation and source features cannot be applied to word-final consonants, and so is probably an oversimplification. What is more, a strength hierarchy makes no sense unless it is applied with reference to the position of the segment in question; for example, we have seen how it is precisely those segments which are suppressed first in final position (the labial among the nasal consonants) which are the 'strongest' in intervocalic position, if we take resistance to elision as a criterion for strength. In fact, weakness is a manifestation of assimilation to surrounding segments; in all cases, the extreme result of this assimilation is loss, but it affects consonants at different ends of the strength scale. We can only reconcile this by reference to the position of the segment within the syllable and/or word.

(b) The educated variety of Castilian is conservative in its preservation of final consonants in comparison with other dialects: standard Castilian admits 'stronger' consonants in this position (see Pensado 1985:313–20).

(c) Optional or variable rules have a clear historical significance, which is not overshadowed by the fact that their operation is normally relegated to a stage after the application of more general obligatory rules.

(d) Surface phonetic constraints are all-important in natural processes: note that a more abstract analysis, be it autonomous phonological or systematic phonological, cannot account in the same way for processes like [b] → [β] → [ɸ] and [d] → [ð] → [θ], [g] → [ɣ] → [x], since while the first represents fairly late and minor ('subphonemic') phonetic adjustments, the latter two involve a neutralization of two underlying phonological segments, /θ/ and /d/ or /ð/, and /x/ and /g/ or /ɣ/.[27]

Notes

1. We may deduce these to have been early pronunciations from the forms in Menéndez Pidal (1972:234). See also Malkiel (1968:44–5).
2. SAL was in fact generally used as a masculine noun in Classical (i.e., literary) Latin, but the widespread uncertainty in use may be seen from the fact that in Modern Castilian **sal** is feminine, while in other parts of the Peninsula (Portuguese-speaking areas, for example) it is masculine.
3. The liquid not found in final position in Spanish is the palatal. When the medieval apocope rule applied to forms in **–lle**, the result was depalatalization of the lateral: MILLE → **mil** 'thousand', PELLE → **piel** 'skin', VALLE → **val** (M.Sp. **valle**) 'valley'. See Menéndez Pidal (1958:169), Alarcos Llorach (1971:182 note 6), Pensado (1985:314), and note 11 below. The only apparent exceptions are the use of the article **ell** before vowels, commonly found until the end of the fourteenth century, and the numeral **mill** in the same phonetic context. This pronunciation was possible, of course, due to their proclitic position (see Corominas and Pascual 1980–, s.v. el, mil; and Frengle 1975:169–70). Cp. the survival of **much** until the thirteenth century mentioned in chapter 4, note 22 below.
4. We cannot here enter into the intricacies of the question of the struggle between regular phonetic change and functions realized morphologically. For a recent treatment of the direction of morphophonemic change, see Hooper (1979) and the references contained therein. Hooper's article, incidentally, reaffirms the importance of the third person verb form as a sort of 'base' element within the conjugation; see also Kiparsky (1973:174). For variability in the loss of contemporary Spanish final [s] and [n], which have important morphological functions, see Poplack (1980a, 1980b) and Lipski (1983).
5. Núñez Cedeño (1980), Poplack (1980a, 1980b), and Terrell (1982) on the varieties of Spanish spoken in the Dominican Republic, in Cuba, and in Puerto Rico, are some of the most interesting articles published in recent years. For the situation in a variety of Spanish

spoken in the Canaries, see Felix (1979). It is impossible here to give anything approaching a complete list of works published: suffice it to say that there is still no general agreement on the way in which the variable rules expressing this process are governed (indeed, this in itself may vary from dialect to dialect), though researchers do agree that variability is clearly there: 'with minor exceptions none of the variants is used categorically by any speaker' (Terrell 1982:49). It does seem, however, that it is not a simple question of a lenition [s] → [h] in all cases.

6. For the apparent paradoxes involved in 'weakening' and 'strengthening', see also Lodge (1986:348–9).
7. Note that, conversely, weak elements in word-initial position (i.e., the strongest) are actually strengthened in some cases in Spanish. Thus the glide [w], as in **hueso** [wéso] 'bone', is pronounced [ɣw] in many dialects; similar strengthening to a fricative or an affricate affects the front glide [j]. There are even sporadic examples of this in internal syllable-initial position: **mangual** < MANUALE, **menguar** < MINUARE. Like so many of these processes, this phenomenon is not yet as fully understood as we would wish, and it is only speculative whether this strengthening is a therapeutic measure against possible loss. See Guile (1973) and Lozano (1979) for further discussion. Incidentally, it is also interesting to note that initial r– in Spanish is always [rr], and other varieties of Peninsular Latin also strengthened initial l– by palatalization: Ct. **llet** 'milk', **lluna** 'moon'; As. **lloco** 'mad', **llobo** 'wolf', corresponding to Cast. **leche, luna, loco, lobo**, respectively. In a smaller area, this palatalization also extended to initial n–. See Menéndez Pidal (1972:239–40). And it is precisely the case that the semivowels are followed in order of increasing strength by the liquids and then the nasals.
8. Lass's proposal is rejected on different grounds by Houlihan (1979).
9. A few monosyllabic forms have retained a nasal to the present day: QUEM → **quien** 'who', TAM → **tan** 'so', CUM → **con** 'with', QUAM → **cuan** 'how'. The reasons for this preservation are not absolutely clear: it may have been a question of accentuation – polysyllabic words ending in [–m] (which was lost; see page 38 above) were not stressed on the last syllable (see Hartman 1974:135–6. For another suggestion, see Hall 1976:180). Or it may be that monosyllables are in general more resistant to loss of phonetic substance: cp. the situation of [–s] in the Spanish of the Canaries (Felix 1979:365–6, 377–8). In any case, there are two points to bear in mind: first, the preservation was not absolutely general (for example, IAM → **ya** 'already'); and second, even when the nasal was preserved, it was converted into a coronal nasal, just as our hypothesis would predict.
10. Cf. Navarro Tomás (1977:112): 'La **n** final ante pausa es, generalmente, una **n** relajada en cuya articulación la lengua suele quedar adherida a los alvéolos más tiempo del que duran la presión

del aire espirado y las vibraciones vocálicas; la articulación, en parte, acaba, por consiguiente, muda . . . muchas personas, acaso por influencia dialectal, pronuncian en estos casos, en vez de la **n** una [nasal] velar'. Similar realizations of final –n are reported from many parts of Spanish America too (see, for example, Hyman (1956), and Bjarkman (1978) for a slightly different interpretation).

11. For further details of this phenomenon, see Harris (1969:16–18). We have not mentioned here the palatal nasal [ñ] (which arose historically in Spanish from the palatalization of [n] in various circumstances), since it has never appeared in word-final position; note the noun **desdén** 'scorn', as compared to the verb **desdeñar** (though this noun may well be a Gallicism; see Menéndez Pidal (1958:233) and Corominas and Pascual (1980–, s.v. digno)), (O.Sp.) **lueñe/luen** 'far away', and **don, duen(de)**, reduced forms of **dueño** 'master'. On the strength hierarchy, the position of [ñ] relative to that of [m] is therefore at the moment an unsolved, though probably trivial, problem. Cf. note 3 above.
12. The following comment by Navarro Tomás is symptomatic: 'Recházase igualmente como vulgarismo la pronunciación de la **s** final como una simple aspiración, y asimismo su eliminación total en determinadas circunstancias, hechos corrientes, según es sabido, en el lenguaje popular de varias regiones de España y América' (1977:110). For the place [s] occupies on strength parameters in relation to other final segments, see Hammond (1980).
13. This is at least true of standard Castilian, but cf. Hammond (1980), especially the comments on Cuban /r/ and Dominican and Cuban /l/. It is also often observed that in regions of Andalusia and Spanish America, final [–l] and [–r] are completely confused; see Navarro Tomás (1977:119), Alonso and Lida (1945), Núñez Cedeño (1980), Lapesa (1981:385, 505–6, 575) and Terrell (1982).
14. We are here omitting any mention of the glides, since their universally accepted midway character between consonant and vowel segments makes their being taken into consideration superfluous.
15. The best recent appreciation of the importance of the apocope rule in Spanish from a theoretical point of view is to be found in Hooper (1976:104–9), on which much of the following material is based. For a somewhat different interpretation of apocope, see Allen (1977).
16. This division of the examples into categories follows that of Hooper (1976:106).
17. In the case of **merced**, the consonant was certainly [ð]. In the earliest cases of apocope, however, it is doubtful that the second consonant shift had taken place (see pages 7–12 above); the consonant was still therefore [d] in forms like **edad**. The date of the spirantization of [d] to [ð] is difficult to establish, but the process had certainly been achieved by the time of the final petrification of forms with [–e] (groups (b) and (c)) and those without (group (a)); see note 25 below, and Alonso (1976:63, 75) and Alarcos Llorach (1971:264).
18. For more details, see the section of Hooper (1976) already cited.

There are two notable exceptions to the restoration of [-e] in verb forms: the infinitive (AMARE → **amar** 'to love') and a few familiar singular imperative forms like **sal** 'go out', **pon** 'put', **ten** 'take, hold', **haz** 'do, make'. See also Vincent (1978:419–20) for further discussion.

19. See the summary and well-reasoned comments in Alonso (1969: 158–72). Also Macpherson (1975:125) and Allen (1977).
20. Though whether or not devoicing actually took place has given rise to some controversy in the past, a glance at Arabic loanwords can hardly leave much doubt: consonants final in Arabic were either given a support vowel or devoiced in Spanish; as apocope in its extreme form began to disappear, even some of these devoiced consonants had [-e] added. Thus we find Ar. **qawwad** → **alcahuete** 'go-between', Ar. **rubb** → **arrope** '(type of) syrup'. For further details, see Pensado Ruiz (1984:71, 150, 211).
21. Hooper (1976:106 note 8) describes final devoicing as 'a process that does not survive in Modern Spanish'. We shall have reason to question this a little later.
22. Escure also notes that the standard hierarchy 'requires some modification in order to apply to final consonants' (1977:61) without suggesting what it might be.
23. For further evidence that [± voice] cannot be incorporated into the strength parameter, see Dekeyser (1978:112–15), and cf. also Escure (1975:33).
24. In an autonomous phonological analysis, [ð] is considered an allophone of /d/; cf. chapter 2, page 16 above.
25. The occasional spirantization of Arabic final stops in words taken into Spanish indicates that this process must have started functioning in the fifteenth century at the very latest, and many other clues point to its being several centuries earlier (Pensado Ruiz 1984:212); the form **alcaide** < Ar. **qâ'id** appears in the variant **alcayaz** in the **Cantar de Mio Cid** (?twelfth century) (Corominas and Pascual 1980–, s.v. alcaide).
26. If indeed devoicing was an optional rule, this may reflect the intrinsic necessity of obligatory rules applying before optional ones. See Sanders (1976). Yavas (1982) suggests that processes adjusting loanwords to native outputs work according to a strength hierarchy, which would fit in well with our findings; but his requirement that the strongest be applied last cannot be upheld in this case, if we take spirantization to be the 'strongest'; i.e., the process applied most generally.
27. For the problem of whether the underlying segment is /d/ or /ð/, etc., in a generative analysis, see chapter 2, page 16 above. Harris (1969) does not in fact posit an underlying segment /x/, but this does not affect the argument here, since some other segment will have to be posited which will surface as [x] in non-alternating morphemes. See Harris (1969: 163–72).

Chapter four

Syllable-Final Consonants

The development of word-internal syllable-final consonants has been considerably more complex than that of word-final segments, mainly on account of the important influence exerted by following, environmentally stronger syllable-initial segments. This influence (largely manifested in assimilation processes) has a very marked tendency to weaken syllable-final consonants: assimilation is in itself a weakening process, since its culmination, when achieved, involves the total coalescence of one segment with another, and hence a reduction to zero; but even the developments not involving assimilation are weakening processes.

Syllable-final is generally recognized as a weak position for consonants universally, in comparison with syllable-initial position. It also seems clear that absolute final position is weaker than word-internal syllable-final position if we bear in mind the evolution described in the last chapter, where we saw how Modern Castilian preserves only [s ð x θ n l r] as absolute finals, and some of these have a fairly precarious existence; while many more consonantal segments are found in syllable-final position within the word, at least in the standard variety of Castilian. We are, however, making no universal claims here; the hypothesis[1] that CV is a universally optimal syllable structure and that phonological conspiracies have such a structure as their goal, does not seem very convincing when applied to the history of Spanish consonantal structure. While it is true (as may be seen from the discussion in the last chapter) that final consonants are weak and many have been suppressed, it is also true that the apocope rule created more final consonant segments than had previously existed.

Let us take a look at the development of Latin syllable-final consonants in Spanish, beginning with the consonants whose resistance to weakening we have already seen to be greatest: that is, the liquids.

As may be expected, the liquid [r] has largely survived unchanged, with the exception of the group –RS–, which was assimilated at an early period in Latin (Menéndez Pidal 1958:136, Hartman 1974:137–8[2]) and gave voiceless [s] in Medieval Spanish:

*VERSURA	→ bas(s)ura	**rubbish**
EXCAR(P)SU	→ escas(s)o	**scarce**
URSU	→ os(s)o	**bear**
CURSU	→ cos(s)o[3]	**arena, bullring**

For the moment we will express this informally as:

16. r → s / ___ s

But [r] was not the only sonorant to be lost before [s]: the nasal [n] was regularly suppressed from a very early date within the Imperial period (Menéndez Pidal 1958:136); there are many inscriptional examples of the type COSUL, SPOSUS, etc. (Grandgent 1908:74; Elcock 1960:26). Spanish examples include:

SPONSU	→ esposo	**husband**
ANSA	→ asa	**handle**
SENSU	→ seso	**sense, brain**
CONSUERE	→ coser	**to sew**[4]
MENSE	→ mes	**month**
MENSURA	→ mesura	**restraint**
INSULA	→ isla	**island**

At first glance, this would seem to have a great similarity with rule 16: the environment is the same, and both involve segments which are [+cor, +ant], but the difference is that while the nasal is totally suppressed, rule 16 is merely an assimilation rule. The fact that [rs] assimilated to [ss] may be seen from the Medieval Spanish results, where the segment involved is [s],[5] written –ss– (Menéndez Pidal 1958:136), whereas the result of [ns] was [z] in Medieval Spanish, written as –s–, indicating a single –s– which underwent intervocalic voicing.

It is important, however, to note that both are assimilations of [+cor, +ant] segments, because there is evidence that this type of assimilation was more widespread. In the case of the group [nf] we have the following correspondences in Latin and Modern Spanish:

INFANTE	→ infante	**infant, prince**
INFERNU	→ infierno	**hell**

but we also find in Old Spanish, among others, the forms **ifante**,

ifierno, cofonder, and **cohonder** 'to confuse, confound' (< Latin CONFUNDERE; see Menéndez Pidal 1958:137; Corominas and Pascual 1980–, s.v. fundir); Modern Spanish **cohechar** 'to bribe' < *CONFECTARE and **cogorza** 'drunkenness', ultimately < CONFORTIARE; and we also have the placenames **Sahagún** (O.Sp. **Safagun(d)** < SAN(CTI) FACUNDI), **Cohiño** (< CONFINIU) and **Sahelices** (< SAN(CTI) FELICIS) (Menéndez Pidal 1958:137), all suggesting a rule of the type n → ø / ___f, informally, which was variable and subsequently lost.[6] The intrusive nasal in the form **invierno** 'winter' (< Latin HIBERNU) is probably an indication of the hesitation over the pronunciation of a nasal before a labial fricative. Menéndez Pidal (1958:137) says that '**ifierno** apenas tuvo vida, sustituído por el culto **infierno**', but **infierno** cannot be seen as a truly learned form because of its diphthong, though the nasal may indeed have been reinserted by learned influence, in this case clearly ecclesiastical. The fact that the rule has been lost may be appreciated from a glance at the numerous forms taken into Spanish in the last centuries: **infarto** '(cardiac) insufficiency', **informe** 'report', **inferir** 'to infer', **inflamar** 'to inflame', **ninfa** 'nymph', etc., all pronounced with a labiodental nasal.

We are dealing, then, with a very general process, since [s] and [f] were the only voiceless fricative consonants in Latin, forming a perfectly defined natural class. A formalization of the rule would be straightforward:

17. $[+\text{nas}] \rightarrow \emptyset\ /\ \underline{\qquad}\ \begin{bmatrix} +\text{cont} \\ -\text{vce} \end{bmatrix}$

  (n → ø / ___s, f).

Here we have further evidence that the [ns] → [s] process is distinct from the [rs] → [ss] development: the group [rf] (unlike [nf]) was totally unaffected, as may be seen from the examples:

ORPHANU → huérfano **orphan**
PERFIDIA → porfía **obstinacy, dispute**

The actual mechanics of the [ns] → [s] process was probably carried out by a nasalization and lengthening of the preceding vowel.[7] The loss of the nasal before a fricative is quite well attested from early periods of Latin: COIUGI, COVENTIO, IFERI (Grandgent 1908:74), though in cases such as these it was generally restored because of the influence of the prefixes CON– and IN– used in other forms. But the fact that this loss always took place before fricatives but never before stops is also a strong indication that the process involved was nasalization. Foley (1977, chapter 4) has shown that in many languages the nasal consonant is effaced before a continuant but not before a stop, and on the scale of implications, in a language where nasal effacement has taken place before a stop, it will also have taken place before a continuant (see also Cohen 1971:321).

The processes [rs] → [ss] and [ns] → [s] then, despite a superficial similarity, are phonetically quite different: though it seems any [+cont] segment in syllable-final position before [s] is in a weak environment, a fact we shall see reflected in other changes. What happened to the [rs] cluster was a straightforward assimilation, while the [ns] cluster was simplified by the loss of the nasal consonant only after it had nasalized and lengthened the preceding vowel.

Having seen, then, that both the nasal and one of the liquids are weakened in the proximity of a following [s], it would establish an interesting pattern if we were to discover that the other liquid, [l], was similarly affected, especially bearing in mind that its point of articulation is again [+cor, +ant], just like the other continuants involved, and like [s].

What we do find is considerable confusion. Judging from an example like INSULSU → **soso** 'tasteless, insipid' (and the placename **La Sosa** < SALSA; see Corominas and Pascual 1980–, s.v. empujar), we seem to be on the right track; Spanish historical linguists, however, are in disagreement on several crucial etymologies.[8] What is clear is that syllable-final [l] was generally lost after a high back vowel, which in itself does not discount our hypothesis, since a rule extension may quite reasonably start in the most favourable phonetic environment and [l] would indeed be most likely to succumb to absorption in such a context as this – cf. the pronunciation of the so-called 'dark l' in some English dialects as a high back vowel (see Gimson 1970:203). The problem is that in the group –ULT–, the [l] did not disappear without trace: it clearly generated a glide which palatalized the following [t] and raised the preceding vowel. Menéndez Pidal (1958:139–40) associates the groups –ULT– and –ULS–, suggesting that the latter also produced a glide, but then he goes on to propose for **empujar** 'to push' (with [-š-] in Old Spanish) the etymology *IMPULSIARE, which seems unnecessary in the light of the association he himself makes; in other words, we expect –ULS– → [ujs] → [uš] without the influence of another glide. Corominas and Pascual (1980–) suggest the more reasonable IMPULSARE, especially if the correct etymology of **pujar** 'to struggle, raise up' is PULSARE (the form **pulsar** was evidently taken from Latin at a later date). This again, then, implies the production of a glide from [l] in order to explain the palatalization and raising of the preceding vowel; the form **soso**, however, manifests neither.[9]

As regards the fate of the same group, –UL–, in the vicinity of other consonants, the evidence is still conflicting: there is raising of the vowel and loss of the [l] in:

| DULCE | → | (O.Sp.) duz (/dulce) | **sweet**[10] |
| CULMINE | → | cumbre | **summit** |

raising but not loss in:

| SULCU | → | surco/sulco | **furrow** |
| DULCE | → | dulce (//(O.Sp.) duz) | **sweet** |

loss but not raising in:

| CULCITA | → | cócedra | **cushion** |
| ULVA | → | ova | **(type of) seaweed** |

and neither development takes place in:

| ULMU | → | olmo | **elm** |

If indeed the regular development of [l] involved the production of a glide, it seems unnatural to separate the group [ls] from the rest in order to make the tenuous connection with the development of [rs] and [ns]; while on the other hand, it seems clear that the complexity and variety of developments in these forms require a lengthy and careful study which we cannot dedicate to them here. The two most relevant examples, IMPULSARE and INSULSU, themselves provide contradictory evidence; research may find indications of complex dialect mixture and lexical spread in the high level of variation in all these forms.

Syllable-final [l] in the Iberian Peninsula in general (indeed, it was probably a feature of Latin itself; see Grandgent (1908:122), Haadsma and Nuchelmans (1963:26)) tended to velarize, which is a weakening process leading eventually to the vocalization of the segment.[11] This velarization is still present in Portuguese and Catalan, but not in Spanish. The fact that it did exist in the early stages of Spanish is clear from the following forms:

ALTERU	→	otro	**other**
SALTU	→	soto	**grove, copse**
ALTERIU	→	otero	**hillock**
BALBU	→	bobo	**silly**[12]
FALCE	→	hoz	**sickle**

CALCE	→ coz	**kick**
SCALPRU	→ escoplo	**chisel**

where the development could only have been [ał] → [aw] → [ow] → [o].[13] In other words, the velar liquid first vocalized:

18. $\begin{bmatrix} +\text{son} \\ +\text{hi} \\ +\text{bk} \end{bmatrix} \rightarrow \begin{bmatrix} -\text{cons} \\ \\ -\text{lat} \end{bmatrix} / \begin{bmatrix} -\text{cons} \\ +\text{bk} \\ +\text{low} \end{bmatrix} \underline{\quad} \$$

(ł → w / a ___ $).

There is one outstanding exception to this process in the form **alto** 'high' (Latin ALTU), for a possible explanation of which see Menéndez Pidal (1972:107–9).[14] The other apparent exception, BALNEU → **baño** 'bath' is in fact, if Menéndez Pidal is right, not an exception at all. He suggests that Sp. **baño**, as well as other Romance forms, derives from a Latin BANEU (documented: see Corominas and Pascual 1980–, s.v. baño) and is therefore perfectly regular. Nevertheless, and in further support of this form's regularity, there are a number of placenames in the Peninsula which indicate a survival of the Classical BALNEU: **Boñar** (< BALNEARE), **Boñuelos** (< BALNEOLOS), and so on (Menéndez Pidal 1972:104–5), clearly manifesting the expected output of rule 18 and the reduction [aw] → [o].

The vital factor in the environment here, then, is not the following consonant but the preceding vowel; note that Foley (1977:44–8) indicates that /a/ is the strongest of all the vowels phonologically, and this may be the reason why its assimilatory influence on the following weak segment (already velarized) was sufficient to vocalize it; though such a hypothesis may not be necessary: see rule 19 below. The coalescence of the diphthong was then undertaken by another rule; compare:

AURU	→ oro			**gold**
CAUSA	→ cosa			**thing**
TAURU	→ toro			**bull**
AMAVIT	→ *amawt	→	amó	**loved (3rd sg. pret.)**
AURICULA	→ oreja			**ear**

and so on. Since medieval times, Spanish has lost the vocalization rule (18), the velarization (compare SOLIDU → **sueldo** 'salary', SOLIDARE → **soldar** 'to solder', etc.) and the vowel rule assimilating [aw]. The fact that the latter was lost at a relatively early period may be seen in the development in which [l] became syllable-final only by the syncope of a medial vowel:

CAL(I)CE	→ cauce	**riverbed, (water)course**
SAL(I)CE	→ sauce	**willow**

(**calze** is documented in Castilian since about 1140, and **calçe** in 1063, according to Corominas and Pascual (1980–, s.v. cauce), and **cauze** since 1475; **salze** appears from the end of the tenth century onwards, according to Menéndez Pidal (1972:311), and **sauze** from the middle of the fourteenth century (Corominas and Pascual 1980–, s.v. sauce).)[15]

The vocalization rule (18) would automatically be bled of all its input by the loss of velarization, so which was lost first chronologically is a trivial question. What is perfectly clear is the lack of any velarization in Modern Castilian.[16]

Although beyond the limits of this study, the history of the rule of monophthongization [aw] → [o] in Spanish would be an interesting one. There is ample inscriptional and other evidence that the pronunciation with [o] was a common one in Latin (though perhaps [o]/[aw] fluctuated on a dialectal basis; see Elcock (1960:25); but the reduction is not common to all the Romance languages: both Rumanian and Occitan maintain –au– (the reflexes of AURU, TAURU are in both languages **aur, taur**); Portuguese long maintained an intermediate stage, still reflected in the orthography, as in **ouro, touro, amou**; while French, Catalan, and Spanish have reduced the diphthong to [o] (see Vidos 1977:20). It appears, however, that at least in a high number of forms, this reduction is autonomous in each language and not commonly inherited from Latin (see Malkiel 1981:553–5): thus in French it took place later than the palatalization of [k] before [a]: CAUSA → (Fr.) **chose** 'thing', CAULE → **chou** 'cabbage', just as CANTARE → **chanter** 'to sing' and CAMPU → **champ** 'field'; this palatalization did not take place before [o]; compare COLORE → **couleur** 'colour', COLARE → **couler** 'to pour, flow'. Vidos (1977:186) fixes the end of the seventh century for this palatalization in French, which presumably gives a chronological starting point for the reduction of the diphthong.

Spanish, however, shows that the situation was probably not so straightforward. As Menéndez Pidal (1958:53) points out, the glide of the diphthong [aw] occasionally prevented the voicing of intervocalic obstruents; thus:

PAUCU	→	poco	**little**
CAUTU	→	coto	**reserve, enclosure**
*SAUP–		(Class. SAPU–) → (O.Sp.) sop–, (M.Sp.) sup–	**knew (pret. stem)**
*CAUP–		(< *CAPU–, Class. CEP–) → (O.Sp.) cop–, (M.Sp.) cup–	**fitted (pret. stem)**

rather than ***pogo**, ***codo**, etc., as would be expected if the obstruent had been preceded by a true vocalic segment (see chapter 2, page 12, rule 2). But we cannot conclude from this that the reduction of the diphthong did not commence before the obsolescence of rule 2, since we have a series of counterexamples in which voicing did take place: (O.Sp.) **yogue** 'lay (1st sg. pret.)', based on IACUI, (O.Sp.) **plogue** 'pleased (1st sg. pret.)', based on PLACUI, **pude** 'was able (1st sg. pret.)', based on POTUI (Menéndez Pidal 1958:141), and so on. The only explanation for this is that the reduction of the diphthong spread gradually through the lexicon, feeding the voicing rule with forms affected early and counterfeeding it in other cases, where the forms still maintained the diphthong.[17]

To return to our topic, however, the only other diachronic process to affect syllable-final [l] to any extent was the palatalization of the group -ULT-:

CULTELLU	→	cuchillo	**knife**
A(U)SCULTARE	→	escuchar	**to listen**
MULTU	→	mucho/muy	**much/very**
VULT(U)RE	→	buitre	**vulture**
VULTURNU	→	bochorno	**sultriness**
CULTRU	→	(O.Sp.) cuitre[18]	**ploughshare, knife**

As may be observed from the examples, two results are produced from the same group, a fact we shall return to later. Initially, the syllable-final –l– in this group was velarized, like all of the others. Since the preceding [+back] vowel [u] then formed an environment for the production of a glide from this velar, it seems likely that the same would have happened after –o–. Unfortunately, we find there are few examples to confirm this hypothesis, but one fact seems to leave the question reasonably clear: the forms cited above had a short –U– in Latin, which in Western Romance lowered to [o] in all cases (see note 23 to chapter 2 above). The reason for the high vowel in Spanish **mucho** and the other examples is that it was closed by the high glide produced by the syllable-final velar. At the time the glide appeared, therefore, the vowel preceding it was [o], not [u] (though Pensado Ruiz (1984:508, 517), for example, seems to prefer to believe Latin –U– was maintained in this context).

This seems sufficient justification for making the generalization that all [+back] vowels induced glide formation in these circumstances, while [−back] vowels had no effect; cf. SILVA → **selva** 'forest, jungle'. But all the evidence suggests that the glide produced in the –ULT– group was a front one. This evidence comes from various sources: first, Modern Spanish forms like

64 Syllable-Final Consonants

muy, buitre (see below);[19] second, the development of parallel forms in other areas of the Iberian Peninsula: Pt. **muito**, Gl. **cuitelo, coitelo**, and in some dialects of Aragonese (Menéndez Pidal 1972:280–1); and third, the great number of documented spellings of the type **muito, (e)scuitare**, even, of course, on Castilian soil, though Menéndez Pidal unnecessarily suspects influence from regions like Navarre and La Rioja, which apparently shared the lack of palatalization with neighbouring Aragón (1972:280–1).

This glide formation can be formalized as:

19. $\begin{bmatrix} +\text{son} \\ +\text{hi} \end{bmatrix} \rightarrow \begin{bmatrix} -\text{cons} \\ -\text{lat} \\ -\text{bk} \end{bmatrix} / \begin{bmatrix} -\text{cons} \\ +\text{bk} \\ -\text{low} \end{bmatrix} \underline{\quad} \begin{bmatrix} -\text{cont} \\ +\text{cor} \\ +\text{ant} \\ -\text{vce} \end{bmatrix}$

$(ɫ \rightarrow j / o, u \underline{\quad} t)$[20]

which could easily be collapsed with rule 18 by the use of angled brackets.

What looks like a rather unlikely process is in fact confirmed by the exactly parallel development of the group –ULS–, mentioned above (on pages 59–60), which naturally enables us to simplify rule 19 by suppressing [–cont] in the following environment. Finally, the glide palatalizes the consonant following it:

20. $\begin{bmatrix} +\text{cor} \\ -\text{vce} \end{bmatrix} \rightarrow \begin{bmatrix} -\text{ant} \\ +\text{hi} \end{bmatrix} / \begin{bmatrix} -\text{cons} \\ -\text{syll} \\ -\text{bk} \end{bmatrix} \underline{\quad} [-\text{cons}]$

$\left\{ \begin{matrix} t \\ s \end{matrix} \right\} \rightarrow \left\{ \begin{matrix} č \\ š \end{matrix} \right\} / j \underline{\quad} V).$

Rule 20 is a relatively late rule[21] which is to some extent essentially characteristic of Castilian as opposed to other Peninsular varieties of Romance, and we shall see more of it shortly (see page 73 below).

The environment ____[–cons] is necessary since, as may be observed from the forms **muy** and **buitre**, the affricate was not produced when it would have been final or followed by a consonantal segment. In adverbial usage, the reflex of MULTU was apocopated (cf. SECUNDU → **según** 'according to') at the stage [mújt(o)] and the resulting final consonant lost (see chapter 3). The explanation of this lack of palatalization seems clear: forms such as **much** or ***buchre** break syllabic structure conditions in Spanish: the affricate [č] may neither be final nor form part of a cluster without a syllable boundary (and even then there are restrictions; see pages 68-9 below), the only exception being the apocopated forms **noch, lech** mentioned on page 46 (chapter 3) as examples of the relaxed conditions on syllable structure applying in Medieval Spanish, and which disappeared, substituted by the full forms **noche, leche**. The attested form **much** would have resulted from the apocope of **mucho** under the same conditions, and existed variably alongside **muy** and **mucho** until the extreme form of apocope was no longer applied.[22] For a discussion of the role played by [č] in Spanish syllable structure, see Hooper (1976:212-14).[23] If syllable structure conditions were included in a diachronic phonology of the type suggested here, and could check the possible output of each rule, the specification [-cons] in the environment of rule 20 would be rendered unnecessary, since forms like **much, *buchre** would be automatically rejected, not undergo the rule, and remain as **muy, buitre** correctly. This seems a much more satisfactory solution, since it explains why Spanish rejected the application of the rule in these cases (see also Cooley 1978). To return to the problematic list of words cited on page 60, the development of **cumbre** would seem to be the expected one, while **dulce** and **surco** are Latinized forms, as is generally accepted (Corominas and Pascual 1980–, s.v. cumbre), and the raising of the vowel is variable.[24]

Thus we see that, with regard to the liquids, syllable-final [l] has had a much more turbulent history than [r], mainly due to the weakening implicit in the velarization of [l] in this position and the participation of the resulting glide in various processes of assimilation involving contiguous segments.[25]

The next block of consonants, the nasals, also weakened in syllable-final position, but in a rather different way. Already in Latin it seems that the syllable-final nasals had a tendency to assimilate their point of articulation to that of a following consonant. This was especially evident in morphological processes: note the variant IM– of the negative prefix IN– used before labial consonants, for instance. This same process has continued throughout the history of Spanish, as may be seen from forms where a nasal became syllable-final only at a relatively late period, as a result of the syncope of an unstressed medial vowel:

LIM(I)TE	→	linde	**boundary**
SEM(I)TA	→	senda	**path**
COM(I)TE	→	conde/(O.Sp.) cuende	**count, earl**

Forms like **semda, comde, limde** appear sporadically in

medieval sources (see page 109 below and Menéndez Pidal 1972:313–14), but we may assume they only existed while the unsyncopated form was still present in the speakers' competence or for a very short time afterwards.

It is normally recognized, therefore, that Spanish has, at the phonetic level, a whole series of nasal consonants in syllable-final position, none of which are autonomously phonemic, since their point of articulation is totally governed by the point of articulation of the following consonant. Thus in each of the following forms, the nasal is realized differently: **cambiar** 'to change', **ninfa** 'nymph', **alabanza** 'praise', **mandar** 'to command', **denso** 'dense', **concha** 'shell', **banco** 'bench, bank', being bilabial, labiodental, interdental, dental, alveolar, (pre)palatal, and velar respectively (Alarcos Llorach 1971:161–2, 181–2; Harris 1969: 8–18).

Incidentally, the controversy pointed out – and aggravated – by Harris (1969:8–18, 1970) about whether it is the palatal [ñ] or an alveolopalatal nasal which is pronounced before [č] is very much a storm in a teacup. First, Harris's statement that 'Informants uniformly assert that the nasal before [č] is **n** and, furthermore, that the cluster [ñč] is impossible' (1969:9) is undoubtedly true, but leads us nowhere if we consider that native speakers unprejudiced by any knowledge of phonetics will also (a) insist that the second nasal of **ninfa** or that of **triunfo** is **n**, that there is no difference between the nasal of **denso**, that of **cuando**, and that of **concertar**; (b) even with some knowledge of phonetics and as second-language learners, have great difficulty in perceiving or producing the difference between English **sin** and **sing**; and (c) will, in the case of semi-literates, spell, for example, **canbiar** for **cambiar**; all proving beyond reasonable doubt that a detailed description of the phonetic articulation of these syllable-final nasals is beyond the capacity of the average untrained speaker. Second, the point is not that these sounds may be exactly identified with others realized in independent circumstances (such as [ñ] in intervocalic position, for example, **niño** 'child', **paño** 'cloth', etc.) but precisely that the nasal loses all autonomy as regards its point of articulation, which is totally subsumed to that of the following consonant; thus it is natural that in an autonomous phonemic analysis like that of Alarcos Llorach (1971, cited in an earlier edition by Harris as Alarcos 1961), the nasal realized before [č] should be grouped with the phoneme /ñ/, while actually the realization of this nasal is much less fully palatal than [ñ], simply because the articulation of [č] is prepalatal rather than palatal too (see Navarro Tomás 1977:

125–6); this, added to the fact that in syllable-final position the off-glide typical of these palatal sounds does not take place, makes the perception of the nasals in **concha** and **paño** rather different.[26]

Thus a very simple rule will reflect the situation of syllable-final nasals in Spanish:

21. $[+\text{nas}] \rightarrow [\alpha \text{ PA}] / \underline{\qquad} \begin{bmatrix} -\text{syll} \\ \alpha \text{ PA} \end{bmatrix}$

given that the 'blanket' feature [PA] will control all those specific features referring to point of articulation (see Cressey 1974).[27]

Modern Spanish also has the same type of rule assimilating laterals to the point of articulation of a following obstruent, with the important difference that, as well as there being no labial or labiodental lateral, there is no velar lateral (Harris 1969:18–20; Alarcos Llorach 1971:161–2, 181–2[28]), the velar lateral having been lost in the history of Spanish. (Velarization was a different type of rule anyway, not depending on assimilation to the following segment, but rather on an across-the-board weakening of the lateral in syllable-final position.) The interesting thing here is that the rule of homorganic lateral assimilation could not have existed while velarization was present in the grammar, since all syllable-final laterals simply underwent this process. This means that the lateral assimilation rule was introduced as a new rule in Spanish; that is, it was not a rule inherited from Latin, as the nasal assimilation rule certainly was. It is thus a manifestation of weakening in syllable-final position which has spread from the nasals to the lateral: another indication of how weakening processes spread in final position.

We have thus established a clear associative pattern between the behaviour of consonants in absolute final position (see chapter 3), and those in syllable-final position within the word. We find that progressive weakening has taken place in both positions, but with a different typology: weakening in absolute final position is typically an independent phenomenon; that is, each segment undergoes what we might denominate 'absolute weakening', perfectly explicable phonetically by the use of a strength hierarchy, while in internal syllable-final position, consonantal segments prone to weakening do so in most cases under the assimilatory influence of neighbouring (generally following) segments.[29] One clear exception we have seen is velarization, with only ___$ as a context: but it is important to notice how even in this case of independent weakening, the velarized lateral, converted into a glide, later appears in assimilatory processes such as that expressed in rule 20.

Bearing this in mind then, and having seen that [s] has been maintained in absolute final position in Castilian Spanish,[30] we should expect the same to have happened in internal syllable-final position, and this is indeed what we find, both in Latin and Romance clusters:

AUGUSTU	→	agosto	**August**
AESTIVU	→	estío	**summer**
NOSTRU	→	nuestro	**our**
VESPA	→	avispa	**wasp**
MUSCA	→	mosca	**fly**
FRAX(I)NU	→	fresno	**ash (tree)**
AS(I)NU	→	asno	**ass**

Only in one very specific position did syllable-final [s] undergo any alteration: in the Latin groups –SC–, –ST– followed by a front vowel or a glide:

*ASCIATA	→	(O.Sp.) açada	→	(M.Sp.) azada **hoe**
CRESCERE	→	(O.Sp.) creçer	→	(M.Sp.) crecer **to grow**
USTIU	→	(Class. OSTIU)	→	(O.Sp.) uço → (arch.) uzo **door**
MISCERE	→	(O.Sp.) meçer	→	(M.Sp.) mecer **to rock, sway**
FASCE	→	(O.Sp.) f-/haç(e)	→	(M.Sp.) haz **bundle**
PISCE	→	(O.Sp.) peç(e)	→	(M.Sp.) pez **fish**

(cf. PISCARE → pescar **to fish**)

where the Old Spanish reflex was –ç– ([tˢ]), later developing into the Modern Castilian –c–/–z– ([θ]).[31] The affrication of the second consonant is perfectly regular within the development of Spanish from Latin, and will be correctly dealt with by the processes described in chapter 2 (see rules 7, 10, and 13).

The suppression or absorption of the syllable-final [s] here seems to be in accordance with the syllable structure constraints of Spanish. Taking the affricate segment [č] in Modern Spanish, we find that it is only preceded by [s] when the syllable boundary between them is also a morpheme boundary (Alarcos Llorach (1971:190–2) cites **deschanzado** 'found out, lost (slang)' based on **chanza**, and **deschuponar** 'to remove suckers from trees' based on chupón), and the intrinsic strength of [č] is demonstrated by the fact that, apart from the cases of –s$č–, the only segments to appear before the affricate are the liquids and a nasal (see Alarcos Llorach 1971:190–2). It seems likely that the same constraint operated in Medieval Spanish too: that the affricate [t^s] was too strong to permit clustering (even with a $ boundary in between) with a preceding segment stronger than a nasal. The picture has unfortunately been obscured by the subsequent development of the Medieval Spanish affricates: the Modern Spanish reflex of [t^s] (and of [d^z]) is [θ]; that is, a fricative, not an affricate, and as a fricative it will group with a wide range of preceding consonants; it is, however, notable that clusters of a stop plus [θ] and [sθ] are learned forms, brought into use since the period of Medieval Spanish, and taken directly from Latin or some other foreign source.

A constraint operative throughout the history of Spanish will impede the grouping $C_1$$$C_2$ where C_2 is an affricate and C_1 is any segment stronger than a nasal, unless $ is also a morpheme boundary. In the diachronic context, this constraint would probably be best interpreted as a rule assimilating C_1 (as a non-nasal segment with the same point of articulation as C_2) to C_2, which will correctly account not only for the development of the examples above, but also for that of MATTIANA → ma(n)çana (see page 23 above). This is a perfectly natural interpretation, for several reasons: first, as may be seen from the above examples, the Medieval Spanish reflex of the palatalization process was a voiceless affricate, which indicates in principle an original geminate or post-consonantal segment; second, the assimilation of a relatively strong syllable-final consonant to the following syllable-initial consonant is amply attested in the history of Spanish (and indeed of Western Romance in general: see below, pages 71–2 for the assimilation of syllable-final stops), especially bearing in mind that we are talking of segments with the same point of articulation.

What is more, the fact that [s] is liable to undergo assimilation to a following syllable-initial consonant is attested by the process which voices [s] to [z] before voiced consonants across a syllable boundary, a process which has apparently always existed in Spanish (see Harris 1969:29–30; Navarro Tomás 1977:108); thus:

mismo	[mízmo]	**same**
desde	[dézðe]	**since**
esbozo	[ezβóθo]	**sketch**

It is interesting to compare this process with the discussion in the previous chapter (pages 47–50, especially 47–8) regarding the devoicing of final consonants (specifically the fricatives). It was pointed out in that discussion that there seemed to be no reason why we should qualify devoicing in final position as unnatural; nor indeed should we wish to describe the voicing of [s] mentioned here as any less natural: moreover, they both seem to be weakening processes, even though the phonetic results of the weakening take a totally opposite course. And we shall see similar evidence provided by the processes undergone by stops a little later.

Of the other fricatives present in Latin, there are only marginal reflexes in Spanish, principally because [s] was the only fricative used in Latin in syllable-final position, with the exception of a few derivative forms with an assimilated prefix, such as AFFLARE (→ Sp. **hallar** 'to find') and SUFFLARE (→ Sp. **(re)sollar** 'to breathe heavily, wheeze'). Hence the only other developments we have at our disposal are those brought about by the syncope of an unstressed medial vowel which in Latin had followed a fricative consonant.

Thus verbs compounded in Latin with –IFICARE give the following reflexes:

SANCTIFICARE	→	santiguar	**to make the sign of the cross**
PACIFICARE	→	(a)paciguar	**to pacify**
*TESTIFICARE	→	(a)testiguar	**to testify**

suggesting that the regular voicing of intervocalic [f] took place before syncope, producing *–**iv(i)gare**, and by vocalization, *–**iwgare**, metathesized as **–igwar(e)** (cf. Hartman 1974:165, 168). This metathesis is not too surprising, given the very general instability of the back glide (cf. the results of SAPUI, *CAPUI, on page 62 above) and the Medieval Spanish tendency to eliminate falling diphthongs (cf. pages 60–2, note 19, and pages 74–5, 78).[32] And the vocalization of –v– is exactly parallel to that of the other labial, written –b– in Medieval Spanish (< Latin –V– and –P–) in the same situation:

CIV(I)TATE	→	(O.Sp.) cibdad	→	(M.Sp.) ciudad **city**
*LEV(I)TU	→	(O.Sp.) l(i)ebdo	→	(M.Sp.) leudo **fermented with yeast**
CAP(I)TALE	→	(O.Sp.) cabdal	→	(M.Sp.) caudal **volume (of river, wealth, etc.)**
CAP(I)TELLU	→	(O.Sp.) cabdi(e)llo	→	(M.Sp.) caudillo **leader**

This is in itself a late development in Spanish, not shared by syllable-final stops inherited in that position from Latin, as we shall see a little further on.

Finally we come to the development of internal syllable-final stops. Since the stops are the strongest segments on the hierarchy and syllable-final position is inherently weak, we should expect this anomaly to resolve itself in processes weakening the stops to a much greater extent than other segments, as we found in the case of absolute final position. And indeed, we find that in general, none of the syllable-final stops found in Latin has survived, at least in its original guise, in Spanish. In order to make the situation clear, we should distinguish between syllable-final stops originally present in Latin, and those which came into final position only in a later period due to the syncope of unstressed vowels.

Already in Latin we find a certain repugnance for syllable-final stops: neither the voiced nor the voiceless dental stop appeared with any regularity, except when AD- was used as a prefix, in which case total assimilation to a following consonant (especially a stop) was a regular process. The same applies to the voiced labial, particularly in combinations with SUB-; and we only find syllable-final –G– in native Latin forms before a syllable beginning with –N–, where it may have been a representation of a velar nasal (Allen 1978:23–5; Kent 1945:54–5; Ward 1944).

It appears, however, that this assimilation was also active from an early date in the case of the voiceless syllable-final stops, with –P– more so than with –C–:[33] the Latin of the Empire had already assimilated –PS– to –SS–, and the parallel reduction of –PT– to –TT– (common to Western Romance and Italian) was probably not much later (Menéndez Pidal 1958:142–3; Alarcos Llorach 1971:241). Thus Spanish has:

IPSE	→ ese	**that (dem.)**
GYPSU	→ yeso	**plaster**
SEPTE	→ siete	**seven**
SCRIPTU	→ escrito	**written**
RUPTU	→ roto	**broken**
CAPTARE	→ catar	**to taste, try**
*CAPTIARE[34]	→ (O.Sp.) caçar →	(M.Sp.) cazar **to hunt**

Neither the intervocalic [s] (transcribed –ss– in Medieval Spanish; cf. page 16) nor the [t] voiced, and the –ç– of the medieval **caçar** was voiceless [t^s], all indicating that in both cases, the syllable-final consonants were not completely lost in Latin, but merely assimilated, producing geminate –SS– and –TT–, as is in fact attested in inscriptions. We therefore have the same process as that which affected the final stops of the prefixes AD- and SUB-, producing in Spanish such forms as:

*AD-/AS-SED(I)ARE³⁴ → asear **to clean, tidy**
SUB-/SUC-CUTERE → sacudir **to shake, beat**

where again the need to postulate a geminate consonant in the etymon is clear in most cases (for example, **sacudir**, not ***sagudir**, as we should expect from a single intervocalic –C–).

Bearing in mind that, as will be discussed in a moment, we do not have the same process in many cases of internal syllable-final –C, we may now formulate a rule in which the stops already mentioned assimilate to a following consonant:

22. $\begin{bmatrix} -\text{cont} \\ -\text{bk} \end{bmatrix}$ $ [+\text{cons}] → C $ C
        1   2   2 2

a rule which must be ordered before rule 3, the reduction of geminate consonants. The $ is necessary here in order to maintain the generality of the process: tautosyllabic clusters such as [pl] etc. do not assimilate, and so if the $ mark is omitted from the rule, we shall have to complicate the expression of the environment in order to account for this: a completely superfluous complication, and yet another indication of the need to recognize the syllable boundary as an important environment in historical phonological processes.

The history of Latin syllable-final [k] has been rather different, however (note that Latin –X– was [–ks–]):

FACTU	→	hecho	**done, made**
LACTE	→	leche	**milk**
TRUCTA	→	trucha	**trout**
LACTUCA	→	lechuga	**lettuce**
PROFECTU	→	provecho	**benefit**
STRICTU	→	estrecho	**narrow**
TECTU	→	techo	**ceiling**
NOCTE	→	noche	**night**
OCTO	→	ocho	**eight**
PECTUS	→	pecho(s)	**chest, breast**
MAXILLA	→	mejilla	**cheek**
COXU	→	cojo	**lame**
TAXU	→	tejo	**yew**
AXE	→	eje	**axis, axle**

Syllable-Final Consonants 73

(The forms with –j– (M.Sp. [x]) had –x– ([š]) in Medieval Spanish.)

All the above examples clearly indicate a palatalization of the following [t] or [s] by the agency of a reflex of the syllable-final [k]. We are fortunate in this case to have abundant evidence of the process: Castilian has added a rule of palatalization to a development common in Western Romance: cf. Fr. **fait, lait**; Pt. **feito, leite**; Ct. **fet, llet** for Sp. **hecho, leche**. What is more, valuable evidence from Mozarabic not only helps with the phonetic development, but also with the chronological aspect of the changes involved: in Mozarabic we find both **nójte** and **nóχte**, **majšéla** and **maχšéla**, as well as **léjte** and **laχtájra** (< *LACTARIA, the plant 'bedstraw' called **cuajaleche** in Modern Spanish) (Menéndez Pidal 1972:284–5; Entwistle 1936:122; Lapesa 1981:126; Galmés de Fuentes 1983:106), suggesting that a fricative reflecting the Latin [k] was still to be heard in the Peninsula possibly as late as the eleventh century (see Sampson 1980:22).

Thus the first step would be:

23. $\begin{bmatrix} -\text{son} \\ +\text{hi} \\ +\text{bk} \end{bmatrix} \rightarrow [+\text{cont}] \ / \ \_\_\$$

$(k \rightarrow \chi \ / \ \_\_\$)^{35}$

As we have seen, the result of rule 23 was still to be found in the Spanish spoken in at least some parts of the Peninsula in the eighth century, and was maintained much longer in Mozarabic.

The subsequent passage from fricative to glide may be expressed as:

24. $\begin{bmatrix} +\text{cons} \\ +\text{cont} \\ +\text{hi} \end{bmatrix} \rightarrow \begin{bmatrix} -\text{cons} \\ -\text{bk} \end{bmatrix} \ / \ \_\_\$$

$(\chi \rightarrow j \ / \ \_\_\$)$

One is immediately struck by the similarity between this process and that formalized in rule 19: both involve the conversion into a glide of velar continuants in syllable-final position, and seem to be parts of the same process. Whether or not this can be shown formally is a question we shall return to later.

First, let us consider forms that emerge from rule 24 such as [lájte], [fájto], or, with vowel adjustments,[36] [léjte], [féjto], (which, with minor phonetic adjustments, would in fact be the Modern Portuguese forms), which will then undergo rule 20, and appear as [léjče], [féjčo], the glide of which is subsequently absorbed by rule 25, necessary also for the reflexes of the forms deriving from -ULT-:

25. $\begin{bmatrix} -\text{cons} \\ +\text{hi} \\ +\text{bk} \end{bmatrix} \rightarrow \emptyset\ / \underline{\quad} \begin{bmatrix} +\text{cons} \\ +\text{hi} \\ -\text{bk} \end{bmatrix}$

(j → ∅ / ___ č)

The correct Medieval Spanish forms [léče], [féčo], are thus produced.[37] From all this it may be appreciated that rule 20 has a larger input than was first indicated, and that the palatalization of the groups –ULT–, –ULS–, and –CT–, which we have seen so far, should not only be considered as the same phenomenon in diverse manifestations, but it should also be made clear that they are natural results of the weakening of the syllable-final consonant, combined with the peculiarly Castilian tendency to palatalize the [t] in these circumstances.

Further evidence that we are dealing with a single phenomenon is given by the exceptions to the general palatalization of the –CT– group. Note the following examples:

LECT(O)RILE   →   (O.Sp.) latril   →   (M.Sp.) atril
                                       bookrest
PECT(O)RALE   →   petral/pretal   **breast-strap**
APPECT(O)RARE →   *apetrar   →   apretar   **to squeeze, press**

In none of these forms has palatalization taken place, simply because the syncope of the unstressed medial vowel left the [t] as part of a cluster and hence in a situation incompatible with the realization of an affricate according to the syllable structure constraints of Spanish (see rule 20 and comments on page 64 above).

The only other exceptions to the palatalization of –CT– are to be found in developments exemplified by:

FRICTU   →   frito   **fried**
FICTU   →   hito   **landmark, boundary post**

which are to be explained in the following way: the passage of these forms through rules 23 and 24 would have produced **frijto, fijto**, at which point their development diverged from that of FACTU, LACTE, etc., since the group [ij] was reduced to the single vowel [i] as a result of the general tendency present in Castilian to eliminate combinations of glides with high vowels and palatals (cf. ALTERIU → **outeiro** → **otero**).[38] This reduction, which we cannot go into any detail about here, may be achieved with the suppression of V and other minor complications in the SD of rule 14 (page 24 above), since it is clearly part of the same process. Note also that rule 25 is doubtlessly implicated in this process too, although it is not necessarily collapsible with rule 14.

In the case of the Latin group –X– ([–ks–]), rules 23 and 24 also apply, producing, for example, **tájso** and **ájse**, and with the appropriate vowel adjustments (see note 36), **téjso** and **éjse**. The [s] then palatalizes by application of rule 20, and with the subsequent absorption of the glide, we have the Medieval Spanish forms, [tés̆o] and [és̆e].

The chronological aspect of this rule leads us to some interesting conclusions. As well as the forms already given, we shall consider the following etymologies:

CASEU	→ queso	**cheese**
BASIU	→ beso	**kiss**
*BASSIARE	→ bajar	**to descend, lower**

Both **beso** and **queso** had [–z–] in Medieval Spanish, while the reflex of *BASSIARE was **baxar** with voiceless [–š–]. The history of all these words is interwoven in a very complex way; let us see a few derivations:

		LACTE	FRICTU	TAXU
		lákte	fríkto	tákso[39]
Rule	23	láχte	fríχto	táχso
	24	lájte	fríjto	tájso
	14	___	fríto	___
Voc. assim.		léjte		téjso
	20	léjče		téjšo
	25	léče		téšo
Med. Sp.		[léče	fríto	téšo]
Orthography		**leche**	**frito**	**texo**

These derivations seem reasonable and uncontroversial. Now let us add those of CASEU and BASIU:

		LACTE	FRICTU	TAXU	CASEU	BASIU
		lákte	fríkto	tákso	kásjo	básjo
Rule	2	___	___	___	kázjo	bázjo
	23	láχte	fríχto	táχso	___	___
	24	lájte	fríjto	tájso	___	___

The fact that rule 2 should be ordered before rule 24 seems clear: although stops did not undergo rule 2 when preceded by a glide in some cases (see page 62 above), it seems that [s] did.[40] Thus Medieval Spanish had [kóza] 'thing' < CAUSA, [pozár] 'to settle, put down' < PAUSARE, [ozár] 'to dare' < AUSARE (see Menéndez Pidal 1958:141); which means that were rule 2 ordered after rule 24, it would incorrectly produce ***tájzo**, leading to *[tézo] instead of [téšo]. So:

	lájte	fríjto	tájso	kázjo	bázjo
Rule 14(a)	____	fríto	____	____	____
Glide attr.	____	____	____	kájzo	bájzo

The displacement of the glide in these forms may now be seen as more natural within the surface phonotactics of the language: the diphthong [áj] already existed as a model, thanks to the effect of rule 24.

	lájte	frito	tájso	kájzo	bájzo
Voc. assim.	léjte	____	téjso	kéjzo	béjzo
Rule 20	léjče	____	téjšo	____	____
25	léče	____	tèšo	____	____
14(b)[41]	____	____	____	kézo	bézo

The curious thing here is that the palatalization rule 20 affects the groups [jt] and [js], but not [jz]. At first sight, this may seem unnatural, but it is possible that the primitive rule affected [js], expanding later to include the stop [t], also [+coronal, +anterior, −voice]. The next logical expansion, which would have been to [z], [+coronal, +anterior, +continuant], may well have been blocked by the spread of the following rule, which reduced [ej] to [e] and so suppressed the palatalizing element.

Support for this hypothesis comes from Portuguese. Interestingly enough, Portuguese does not reduce the diphthong [ej], nor does it palatalize the group [jt], thus LACTE → **leite**; on the other hand, [js] does palatalize (TAXU → **teixo**), suggesting that the primitive segment affected in the Peninsula was the voiceless fricative. But Portuguese, which, as we mentioned above, maintains [ej], also palatalizes the group [jz].

The other problem is the derivation of *BASSIARE → (O.Sp.) **baxar** (→ **bajar**). If *BASSIARE followed the same process of glide attraction as, for example, BASIU, we should expect (bearing in mind the presence of −SS− in the etymon) a form *[bešár] rather than the correct [bašár]. The only way of deriving **baxar** correctly is the following:

	LACTE	TAXU	CASEU	BASIU	*BASSIARE
	lákte	tákso	kásjo	básjo	bassjáre
Rule 2	___	___	kázjo	bázjo	___
23	láχte	táχso	___	___	___
24	lájte	tájso	___	___	___
Glide attr.	___	___	kájzo	bájzo	___

The reason why the glide of **bassjáre** is not attracted to the preceding syllable is quite plausibly because of the presence of the intervening geminate –ss–. The attraction of the glide would therefore produce not simply the diphthong [aj], familiar, as pointed out above, from the effects of rule 24, but the more complex VGC group [ajs$], both the glide and the consonant being postnuclear.

	lájte	tájso	kájzo	bájzo	bassjáre
Rule 3	___	___	___	___	basjáre
Voc. assim.	léjte	téjso	kéjzo	béjzo	___
Glide attr.	___	___	___	___	bajsáre

The attraction of the glide in **bajsáre** may now take place, since the loss of the geminate resulting from rule 3 eliminated the syllable-final consonant.[42]

	léjte	téjso	kéjzo	béjzo	bajsáre
Rule 20	léjče	téjšo	___	___	bajšáre
25	léče	téšo	___	___	bašáre
14	___	___	kézo	bézo	___
Med. Sp.	[léče	téšo	kézo	bézo	bašár]
Orthography	**leche**	**texo**	**queso**	**beso**	**baxar**

We therefore have to accept that the attraction of the glide could still be exerted in **basjáre** some time after it had taken place in **básjo**, etc. As for the assimilation of [áj] to [éj] in **bajsáre**, we know that this process was lost in Spanish in the medieval period from the preservation of the diphthong in loanwords; for example, **fraile** 'friar' (from Occitan; first documentation 1174 according to Corominas and Pascual 1980–), **bailar** 'to dance' (also from Occitan; first documentation c.1270, see Corominas and Pascual 1980–), and in **aire** 'air' (< Latin AERE), where the diphthong is a late development from the primitive form **aer(e)**.[43]

The only alternative would be to postulate some extraneous origin for **bajar** in the same way that **caja** (O.Sp. **caxa**) 'box' is undoubtedly a borrowing from Catalan, not only because of the typical Catalan development of CAPSA → **caixa** (cf. IPSE → **eix** 'that (dem.)' etc.),[44] but also because of its late documentation: Corominas and Pascual (1980–, s.v. caja) only find three trustworthy citations before the last decade of the fifteenth century. For the moment, however, this postulation would appear gratuitous. Moreover, there is evidence of a similar development to that of **bajar** in **rojo** (< RUSSEU) 'red' and in the Castilian dialect forms **caja, cajilla**, and standard **quijada** 'jaw(bone)' from *CASSEU (*CAPSEU), an adjectival form based on CAPSA (see Corominas and Pascual 1980–, s.v. caja).[45]

The condition in rule 20 that a [–cons] element should follow the segment palatalized, which, as we saw, was necessary for the correct derivations of **leche/atril, pecho/petral**, etc., is also correct in the development of the [–ks–] group:

FRAX(I)NU → freisno → fresno **ash(tree)**
*SEX(I)MA → seisma → sesma **one-sixth**

(see Menéndez Pidal 1972:85). Thus a typical derivation would be:

		FRAXINU
		frákseno
Rule	23	fráχseno
	24	frájseno
Voc. assim.		fréjs(e)no

and the posttonic medial vowel will disappear before the application of rule 20 (see chapter 5 below), leaving the correct form **freisno**, whose diphthong would be reduced like all the others, giving the modern form **fresno**.

The only other case to be considered involving a Latin syllable-final consonant is that of the group –GN–. Consider the following examples:

LIGNA → leña **firewood**
SIGNA → seña **sign, mark**
PUGNU → puño **fist**
STAGNARE → (re)stañar **to stop (the flow of)**

This development of –GN– to [–ñ–] is open to two interpretations: first, if the –G– in the Latin spelling represented a velar nasal, as maintained by most classical scholars (see page 71 above), then nasal assimilation (pages 65–7 above) will produce a geminate, whose later development will be the same as that observed in PANNU → **paño** 'cloth' and CANNA → **caña** 'reed'. On the other hand, if –GN– did not represent a totally nasal group (a possibility considered by some; for example, Ward (1944)), we may assume the development to have been parallel with that of syllable-final [k] in the groups –CT– and –X–; that is to say, spirantization of the syllable-final velar, and later glide formation leading to palatalization of the following nasal. Rules 23 and 24, as formalized, will convert the velar into the front glide; let us compare the derivations of LACTE, LIGNA and STAGNARE:

	LACTE	LIGNA	STAGNARE
	lákte	légna	stagnáre
Rule 23	láχte	léɣna	(re)staɣnáre
24	lájte	léjna	(re)stajnáre

So far, so good; but here we begin to encounter problems. First, according to our previous derivations, these forms now undergo vocalic assimilation, leaving **léjna** untouched, and producing **léjte** and **(re)stejnáre**, the latter being manifestly incorrect, given the correct output [rrestañár]. Second, rule 20, which, as we have seen, palatalizes [t] and [s] in these conditions (but not [z]), cannot in its present form be extended to include [n], since it would be necessary to remove the feature [–voice], and thus it would include, incorrectly, [z]. Something is therefore seriously wrong, and it seems once again that the problem is one of chronology.

In order to take in the wider panorama of this problem, we should begin by looking into the question of syllable-boundary clusters which arose by syncope in the Latin period, since they are also implicated. Consider the following examples, in which –j– represents Old Spanish [ž], Modern Spanish [x]:

APICULA	→	abeja	**bee**
OCULU	→	ojo	**eye**
LENTICULA	→	lenteja	**lentil**
FENUCULU	→	hinojo	**fennel**
MANUCULU	→	manojo	**handful, bunch**
REGULA	→	reja	**harrow**
TEGULA	→	teja	**tile**
COAGULU	→	cuajo	**rennet**

The groups –CUL– and –GUL– were reduced by syncope of the unaccented vowel at an early period (see chapter 5, below), and the otherwise unknown group –T'L– (resulting from syncope in forms like VETULU → **viejo** 'old', *AD-ROTULARE → **arrojar** 'to throw') was absorbed in part into the –C'L–, –G'L– result: the *Appendix Probi* points out VECLUS as an incorrect form of VETULUS (Elcock 1960:30).

The point is that in these groups the velar stop again

spirantized, and the glide subsequently palatalized the following lateral. So the development of –G'L– (and –C'L–, the first element of which would voice in any case) was totally parallel with that of –GN–.[46] What is quite clear is that these palatalizations (along with another which does not strictly concern us here, [–lj–] as in FILIU → (O.Sp.) **fijo** → (M.Sp.) **hijo** 'son') took place at a much earlier date than those of –CT– and –X–. The examples collected by Menéndez Pidal (1972: 274–80) demonstrate that not only had the [l] been palatalized by the time Castilian emerged as a written language, but also that the palatal result was already being delateralized by the tenth century, a period when the palatalization of –CT– and –X– was still being completed (Menéndez Pidal (1972:82–3) and, for aspects of chronology, see Pensado Ruiz (1984:440–2)). Moreover, while the palatalization of –GN–, –G'L– is common to Western Romance, that of –C'T– is peculiar to Castilian.

The similarity between the palatalizations of –G'L–, –GN– on the one hand, and –CT–, –X–, –ULT–, –ULS– on the other, is of course very attractive, but for all their similarity, there is no possibility of collapsing these processes into a single rule, partly for reasons of chronology, as was shown. We have to recognize that the palatalization of the sonorants took place much earlier and reflect this chronological difference in the rules.[47] We therefore need a rule:

26. $\begin{bmatrix} +\text{son} \\ +\text{cor} \\ +\text{ant} \\ -\text{vib} \end{bmatrix} \rightarrow \begin{bmatrix} -\text{ant} \\ +\text{hi} \end{bmatrix} / \begin{bmatrix} -\text{cons} \\ -\text{syll} \\ -\text{bk} \end{bmatrix} \_\_\_$ [48]

$\begin{Bmatrix} l \\ n \end{Bmatrix} \rightarrow \begin{Bmatrix} \tilde{l} \\ \tilde{n} \end{Bmatrix} / \text{ j}\_\_\_)$

A degree of similarity with rule 20 is obvious (the context here could also be completed as ___[–cons], but this is unnecessary since these groups were always followed by a vowel), but it is not possible to claim any formal advantage of simplicity from this similarity: the operation of rule 26 took place a great deal earlier than that of rule 20. What could be claimed, and with some conviction, is that the process expressed in rule 20 is an extension of the palatalization reflected in rule 26. Such an extension would indeed correspond with what we would expect to happen naturally: for the segments affected ([n], [l], and later [s], [t]), the palatalization is an assimilation process, natural enough in syllable-initial position when carried out at the expense of a preceding syllable-final element. Having begun with the sonorants, the palatalization may well have extended to affect fricatives and stops with the same [+coronal, +anterior] point of articulation. This would support our hypothesis that palatalization affected [s] before [t], but it would still not explain the lack of palatalization of [z] in Spanish, unless the tentative suggestion we have already made (see above, page 76) will hold water.

In any case, rule 26 will certainly solve the problem of the derivations, as may be seen here:

		LACTE	LIGNA	STAGNARE	OCULU	REGULA
		lákte	légna	stagnáre	óklo	régla
Rule	2				óglo	
	23	láχte	léɣna	(re)staɣnáre	óɣlo	réɣla
	24	lájte	léjna	(re)stajnáre	ójlo	réjla
	26		léjña	(re)stajñáre	ójl̃o	réjl̃a
	25		léña	(re)stañáre	ól̃o	rél̃a
Voc. assim.		léjte				
	20	léjče				
	25	léče				

And so we have the medieval forms [léče], [léña] and [rrestañár(e)]. The palatal lateral of the reflexes of OCULU and REGULA, as we have already mentioned, underwent delateralization unconditionally, thus producing the medieval forms [óžo] and [rréža].

We find, then, that there are essentially several processes taking place over a considerable period of time – several centuries – involving an ever greater number of segments. The first of these processes, the weakening of syllable-final velar consonants via spirantization and glide formation, may have been sparked off by the syncope of unstressed internal vowels in the groups –CUL– and –GUL– (for which, see the next chapter), leaving the velars in syllable-final position.[49] These velars weakened, and were followed by those velars preceding a syllable-initial nasal (the next segment to the lateral on the strength parameter). At this point Latin had among its syllable-final continuants the velar lateral, which already existed, and [ɣ], which must have been sufficient for the spirantization process to affect the other syllable-final velar, [k], first before [s] and later before [t], which had existed as the clusters –X– and –CT– in Latin before syncope took place.

After the formation of the glide from the velar fricative (which we would expect to have taken place earlier in the case of [ɣ χ] than in that of the velar lateral, given the latter's greater stability in syllable-final position), the following syllable-initial palatalized. This palatalization, having begun at an earlier period with the lateral and nasal, thus presumably spread to the fricative [s], and finally to [t].

There are several factors in favour of the interpretation of these processes as spreading gradually from one segment to another. First, all the available evidence shows that the palatalization of –G'L– and –GN– took place considerably earlier than that of the other groups. Second, some palatalizations are much less common features of Western Romance generally (the production of an affricate from –CT– is purely Castilian, for example) than others, suggesting that, by the implication of the wave model of the spread of historical change, the former were later innovations in smaller areas. Third, while the palatalization of the syllable-final obstruents is unconditional, this is not the case with the lateral, from which the formation of a front glide with its palatalizing effect only took place under restricted conditions. Clearly, the sonorant quality of the lateral helped it resist change in this weak position more successfully than its fricative companions.

In short, the weakening of all these syllable-final elements was closely related, but it cannot be expressed as a single phenomenon in generative formalism: partly, as we have seen in the derivations above, because the various processes interact in such a way as to make telescoping impossible; and partly because the variety and type of segments involved, both those which are palatalized and those which appear in the respective environments, would make the formalization of a single palatalization rule virtually impossible, or at least monstrously ad hoc.

As regards other syllable-boundary consonant clusters formed in the Romance period, their development essentially demonstrates that rules operative in the Latin period no longer had effect some centuries later (*pace* Foley 1971). There is clearly a similar aim: the weakening of strong syllable-final consonants; but it is achieved in a different way. Let us look at a few examples in detail.

With the labials, it is again a question of the formation of a labialized glide:

CAP(I)TELLU	→	(O.Sp.) cabdi(e)llo	→	caudillo	**leader**
CAP(I)TALE	→	(O.Sp.) cabdal	→	caudal	**volume**
*CUP(I)DITIA	→	(O.Sp.) cobdicia	→	codicia	**greed**
DEB(I)TA	→	(O.Sp.) debda	→	deuda	**debt**

CUB(I)TU → (O.Sp.) cobdo → codo **elbow**
CIV(I)TATE → (O.Sp.) cibdad(e) → ciudad **city**

Thus, syncope of the medial vowel does not take place until after the operation of rule 2, which voices the intervocalic stops (see chapter 5, below). The syllable-final labial was maintained for many centuries: though Menéndez Pidal (1972:314) finds examples of vocalization dating from the eleventh century (**fraucato** < *FRABICATU (?) 'made, built'), the change took a century or more to establish itself, and forms with –b– are still to be found, though clearly becoming obsolete, in the sixteenth century (Menéndez Pidal 1958:161; Macpherson 1975:152, 155). Notice that when the glide is produced after a non-low back vowel, the resulting group [ow] is reduced to [o] (see pages 61–2 above), while the group [aw] is maintained, having been produced after the disappearance of the rule reducing Latin –AU– to [o] (cf. CAL(I)CE → **cauce**, SAL(I)CE → **sauce**, while AURU → **oro**, CAUSA → **cosa**, etc. (pages 61–2 above).

The development of the Romance group is therefore fundamentally different from that of the Latin group –PT–, in which the labial simply assimilated completely to the following syllable-initial consonant. This may be due to the fact that, almost certainly in the case of **debda, cobdo,** and **cibdad**, the labial was a fricative and not a stop, having undergone the first consonant shift while still in intervocalic position (see chapter 2 above). This of course is unthinkable in the case of the Latin group, where the labial had never been intervocalic. The same may be true of **cabdillo, cabdal,** and **cobdicia** too, since, although the first consonant shift would merely have effected the change [p] → [b], the existence of [β] from other sources and the Spanish aversion to stops in syllable-final position may well have given rise to the spirantization of the stop.

A similar problem is involved in the development of Romance groups with a syllable-final dental stop:

PORTAT(I)CU → (O.Sp.) portadgo → portazgo
toll
IUD(I)CARE → (O.Sp.) judgar → juzgar
to judge

Here, the same conditions apply: syncope did not occur until after the operation of rules 1 and 2, thus producing the Old Spanish form **judgar** with [–ð–]. The form **portadgo** was clearly pronounced in the same way, though it is doubtful that the second consonant shift had taken place beforehand. The later orthographical change **portadgo** → **portazgo** and **judgar** → **juzgar** indicates a devoicing, as well as a minor articulatory shift.⁵⁰

The most coherent explanation of this is that what still happens in word-final position (see chapter 3, pages 50–1 above) also took place in word-internal syllable-final position; that is, that stops, not being tolerated, are spirantized, bearing in mind that the segments [β], [ð], and [ɣ] already exist in the language, thanks to the action of rule 1 in the first consonant shift. What is more, it seems that the fricative subsequently devoices, just as in word-final position, though this development is somewhat later, and has more relation with the syllable-structure constraints applying to Modern Spanish (see below).

Thus, there seems to be a constraint operating in Spanish since the earliest manifestations of the language, impeding the appearance of stops in syllable-final position and automatically spirantizing any stop which by the operation of a historical rule (in this case syncope) attempts to break it.

Finally, the development of forms like PLAC(I)TU → (O.Sp.) **plazdo** → **plazo** 'period of time' and REC(I)TARE → (O.Sp.) ***rezdar** → **rezar** 'to pray' is rather different in that the segment which by syncope falls into syllable-final position is not a stop, but an affricate [dᶻ], and eventually it is the affricate in the complex group [–dᶻd–] that wins out, despite its weak position. This reduction is largely ignored by the manuals, which mention it without commenting on the unusual outcome (Otero (1971:55), for example, refers to it merely as a 'simplification'): the examples are too scarce to risk any firm hypothesis, but this may well be linked with the reduction of the groups in MATTIANA → (O.Sp.) **mançana**, CRESCERE → (O.Sp.) **creçer**, etc. (see page 69 above), extended to a mirror-image process, as suggested by Hartman (1974:171).⁵¹

The spirantization of syllable-final stops, which we have seen to be so active in the history of Spanish, is clearly reflected in their behaviour in Modern Castilian: nowadays, after several centuries of accepting learned forms, taken principally from Latin and Greek, but also from other languages, the typical syllable structure of Modern Spanish is rather different from that of the medieval language. Word-internal syllable-final consonants are relatively common (with the evident exception of the palatals; cf. notes 3 and 11 to chapter 3, and pages 64–5 and 74), but certain conditions apply to them. Consider the pronunciation of the following forms, which may be described as andante/allegretto (Harris 1969:7), colloquial, subjectively considered by native speakers as neither racy nor pedantic:⁵²

apto	[áβto]	**suitable**
recepción	[rreθeβθjón]	**reception**
obtener	[oβtenér]	**to obtain**
objeto	[oβxéto]	**object**
fútbol	[fúðβol]	**football**
atmósfera	[aðmósfera]	**atmosphere**
advertir	[aðβertír]	**to warn**
adquirir	[aðkirír]	**to acquire**
actor	[aɣtór]	**actor**
técnico	[téɣniko]	**technician**
signo	[síɣno]	**sign**
ignorante	[iɣnoránte]	**ignorant**

There is obviously a constraint at work here which ensures that any underlying stop in syllable-final position is voiced and spirantized. It cannot be designated a process of assimilation, since in many cases, as may be observed above, the following consonant is voiceless and a stop: it is an independent manifestation of weakening brought about merely by the weak environment in which the segment is found.

Of these three segments, [β ð ɣ], the only one permitted in absolute final position, it will be remembered, is [ð] (see chapter 3, pages 47, 49–50), which is devoiced by many speakers, if realized at all, in this position. The same speakers appear to extend the devoicing rule to [ð] in word-internal syllable-final position too, producing forms like [aθβertír], [aθkirír], etc. Of course, we are talking here about low-level rules which may or may not be applied with a good deal of freedom, and the process described here is typical only of certain styles of speech: in varieties considered 'non-standard', the syllable-final segment may be effaced altogether; on the other hand, in deliberate, emphatic speech not only does spirantization not apply, but the segments may also be devoiced, whether or not they are voiceless in the underlying representation:

apto	[ápto]	obtener	[optenér]
atmósfera	[atmósfera]	advertir	[atβertír]
actor	[aktór]	signo	[síkno]

(Alarcos Llorach 1971:184; Navarro Tomás 1977:83–4, 97, 137, 140).

In the case of the labials, moreover, there is still another possibility: glide formation (see pages 82–3 above) is still present in Modern Castilian, at least in the case of some speakers' pronunciation of late loanwords; the pronunciation of **cápsula** as [káwsula] or **objeto** as [owxéto] (Navarro Tomás 1977:83, note 1; Hooper 1976:216) is fairly common in 'non-standard' varieties of the language, though such pronunciations are often frowned upon for sociolinguistic reasons.

In conclusion, then, we find that Spanish has throughout its history striven to rid itself of syllable-final consonants, and the stronger the consonant, the more immediate and drastic has been the solution; though it is also true that due to the influx of learned or foreign items at various periods, Spanish has never developed a truly typical CV syllable structure. We have seen how stops began to disappear from the Latin period onwards, and the tendency to weaken them still persists today, though the processes are rather different: in Latin and Early Romance, the existence of geminate consonants meant that many stops simply assimilated their point of articulation to that of the following syllable-initial element, while, since the reduction of geminate consonants, Spanish has not had this possibility, and so has produced other ways of absorbing or weakening the syllable-final stops: by palatalization[53] (and later effacement), spirantization, or vocalization. The presence of large numbers of learned words in Modern Spanish has meant the frequent appearance of stops in syllable-final position in underlying representations, and a variety of variable rules that may be used to weaken them. These processes, though variable, seem to function hierarchically, with spirantization first (normally with automatic voicing: we have already suggested that the feature [±voice] may have to be extracted from the hierarchy; see page 48), then vocalization if applicable (as it normally only is in the case of the labials, precisely because of their labiality and that of the back glide), and complete suppression, which is not common even in allegretto speech. Certainly it seems Spanish nowadays has a greater tolerance towards consonants in syllable-final position than it did in the sixteenth and seventeenth centuries: the forms **dino** 'worthy', **conceto** 'concept', **seta** 'sect', common among other words introduced by Classical Spanish writers (Lapesa 1981:390–1), have been replaced not only in the orthography (M.Sp. **digno, concepto, secta**), but also in the pronunciation, where a fricative is now much more common: [díɣno], [konθéβto], [séɣta] (see also Pensado (1985:317)).

We have also found further evidence that historical rules do not work in blocks: many processes, such as that of palatalization, begin with one or two segments and only later do they generalize and spread to affect others. We have shown how this may be proved by appealing to chronology and attempting a cross-plot of rules: many seemingly exceptional circumstances can be explained perfectly well if we accept that processes like palatalization are not 'block phenomena', but begin with segments which, both by their inherent phonetic character and their situation, are most susceptible to the process, and then spread to others naturally (that is, phonetically) related. This rule extension may in some cases take centuries to complete, and interference with other historical rules is logical and unavoidable. It is normal, therefore, to find some processes truncated or deviated when they come into conflict with others; and in any case there is a clear necessity to establish surface structure constraints (in most cases specifically associated with syllable structure and the strength of elements on a hierarchy), which, in cases of conflict, will have the power to override the regular operation of historical rules, thereby in many cases simplifying what would otherwise be unnaturally complex formulations. There is considerable evidence that large areas of language history can be best described by means of changes in phonotactic admissibility. These constraints will, in principle, be language-specific and may be relaxed or tightened up over periods of time, as we have seen, though this does not mean that they will be totally unrelated from one language to another.

It is certainly clear that the categorical historical rule itself is insufficient from many points of view: it reflects a simplistic reduction and even manipulation of the facts. As we have demonstrated in the question of the weakening of stops in syllable-final position, such processes may be interpreted and carried out in different ways. We have used the blanket term 'weakening' to cover such diverse phenomena as voicing, assimilation, vocalization, etc; in a way, this is a diachronic equivalent of 'conspiracies' (see Kisseberth 1970). But it is not enough to seek the use of greater semantic generalizations: it will be necessary to formalize with greater accuracy the function of the phenomena involved.

Notes

1. See, for example, Hooper (1976:199).
2. Hartman's is yet another attempt to collapse syllable-final consonant assimilation into one rule without showing any phonetic plausibility.
3. For the orthography, see chapter 2, page 16 above.
4. Examples such as INSIGNARE → **enseñar** 'to teach' indicate that a morpheme boundary may have blocked the fall of the nasal. If this is so, CONSUERE must clearly have lost its status as a prefixed verb.

5. For the reduction of the geminates to single voiceless consonants, see page 12, rule 3, above.
6. For a detailed study of the loss of the nasal in this group, see Catalán Menéndez-Pidal (1968), and cp. the comments of Badía Margarit (1972:147–8). For further comments on this rule, see the Conclusion, pages 121–3 below.
7. The loss of the nasal under such conditions seems to be a relatively common phenomenon in many languages; cf. some varieties of Germanic. See, for example, Tiersma (1980:14–15), and, for English, Strang (1970:385).
8. See, for instance, Zauner (1929, 1930), Brüch (1930), which contain some rather picturesque proposals; and Malkiel (1960b).
9. Menéndez Pidal (1958:140) also cites PULSU → **poso** 'dregs', but he is clearly mistaken here, given the semantic difficulties involved and the obvious connection of **poso** with **posar** 'to put down, rest', from Latin PAUSARE. Otero (1971:297 (P13)) also gives PULSU → PUSSU, probably following Menéndez Pidal. Once more, Otero's rule 13, which it exemplifies, is obviously a gross generalization, as may be seen from the discussion here.
10. There has been considerable argument over whether **dulce** is really a borrowing from Latin; for one of the latest explanations of 'popular' development, see Hartman (1980); while for an explanation based on multiple causation, see Malkiel (1975).
11. This may be another manifestation of the relative weakness of velar-articulated consonants generally; see chapter 3, page 42 and chapter 2, page 14 above.
12. On the basis of this example (which is in itself unobjectionable), Hartman's (1974:152) rule cannot be correctly formulated, since it requires the segment following the lateral to be voiceless. Cf. the placename **Oviñana** (Asturias) < ALBINIANA.
13. The reduction of this diphthong was relatively late in Castilian (see Menéndez Pidal 1972:105–7): some dialects of Portuguese still retain the diphthong, and Catalan has not vocalized the velar.
14. To be more precise, the form ALTU itself was not an exception to the process, as the expected result **oto** is found widely in placenames such as **Colloto, Villota** and **Montoto** among others, as Menéndez Pidal points out (see also Corominas and Pascual 1980–, s.v. alto); **alto** was apparently a parallel form whose use and later complete imposition perhaps involved sociolinguistic factors. See also Badía Margarit (1972:139). As well as **alto**, there are in fact numerous other cases in which the [l] remained: SALTU itself gives not only **soto**, but also **salto; calzar, alzar, calcar** are just a few among them which cannot convincingly be explained away as 'semi-learned'.
15. There are areas in the north of Spain where the vocalization rule had already been lost, and which therefore preserve **calce, salce;** see Lapesa (1981:480), Corominas and Pascual (1980–, s.v. cauce). The other possibility, of course, is that certain northern dialects never

had this rule, which would account for the appearance of many of the 'anomalous' forms we have seen. This would certainly be worth investigating. The vocalization rule did not in any case remain in the grammar of Spanish for very long, as may be seen from its non-occurrence in Arabic and Germanic loanwords, and even in some groups produced by syncope; see **sueldo** above, page 61.

16. With reference to syllable-final [l], Navarro Tomás says: 'final de sílaba o de palabra, y sobre todo en posición acentuada, [la lengua] se hace ligeramente cóncava; pero sin llegar en ningún caso a la articulación hueca o velar de la **l** inglesa o catalana, cuyo uso debe evitarse cuidadosamente en español" (1977:114).

17. Otero (1971) does not take this into consideration, and groups the reduction of au → o with that of ae → e at a very early stage (1971:294). The examples he gives, PAUPERE and AURICULA (Sp. **pobre** 'poor' and **oreja** 'ear'), were probably two of the forms inherited from Latin with –o– rather than –au–: see Menéndez Pidal (1958:141), Vidos (1977:20–1), and Pensado Ruiz (1984:428–9). This in itself supports our hypothesis of gradual spread, as does the fact that Rumanian, a language which, as we have indicated, maintains the diphthong, shows **ureche**, suggesting a Latin base ORIC(U)LA, rather than AURICULA. Cp. Corominas and Pascual: 'en castellano y catalán la monoptongación total de AU fue tardía, no anterior al S.XI' (1980–, s.v. loro II).

18. See Corominas and Pascual (1980–, s.v. cutral) for the history and geographical extension of this form.

19. The modern pronunciation of these forms as [mwí], [bwítre] is innovative: they were formerly pronounced [múj], [bújtre], forms which may still be heard (especially [múj]) as one of the many archaic features of the Spanish spoken in Asturias (see Navarro Tomás 1977:166).

20. It seems unnecessary (and unnatural) to postulate, as Menéndez Pidal (1958:140) does, a palatalization of the syllable-final lateral as an intermediate stage between [l] and the front glide. If we were correct in suggesting in chapter 3 that the palatal lateral is too strong to appear in word-final position (see chapter 3, note 3), it would be unexpected, to say the least, to find palatalization in internal syllable-final position. Moreover, though [ĺ] → [j] is a process well known in Castilian in other contexts, it would be difficult to explain the Portuguese and Galician forms in the same way.

21. Though general by the eleventh century, according to Menéndez Pidal (1972:282).

22. The form **much** appears in thirteenth-century texts in contexts where it is followed by a word beginning with a vowel. Clearly, its ultimate rejection had much to do with the disappearance of **noch**, **lech**, and similar apocopated variants.

23. Incidentally, Hooper comments that 'the hypothetical cluster ?/ktr/ would give in Modern Spanish ?/ytr/, not */čr/' (1976:213); the question mark may be removed from /ytr/, since this was indeed the

result of the process under discussion here. Hooper only considers the development of the Latin –CT– cluster, though that of –ULT– is totally parallel. The only proviso to be made is that already pointed out in note 19, viz, that Modern Spanish has shifted the accent from [–újtr–] to [–wítr–].
24. Hartman's (1980) solution (see note 10 above) is attractive but rests on the assumption of a syllable-final palatal lateral at a time when, as we have seen, it is more reasonable to assume that all syllable-final laterals were velarized.
25. In other dialects of Spanish, syllable-final [r] is also subject to weakening processes; see Lapesa (1981:385–7, 564, 575).
26. This was already pointed out by Navarro Tomás (1977:133).
27. It is not our intention here to go into the question of whether such features are valid in the theory; we are merely using [PA] as an abbreviatory device: there is no doubt the rule can actually be expressed in terms of real features (see, for example, Harris 1969:12, 1970:36). For further comments on this rule, see Basbøll (1981).
28. The reason why Alarcos Llorach lists an interdental nasal and lateral while Harris does not, is simply that Alarcos Llorach is describing standard Castilian as spoken in the Peninsula, while Harris's study is of the speech of Mexico City, which lacks the interdental fricative [θ], present in Castilian, and so clusters of nasal/lateral plus interdental also.
29. This is not to say that the weakening of word-final consonants was not helped along by the presence of following word-initial consonants; but their influence was not exerted in the form of specific assimilations, as in the case of internal syllable-initial consonants.
30. As with word-final [s], internal syllable-final [s] is also aspirated, otherwise weakened, or lost under various conditions in many other dialects of Spanish. See the works mentioned in chapter 3 above (note 5).
31. This is a peculiarity of Castilian within the dialects of the Peninsula: Galician, Portuguese, Astur-Leonese, Aragonese, and Catalan, as well as Mozarabic, have or had [š] as a result of this group; see Lapesa (1981:178) and Menéndez Pidal (1958:150; 1972:307-8).
32. It may also be that the group [gw] was more favoured than [wg], cf. *FRAB(I)CA (Class. FABRICA) → (O.Sp.) **frauga** → (M.Sp.) **fragua** 'forge'. See Pensado Ruiz (1984:325, 333).
33. This could be interpreted as yet another indication of the greater strength of labials than of velars in Spanish and perhaps in Western Romance in general.
34. For these etymologies, see Corominas and Pascual (1980–).
35. This rule, of course, includes other segments, whose development we shall be commenting on in due course.
36. Both the back and the front glide induced immediately preceding vowels to raise in many cases. Thus the same phenomenon witnessed

by these examples may be seen in MULTU → *mójto → mújto and presumably also in ALTERIU → awtéjro → owtéjro; see Menéndez Pidal (1958:44-50, especially 48).
37. The initial f- of fecho in Castilian developed into an aspirate [h-], later totally lost from pronunciation though it is still maintained in the spelling; see Menéndez Pidal (1958:121-4).
38. The participle dicho 'said' < DICTU is anomalous either because of the [č] or because of the [i]. The form decho is documented in León, and it seems the particularity resides in the high vowel of dicho, probably imported from other parts of the conjugation (digo, dices, dije, dijiste, etc.). See Corominas and Pascual (1980-, s.v. decir).
39. This first stage resumes, for ease of exposition, the various vowel adjustments which took place (see chapter 2, note 23), as well as rule 7 (chapter 2, page 17).
40. Once again, we find that historical processes are in fact considerably more complex in many cases than categorical generative rules (such as our rule on page 12) would suggest. If we are right in that the fricative voiced in a greater diversity of environments than the stops, it may be the case, by implication, that the voicing of fricatives was the earlier process. Given the limitations of Latin orthography, however, we cannot be sure.
41. Since we cannot discuss all the questions involved in the development of vowels, we are taking for granted here that the general reduction of [ej] to [e], even before non-palatal segments, may be expressed as an expansion of part of rule 14, as suggested on page 75 above.
42. Note also Corominas and Pascual's (1980-, s.v. lagarto) comment that 'El cat. pixar, cast. pija, de *PISSIARE, muestran . . . que en –SSI– la S ya estaría algo palatalizada antes de consumarse del todo la trasposición de la yod.'
43. Cf. the derivation discussed by Otero (1971:52-4), in which he reaches similar conclusions. It is, incidentally, unlikely that bajo (O. Sp. baxo) 'low' should have *BASSIU as its etymon, bearing in mind the Fr. bas, It. basso, and the attested Latin BASSU. It is more probable that the primitive reflex of BASSU, *[báso], was influenced by the fricative of the verb [bašár(e)], as suggested by Corominas and Pascual (1980-, s.v. bajo).
44. The form capsa is not the popular Catalan reflex of CAPSA, despite Bergquist (1981:51).
45. Pensado Ruiz's (1984:497, 511-12) comments on bajar are confused and unhelpful, though she eventually concedes the possibility of differing chronologies too.
46. As Corominas and Pascual (1980-, s.v. cuchara) point out, and despite the existence of initial stop plus liquid groups in Latin, the stops which came into contact with the lateral after syncope remained syllable-final. Only in this way can their development be understood; and, as we have seen, there is sufficient independent justification for this type of development. In this sense, it is interesting to note the considerable degree of variation in the result

of the labial plus liquid cluster (see Menéndez Pidal (1958:158) and Corominas and Pascual (1980–, s.v. chopo).
47. For a more detailed consideration of the effect and validity of expressing long-term diachronic change in telescoped rules, see the Conclusion, below.
48. We are using the feature [± vibrant] to distinguish [r] from [l]. We have seen from this chapter and the previous one that the two liquids do not behave in the same way; they are on different positions in the hierarchy. Despite the fact that, for this reason, we should expect the nasals and the lateral to take part in processes from which [r] is excluded, there is no satisfactory way of expressing this without a feature peculiar to [r] (just as [+lateral] distinguishes [l] from [n, r] and [+nasal] [n] from [l, r]), such as the one suggested.
49. It has already been pointed out (see note 46 above) that the velars did not form syllable-initial groups with the following liquid, despite the existence of such groups in Latin at that time. We cannot postulate any clear non-ad hoc reason here why this should have been so, but the development of the segments makes this fact clear.
50. The fact that the syllable-final dental was unstable may be appreciated from the numerous orthographical variants: **jugdar, jubgar**, etc. See Macpherson (1975:151), and for further details, Pensado Ruiz (1984:325–30).
51. The other possibility is that forms like ***rezdar** underwent metathesis (→ ***redzar**), thus shifting the over-strong affricate out of syllable-final position. The reduction of the cluster would then be exactly parallel to that of **ma(n)çana**. See Corominas and Pascual (1980–, s.v. rezar).
52. For further details of the pronunciation of stops in syllable-final position, see Alarcos Llorach (1971:184–5), and Navarro Tomás (1977:78, 83–7, 97, 100, 139–41, 143–4). See also comments on the context of spirantization in Pensado Ruiz (1984:181).
53. The processes of palatalization described above, although present in the early stages of Spanish, have also since disappeared, of course.

Chapter five

The Consequences of Syncope

Up to this point, we have looked at processes of weakening which have affected Spanish consonants in their development from Latin, and have used these processes to illustrate the hypothesis that the standard generative theory of historical change cannot be maintained in its extreme requirements. Change cannot be elucidated without careful reference to phonetic fact, nor can it be reduced to categorical rules to be added on to the end of the grammar (whether or not subsequent reordering is permitted), without reference to the surface forms they are destined to produce.

We have attempted to show that a single rule will not necessarily be capable of reflecting what is considered to be a unitary process: changes start with specific segments in specific environments, and, if circumstances are favourable, spread to phonetically related segments in similar environments. Hence the importance of hierarchies in our understanding of the paths given changes will follow in given languages.[1]

It seems likely from the evidence we have considered that if important phonological change in the development of a language can be expressed formally as one rule, categorical and unconstrained as well as phonetically plausible, it is nothing more than a startling stroke of good luck for the language historian who derives esthetic pleasure from formal neatness. It is improbable, however, that such cases will achieve anything other than a simple formalistic reduction of a result: generative rules tell us nothing about the mechanism or implementation of change, nor indeed any other aspect which would give us some insight into such processes.

This chapter will deal with a topic in the history of Spanish which has been discussed many times before, though not perhaps from quite the same point of view. Newton (1971) pointed out that the necessary 'interdigitation' of rules historically was not concordant with the theoretical requirements of generative theory; in a later article (Newton 1972) he demonstrated how syncope must be interdigitated with other rules in the history of French in order to explain the development of a number of forms;[2] Bley-Vroman (1975) brought similar cases in Old Norse to light; and we suggest that the early history of Spanish presents a similar picture. Unlike the topics discussed in the rest of this book, syncope is not directly concerned with consonantal weakening; it involves, nevertheless, a pattern of deletion (though there may be a difference between weakening and deletion, as pointed out by Lass (1971:23), who suggests they are separate processes that move along different strength scales), and it does play an important role in the development of consonantal clusters and the surface configurations of these clusters.

It would not be difficult to formalize in generative terms a rule of syncope applicable to the history of Spanish following the summary description given by many manuals, which characterize syncope as the loss of any internal unstressed vowel (if there is more than one of these in either pre- or posttonic position, the vowel nearest to the primary stress is lost), with the exception of [a] (see, for example, Menéndez Pidal 1958:73–8); exceptions are typically described as learned forms.

But our aim here is to show that while a rule formulated in this way would more or less accurately describe the outcome of forms syncopated between the Latin and the Medieval Spanish periods, it will not only fail to work from a practical point of view as a single rule, but also give no indication about the process of syncope itself or its implementation. (This is, of course, true of categorical generative rules in general, since 'explanation' to generativists has tended to mean little more than 'reduction to a formal schema'; see Lass (1976), and the Conclusion, below.) Moreover, it is evident that a single rule of syncope never appeared at any point in the history of Latin or Spanish.[3] More precisely, it would simply be a convenient summary of a series of syncope rules operating over a span of more than a thousand years, each rule with an input or an environment more extensive than the previous one (though not necessarily following the same pattern, as we shall see). We shall attempt to demonstrate how syncope spread in this way and why it cannot be condensed into one historical rule.[4]

The first fact about syncope of which we can be absolutely sure is that it dates back at least as far as the Latin period. One of the most valuable indications we have of this is the list of forms mentioned in the *Appendix Probi*.[5] Among them, we find:

SPECULUM	non	SPECLUM
MASCULUS	non	MASCLUS
VETULUS	non	VECLUS
VITULUS	non	VICLUS
VERNACULUS	non	VERNACLUS
ARTICULUS	non	ARTICLUS
ANGULUS	non	ANGLUS
OCULUS	non	OCLUS
IUGULUS	non	IUGLUS
CALIDA	non	CALDA
VIRIDIS	non	VIRDIS
STABULUM	non	STABLUM
BACULUS	non	VACLUS
CAPITULUM	non	CAPICLUM
VAPULO	non	BAPLO
TABULA	non	TABLA
TRIBULA	non	TRIBLA
FRIGIDA	non	FRICDA
AURIS	non	ORICLA
FAX	non	FACLA
NEPTIS	non	NEPTICLA
ANUS	non	ANUCLA

The majority of these forms show a reduction of the Latin ending –ULUS, normally (though not exclusively, by any means) a diminutive suffix, but which for various reasons had widely extended its use in the late Latin period: note that the last four examples condemn not only the syncope of the vowel, but also the use of the suffix itself. It is important to note that of those words on the list which have survived in Spanish, all of them have done so in the syncopated form. The peculiar form FRICDA, whose pronunciation must be left open to speculation, seems to suggest that the Classical form FRIGIDA had two possible outcomes: loss of the medial –G– (as would be indicated by our rule 11 on page 21 above) and collapse of the two vowels; or loss of the posttonic –I– before that of –G–, thus leaving some remnant (probably fricative, and therefore comparable with the developments we saw of –CT–, –X–, and –GN– in the preceding chapter) of the –G– clustered with the following –D–. This suggests that syncope at this stage was not only variable, but also already interacting with other processes.[6]

Leaving aside the case of FRICDA, the pattern is perfectly clear. All the cases involve the same type of reduction: the loss of a high vowel (necessarily short in Latin, or as a penultimate it would have carried primary stress), bringing together a stop and a liquid, in one order or the other. Groups of stop plus liquid were already well represented in Latin in forms in which there had been no syncope of an intervening vowel; forms containing a liquid and a stop spread over a syllable boundary were also frequent. In other words, this syncope did not break any type of syllable-structure constraint in Latin; it merely increased the frequency of certain types (see Anderson 1965).[7]

We should therefore suggest that syncope began in Latin as a rule affecting primarily the high back vowel of the unaccented ending –ULU, –ULA in its initial and most highly restricted form (see also Gaeng 1968:268, note 12).

There is no doubt that this part of the series of syncope rules, even if it started as a variable process, became categorical within the Latin period. As well as the examples from the *Appendix Probi*, we also have (where –j– represents Old Spanish [ž], modern [x]):

APICULA	→	abeja	bee
CONC(H)ULA	→	concha	shell
COAGULARE	→	cuajar	to clot, set
FABULARE	→	hablar	to speak
*MANCULA (Class. MACULA)	→	mancha	stain
NEBULA	→	niebla	fog
OVICULA	→	oveja	sheep
REGULA	→	reja	harrow
SINGULOS	→	seños/sendos	one each
TEGULA	→	teja	tile
UNGULA	→	uña	(finger)nail

and many other forms.[8] All Western Romance languages show syncope in these forms: compare Fr. **vieil** and Pt. **velho** with Sp. **viejo**; Fr. **ongle** and Pt. **unha** with Sp. **uña**; and there appear to be no exceptions, unless the placename **Ontígola** is derived from FONTICULA, as Menéndez Pidal (1972:227) suggests. Place-names, however, are not reliable examples, and Menéndez Pidal himself labels this form as a 'semicultismo', though it is difficult to envisage in this case how this could be so (see also Badía Margarit 1972:141–6).

Owing to the obvious lack of documented evidence, the early history of syncope in Latin is otherwise extremely difficult to trace. It appears, however, that the loss of the vowel in the above examples took place before the voicing of the intervocalic voiceless obstruents (rule 2, page 12 above), though, in fact, when the group –C'L– or –G'L–, resulting from syncope, was in an intervocalic position, this would have made no difference, since –C'L– would subsequently have been voiced in any event (see pages 79–80).[9]

Let us now turn to another set of examples for comparison:

CABALLICARE	→	cabalgar	**to ride**
FOLLICARE	→	holgar	**to rest, be idle**
DELICATU	→	delgado	**thin**
FAMELICU	→	jamelgo	**nag, useless horse**
GALLICU	→	galgo	**greyhound**
*PULICA (Class. PULICE)	→	pulga	**flea**
POLLICARE	→	pulgar	**thumb**
ALIQUOD	→	algo	**something**
CALIDU	→	caldo	**broth**
SOLIDU	→	sueldo	**salary**
VIRIDE	→	verde	**green**

In all these forms, the vowel lost by syncope was short –I–. CALIDU, SOLIDU, and VIRIDE had already lost the vowel in Latin: note that CALDA and VIRDIS are cited in the *Appendix Probi* (see page 95 above). These forms, however, seem to have had a considerable head start over the others, perhaps thanks to the articulatory similarity of the stop and liquids brought together: they are all [+coronal, +anterior];[10] which, if true, would provide further support for our contention that sound change of this type, at least at its initial point of departure, is essentially phonetic, or more specifically, moves along phonetic parameters.

The development of the other forms, however, needs a different explanation. The consonants brought together by syncope in this case were a (single or geminate) liquid and a voiceless velar, a context in which, in original Latin forms, the stop never underwent the voicing process, as testified by examples like SALTU → **soto/salto** 'jump', ARCU → **arco** 'bow', PORCU → **puerco** 'pig', etc. Despite this, in the examples above we have a voiced stop everywhere after the [l], the only explanation for which is that these forms underwent the voicing rule before being affected by syncope. It seems there is a clear chronological difference between these forms and those we saw earlier, in which syncope was already categorical in the Latin period: we shall see evidence of this shortly. There are two structural differences between this group of examples and the previous one: the reversed position of the consonant and the liquid, and the vowel which is lost. Bearing in mind that the forms CALDA and VIRDIS appear along with OCLUS, etc., in the *Appendix Probi*, the relative order of the stop and liquid seems of little or no importance: neither order contravened the surface phonetic structure of Latin. So for the present we will assume that the criterion on which the time difference was based is the vowel that was lost.[11]

In other words, we have an extension of the first syncope process to include both vowels: –U– and –I–. They may have lowered at this point to [o] and [e] (cf. above, note 23 to chapter 2). This is important, because although the rule will presumably apply vacuously to –U–, which would have been syncopated by the earlier rule, it will now apply in addition to [o] originating from Classical –O–, as well as [e] from –E–.

This will account for the forms given in the group of examples above, as long as it is applied only after voicing has taken place:

	APICULA	DELICATU	*PULICA
Syncope (i)	apíkla	___	___
Vwl adjs	apékla	delekáto	púleka
Rule 2	abégla	delegádo	púlega
Syncope (ii)	___	delgádo	púlga
Rule 23[12]	abéɣla	___	___
24	abéjla	___	___
26	abéjĺa	___	___
25	abéĺa	___	___
Delateralization	abéža	___	___
Medieval Spanish	**abeja**	**delgado**	**pulga**

As well as purely historical indications, there is also evidence to be drawn from comparative investigations to show that we are correct in suggesting that this second part of syncope was later than the first. It is a commonplace in Romance linguistics that Rumanian and Italian[13] differ from Western Romance (in the most extreme case, French) in the configuration of their preferred surface structure for morphemes: Rumanian and Italian have preserved a considerable number of Latin forms with proparoxytonic accentuation, forms which were normally syncopated in the west (and in French often later converted into oxytones by the loss of final vowels).

Italian, however, underwent the first syncope just as Western Romance did; so the forms corresponding to Spanish **ojo, viejo, oreja, macho, mancha, niebla,** and **uña** are respectively **occhio, vecchio, orecchia, maschio, macchia, nebbia,** and **unghia**. On the other hand, the second syncope rule was clearly non-categorical in Italian; while some forms underwent the process (producing **cavalcare** < CABALLICARE, **pulce** < PULICE), others did not:

CARRICARE → (It.) caricare, (Sp.) cargar **to load**
SALICE → (It.) salice, (Sp.) sauce **willow**

and Old Italian had **pulice**, cognate with Spanish **pulga**.[14] The examples **cargar** and **sauce** provide us with evidence from various other sources that the loss of their vowel took place relatively late – certainly not in the Latin period. First, we find that Spanish is the only language in the Peninsula to have produced syncope in the development of CARRICARE: compare both Pt. and Ct. **carregar**. Second, the form **sauce**, and similarly

CALICE → cauce **riverbed, (water)course**

both show a vocalization of the resulting syllable-final lateral to [w], as formalized here in rule 18 (page 61 above). Nevertheless, the diphthong [aw] is maintained, and not reduced to [o] as was the case with Latin forms having -AU- (for examples, see page 61). The form **salce** or **salze** is documented from the tenth century, but certainly does not represent a Latin syncope. Indeed, in Mozarabic, the name of the willow was represented as **šálich, šálicho**, or **šalcho** (Sampson 1980:23). Note, incidentally, that the Old Spanish **salze, calze**, in which the orthographic –z– represents a voiced affricate of the type [d^z], indicate that the Latin intervocalic obstruent had again voiced, as in the case of **delgado, pulga**, etc.

Exceptions to this type of syncope are cases such as:

AFRICU → ábrego **south-west wind**
LUBRICU → lóbrego **dark, gloomy**
PETRICOSU → pedregoso **stony**

Of course, the application of syncope to these forms would have given rise to consonant clusters which were totally unacceptable in the phonetic structure of Latin or early Spanish. The necessity to complicate the grammar with restrictions on syncope rules would be obviated by a general set of phonotactic redundancy rules which would simply reject those outputs of the syncope rules which were ill-formed in terms of surface structure.

Finally, in support of the hypothesis that the second syncope rule was applied later than the first is the fact that in Old Spanish it does not seem to have achieved a fully categorical state. Menéndez Pidal (1972:163, 254) cites the documented forms

galigos (for **galgos**) and **pulicar** (for **pulgar**). Naturally, not much attention should be paid to the documented forms of early texts, because of the Latinizing tendency of the scribes, but it may be of some significance to note in this case that **Gállego** has survived in Modern Spanish as a geographical and personal name.

As we pointed out above, the form of the second syncope rule will cause the syncope of [e] and [o], as well as [i] and [u], in the correct environment, producing forms such as the following:

ALTERU	→ otro	**other**
APERIRE	→ abrir	**to open**
HEDERA	→ yedra/hiedra	**ivy**
IINIPERU (Class. IUNIPERU)	→ enebro	**juniper**
LIBERARE	→ librar	**to free**
RECUPERARE	→ recobrar	**to recover**
SUPERARE	→ sobrar	**to surpass, be left over**
ANCORA	→ ancla	**anchor**
LABORARE	→ labrar	**to farm**
PECTORALE	→ petral/pretal	**breast-strap**
ROBORE	→ roble	**oak**
TEMPORANU	→ temprano	**early**
COLLOCARE	→ colgar	**to hang**

In most of these examples it is more difficult to establish a chronology, but there are still certain indications which support our hypothesis that syncope in these forms took place later than in those affected by the first syncope rule. Unfortunately, the voicing of the stop in **abrir, enebro, recobrar,** and **sobrar** tells us nothing, since it would have been voiced before or after syncope (cp. CAPRA → **cabra** 'goat');[15] the case of **colgar**, however, is rather different. A stop in this context did not undergo voicing (see examples on page 97 above), which again points to syncope having taken place here only after the action of rule 2, as we should expect if this group of examples is to be derived by the second syncope rule.

In the same way, evidence from other Romance languages testifies to the fact that the reduced forms were not common to the Latin of all the Empire. Italian, to continue with the same comparison, again syncopated some of these forms; thus, **altro, aprire,** and **ginepro** correspond to Spanish **otro, abrir,** and **enebro**; but this was not always the case: we also have It. **àncora, rovere,** and **coricare** parallel to Sp. **ancla, roble,** and **colgar**.[16]

Forms which did not undergo the rule follow a clear pattern, just as the exceptions with Latin –I– and –U– did:

STERCORE	→ estiércol	**dung**
ARBORE	→ árbol	**tree**
MARMORE	→ mármol	**marble**
CARCERE	→ cárcel	**prison**

In this case it seems the surface structure constraints avoided an agglutination of rCr – the dissimilation of the second liquid is considerably later; the first documentation of most of these forms shows a final –re (see the relevant entries in Corominas and Pascual (1980–)).

Up to this point, then, we have seen how high and mid vowels were lost in the period between Latin and early Old Spanish in certain contexts: specifically, those involving a stop and a liquid; and how this syncope was not a unitary process, but rather, as empirical evidence suggests, a series of successive expansions of an original rule which affected only the high back vowel. From the high back vowel, syncope spread to the high front one, and from there, either by subsequent expansion or because of factors external to syncope itself (that is, the lowering of short high vowels to mid), or by a combination of the two, it also affected the mid vowels [e] and [o].

At this point we find that the series of syncope rules dies out without attacking [a]:

(A)SPARAGU	→ espárrago	**asparagus**
PASSARE (Class. PASSERE)	→ pájaro	**bird**
RAPHANU	→ rábano	**radish**
ORPHANU	→ huérfano	**orphan**

Counterexamples to the preservation of [a] are extremely rare: the form **comprar** 'to buy' is most likely to have developed from a Latin *COMPERARE, rather than the Classical COMPARARE, and so would not constitute an exception (see Corominas and Pascual (1980–, s.v. comprar); and also the question of weakening in Latin vowels on page 103 below).

Up to now, we have established that syncope, in its various aspects, must have taken place at different times; initially, without doubt, in the Latin period, and again later, in a different context, in a smaller area of Western Romance; hence the disagreement in the treatment of many forms between Italian and Spanish.[17]

Taking Italian, for the reasons already given, as a point of comparison, let us now consider in some detail the progressive structure of the syncope 'rule' in the history of Spanish. The discussion will take the form of an examination of elements from both languages and we shall attempt to establish the manner in which syncope spread from one context to another.

We have already seen that the first major context in which syncope seems to have taken place was in that illustrated in the following forms (after the Latin etymon, the forms given are those of standard Italian and Spanish in that order):

OCULU	→ occhio, ojo	**eye**
VETULU	→ vecchio, viejo	**old**
NEBULA	→ nebbia, niebla	**fog**
UNGULA	→ unghia, uña	**(finger)nail**

The context is quite straightforward:

$$27. \quad \begin{bmatrix} -\text{son} \\ -\text{cont} \end{bmatrix} \quad V \begin{bmatrix} +\text{hi} \\ +\text{bk} \end{bmatrix} \quad \begin{bmatrix} +\text{cons} \\ +\text{son} \\ -\text{nas} \end{bmatrix}^{18}$$

It also seems quite clear that the syncope in the following forms dates back to Latin:[19]

POSITU	→ posto, puesto	**put (past part.)**
CONSUTURA	→ costura, costura	**seam**
PERSICA, -U	→ pesca, prisco	**peach, apricot**

Note that the early dating of these examples is supported by the voicelessness of [k] in Spanish **prisco** and [t] in **puesto**. Here, the context is:

$$28. \quad \begin{bmatrix} -\text{son} \\ +\text{cont} \\ +\text{cor} \end{bmatrix} \quad V [+\text{hi}] \quad \begin{bmatrix} -\text{son} \\ -\text{cont} \\ -\text{vce} \end{bmatrix}$$

So far the inference to be drawn is perfectly clear: Latin admitted the syncope of the vowel between consonants which were allowed to form syllable- or word-initial clusters. Latin allowed in initial position clusters of stop plus liquid, with the exception of *tl– and *dl–: such forms as VETULU, swept along by the tide of syncope in all other –ULU forms, were rapidly assimilated (note the spelling VECLUS for VETULUS in the *Appendix Probi*, quoted on page 95 above). Latin also permitted initial [s] plus a voiceless stop, and this is precisely the context we have in (28). In this case, the vowel syncopated in this context was either [u] or [i]; the effect of the rule is thus expanded from [+high, +back] to any [+high] vowel.

This expansion has a perfectly natural explanation, as we have already mentioned above. In further support of it, it is not difficult to find external evidence that in Latin the high vowels were the weakest: this is patent in the weakening of the vowel involved in compounded verbs: FACIO 'do, make' but CONFICIO, PERFICIO; TENEO 'hold' but CONTINEO, PERTINEO; LEGO 'gather, choose' but ELIGO, CONLIGO, DILIGO; CAPIO 'take' but RECIPIO, PERCIPIO, etc.[20] We should therefore expect syncope to have affected the high vowels first.

What cannot be explained as rule extension, however, is the context surrounding the vowel in (28) as regards that of (27) (or, for that matter, vice versa). In (27) we have a preceding stop and a following liquid; in (28) a preceding fricative and a following voiceless stop. It is evident that by no stretch of the imagination or the formalism can this be called a rule extension. In fact, what is important here is that there is no way of associating these two descriptions of syncope without reference to surface structure. Once we take the surface structure into consideration, it is quite clear what is happening here: the rules which drop the vowels in contexts 27 and 28 are part of a 'conspiracy' (to use the terminology of Kisseberth (1970)) whose formulation is simply: the weakest vowels drop, but only in those environments between two segments which, as a cluster, are permitted in initial position. The fact that syncope operates in two contexts which underlyingly show no mutual relationship means that it is nonsense to talk in the orthodox way of 'rule generalization', and much less of 'simplification', since the contexts for syncope are so very different. We are obliged, then, to recognize the existence of two separate rules of syncope, despite the fact that there is a clear surface structure relationship between the two.

From this point on, Spanish and Italian begin to diverge: in principle, it would seem that (27) is expanded by permitting more vowel segments to undergo syncope within the same surrounding context; this expansion, however, is not applied equally in both languages. Consider the following examples, given previously:

ALTERU	→	altro, otro	**other**
APERIRE	→	aprire, abrir	**to open**
IINIPERU			
(Class. IUNIPERU)	→	ginepro, enebro	**juniper**

in which the mid vowel is syncopated in the same context as (27). This suggests firstly that this syncope took place later than that described in (27), where it is more restricted; and secondly, that the description of the vowel, by virtue of the examples above, should now become [−low]. But this latter expansion is not quite so straightforward. Let us look at some further examples:

ANCORA → àncora, ancla **anchor**
ROBORE → rovere, roble **oak**

Here, syncope has taken place in the Spanish forms, but not in the Italian ones;[21] and the only difference between these examples and the previous ones is that the vowel which was suppressed was, at least originally, [+back]. This points to a more gradual spread of syncope than has generally been supposed: it seems the first area of spread from high vowels was towards mid front vowels; mid back vowels were only affected later, with Italian being virtually untouched by this last extension.[22]

This implies that in Italian environment 27 must be expanded to include the vowel [e], that is, to [−low, −back]; but it is difficult to see how this can be done formally, although we have seen that the progress of syncope, which may be schematized as follows:

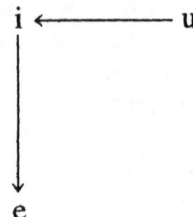

is perfectly natural. Spanish, on the other hand, continues this progression, and, as we have seen, syncopates [o] too; thus:

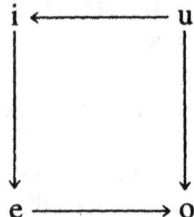

eliminating the feature [−back] and therefore making it possible to collapse (27) and these two subsequent expansions into one environment:

29. $\begin{bmatrix} -\text{son} \\ -\text{cont} \end{bmatrix} \quad \begin{matrix} V \\ [-\text{low}] \end{matrix} \quad \begin{bmatrix} +\text{cons} \\ +\text{son} \\ -\text{nas} \end{bmatrix}$

This would satisfy the canons of orthodox generative theory, since it involves a 'simplification' of the original syncope rule in formal terms, despite the fact that this simplification in real terms distorts the idea of gradual spread along phonetic parameters inherent in the process, a situation which generativists are presumably quite happy with, since the rule produces the correct results.

The next stage in the spread of syncope appears to have been the application of context 29 as a mirror-image environment to the syncope rules. We base the hypothesis that this stage came next on the fact that (29) used as a mirror-image was applied generally in Spanish but only sporadically in Italian. This indicates that it was certainly later than the types of syncope mentioned above, while on the other hand it is unlikely that it was sufficiently late to be considered an independent development in each language: recall that 'VIRIDIS non VIRDIS' and 'CALIDA non CALDA' appear in the *Appendix Probi* (see pages 95 and 97 above), although it is likely that these forms were among the earliest to undergo syncope, thanks to the phonetic characteristics of the segments in the environment. Other forms reduced in both languages include:

VERECUNDIA	→ vergogna, (O.Sp.) vergüeña	**shame**
CABALLICARE	→ cavalcare, cabalgar	**to ride**
PULICE, -A	→ pulce, pulga	**flea**

(but cp. O. It. **pulice**).

In other forms, only Spanish has dropped the vowel:

CARRICARE	→ caricare, cargar	**to load**
SALICE	→ salice, sauce	**willow**
COLLOCARE	→ coricare	**to lay down**, colgar **to hang**[23]

At this point it seems that the spread of syncope, after having been merely sporadic in the forms given above, finally died out in Italian, with the exception of a few other minor environments. Certainly, despite the fact that VIRDIS and CALDA are already attested in the *Appendix Probi*, this type of syncope continued over several centuries; it is important here to bear in mind that CARRICARE, for example, is not even reduced in the Peninsular languages other than Spanish: both Portuguese and Catalan have **carregar**.

One of the contexts in which Spanish has regularly lost the posttonic vowel while Italian has preserved it has a marked similarity to (28). In fact, the preceding segment is the same. The following segment in (28) was a voiceless stop, that is to say, the only type of segment permitted to form an initial cluster with [s] in Latin. The voiced stops, fricatives, nasals, and liquids were unknown in this position, with the exception of a few borrowed forms, mainly of Greek origin. We should therefore expect that any generalization of this rule could naturally only expand the following segment by including the sonorants; that is, the most vowel-like consonantal segments. This is precisely what we find. Examples such as

INSULA	→	isla	**island**
ASINU	→	asno	**ass**
ELEEMOSINA	→	limosna	**alms**
FRAXINU	→	fresno[24]	**ash (tree)**

indicate that we need a further context for syncope:

30. $\begin{bmatrix} -\text{son} \\ +\text{cont} \\ +\text{cor} \end{bmatrix}$ $\begin{matrix} V \\ [-\text{low}] \end{matrix}$ $\begin{bmatrix} +\text{son} \\ +\text{cons} \\ +\text{cor} \end{bmatrix}$

Italian did not take part in this new application of syncope: the Italian reflexes of the examples above are **isola, asino, elemosina,** and **frassino**. This in itself may seem curious, since Modern Italian admits initial groups of [z] plus nasal or liquid: **smentire** 'to deny', **snaturare** 'to pervert', **sleale** 'disloyal'. But this is a much later process, in most cases involving the reduction of a prefix: compare Sp. **desmentir, desnaturalizar, desleal**.

Extracting the segments involved in the last part of the contexts of (28) and (30), we can see that [p t k] on the one hand, and [n l r] on the other, conform to any phonologist's idea of natural sets; but any attempt to collapse them into one would mean losing all naturalness. Why should the voiceless stops and the sonorants associate to the exclusion of the voiced stops and the fricatives? This inexplicable jumble can only be sorted out, once more, by reference to surface structure constraints.

We have already noted that it seems in principle that Latin began by applying syncope between those consonants which, as a cluster, were admissible in initial position; (28) faithfully reflects this principle as a context for one of the early syncope rules. As the phenomenon of syncope began to gather momentum, however, the contexts in which it was permitted began to spread; in some cases by applying to more vowels, in others by allowing already existing contexts to apply in mirror-image; and in others by starting to include in the surrounding environment elements which were not embraced by the original principle. We have already adduced evidence to demonstrate that many historical changes begin with a very limited phonetic environment, only outgrowing that initial environment when their stronghold is firm enough. This expansion is not, of course, erratic, but rather follows phonetic parameters. The point is that these phonetic parameters are not entirely autonomous, and we cannot always predict the exact course a developing change will take; but more importantly, this application of parameters cannot be understood simply from the formalisms of generative rules – indeed, such rules, as we have repeatedly seen, often present a distorted view of the process. The spreading of rules is often determined by surface phonetic structures and their characteristics, and without constant reference to this surface structure, we cannot explain these phenomena adequately.

Thus, in the case which concerns us here, the form of (28) is directly determined by the presence of such clusters already in certain surface contexts. The form of (30) on the other hand is indeed an extension of (28) in the sense that one part of the environment is the same; the extension, however, is carried out at the 'weakest point', as it were: by using those consonantal segments most similar to vowels.[25]

To what extent can we justify this as a 'natural' extension of the rules? For the moment the explanation that immediately suggests itself is the following: an incipient historical change is always limited by certain constraints, which, it seems, have a direct relationship with existing surface-structure constraints (cp. Vincent 1978:425-6); by the time the change reaches its maximum potential within these limits (supposing it actually does – what stops a sound change is still rather an open question), it may or may not have taken root strongly enough in the speech habits of the community to 'outgrow' its original restrictions. If it has, the constraints must be broken, and it seems most natural from an intuitive point of view that they will break most easily at their weakest point.[26] By 'weakest' here, we understand the nearest type of segment on a phonetic parameter to those which are already recognized as acceptable by the constraint in question.

In the case which concerns us here, this segment could be a voiced stop (or perhaps a fricative – the function of [± voice] on the parameter is not always as clear as has sometimes been suggested; see page 48 above) or a liquid. It seems that the latter route was the one taken by the spread of syncope, which then naturally went on to include the nasals.

Further evidence for this type of spreading is found in the next context in which we find syncope in Spanish. In contexts 27, 29, and 30, we have seen how the liquids formed part of the required environment for syncope in its initial stages, first as a following segment, but later as a preceding one too. We have also seen in (30) how this tendency began to spread to the nasals; and we now find these segments alone forming an appropriate environment for syncope in Spanish:

TREMULARE	→	temblar	**to tremble**
GENERU	→	yerno	**son-in-law**
TENERU	→	tierno	**tender**
HUMERU	→	hombro	**shoulder**
ANIMA	→	alma	**soul**
FEMINA	→	hembra	**female**
HOMINE	→	hombre	**man**
MINIMARE	→	mermar	**to reduce**
SEMINARE	→	sembrar	**to sow**
*VIMINE	→	mimbre	**wicker**

where we clearly need a context:

31. $[+\text{nas}] \quad [-\text{low}] \quad \overset{V}{} \quad \begin{bmatrix} +\text{cons} \\ +\text{son} \end{bmatrix}$

(Italian, of course, took no part in this type of syncope, and produced reflexes such as **tremolare, genero, tenero, omero, anima**, etc.[27])

What we referred to above as the momentum of a change permitting it to outgrow its original constraints is now clear. This case of syncope must have taken place relatively late; certainly after the reduction of geminates (see rule 3, page 12 above) and the palatalization of geminate nasals and nasal clusters: compare the results of HOMINE or SEMINARE with those of SCAMNU → **escaño** 'bench, seat' or SOMNU → **sueño** 'sleep'. (These palatalizations, as well as the syncope, are unknown in Italian, cp. **scanno, sonno**.) The loss of the vowel, therefore, was by now such a powerful process that it could take place even if this meant introducing into the surface structure clusters otherwise no longer admitted. The result of this can be seen above. The clusters of two nasals or nasal plus liquid were obliterated by different means: metathesis (as in **yerno, tierno**), substitution of the syllable-final nasal (i.e., the weaker of the two) by a liquid (**mermar**), or more commonly by the intercalation of a transitional epenthetic stop with articulatory characteristics of the preceding nasal (**temblar, hombro**, etc.).[28]

The postvocalic context of (31) was eventually relaxed to include any consonant, even stops:

MANICA	→	manga	**sleeve**
COMMUNICARE	→	comulgar	**to take communion**
SEMITA	→	senda	**path**
LIMITE	→	linde	**boundary**

Thus:

32. $[+\text{nas}] \quad [-\text{low}] \quad \overset{V}{[+\text{cons}]}^{29}$

which also became operative as a mirror-image rule:

SEPTIMANA	→	(O.Sp.) sedmana	→	semana	**week**
*RETINA	→	rienda			**rein**
RICINU	→	rezno			**bott (larva)**
PECTINE	→	peine			**comb**

The hypothesis that this type of syncope is relatively late, already supported by the comparative evidence, is also verified by the fact that in many of the forms given above and similar ones, the first written evidence from medieval documents shows hesitation in the normal assimilation of the point of articulation of the nasal to the following stop in **semdero, limde** (see rule 21 on page 67 above); lack of transition consonant in **omre** (Menéndez Pidal 1972:309–10); and even the preservation of the vowel in **semedeiro** (1972:167).[30]

So syncope had finally shaken itself loose of most of its constraints; not only was it no longer restricted to producing a limited typology of consonant clusters: it now operated in the configuration of clusters which subsequently had to undergo further processes in order to fall in with Old Spanish syllable structure.

The final expression of this freedom with which syncope operated in early Old Spanish was the fact that it eventually took place between two stops (maximally: fricatives and affricates were also involved; see below), thereby bringing one of them into syllable-final position, a distribution totally unnatural in terms of Old Spanish syllable structure, as may be seen from chapter 4. This offensive against established surface constraints was dealt with in several ways. Let us consider some examples:

VINDICARE	→	vengar	**to avenge**
UNDECI(M)	→	once	**eleven**
TREDECI(M)	→	trece	**thirteen**
CAPITELLU	→	caudillo	**leader**

RAPIDU	→	raudo	**swift**
RECITARE	→	rezar	**to pray**
IUDICARE	→	juzgar	**to judge**
DEBITA	→	deuda	**debt**
CUBITU	→	codo	**elbow**
BIBITU	→	beodo	**drunk**

Not all of these examples involve an environment of stops: in the reflex of RECITARE the segment preceding the lost vowel was the affricate [d^z] (see page 84 above); in other cases (IUDICARE, DEBITA, CUBITU, etc.), one of the consonants was a fricative, as a consequence of the rule spirantizing intervocalic voiced stops (rule 1, page 12); and in others (RAPIDU, CAPITELLU) the Latin voiceless intervocalic stop, as well as having been voiced by rule 2 (page 12), may also have spirantized by rule 4 (page 12), though the chronology of this second shift is difficult to establish, as Spanish has never made any orthographic difference between the stop and the fricative. What we are suggesting is that if two stops were allowed to fall together in this way, the same tolerance would naturally be granted, by virtue of the optimal strength position occupied on the hierarchy by stops, to any other obstruent segment.

Syncope had, by this time, achieved its maximum extension in Spanish. An unstressed non-low vowel between any two consonants would drop as long as the first was preceded by a sonorant, whether consonant or vowel,[31] with the sole restriction that a canonical surface structure could be recuperated.

The problem of the consonant cluster was again solved in various ways: between a nasal and an obstruent, the medial consonant was lost, as in **vengar** and **once**; in **trece** (first documented as **tredze**) and **rezar**, the cluster [ðd^z] or [d^{z}ð] was soon resolved to [d^z] (see page 84); in **juzgar** (first documented as **judgar**) the original cluster has been permitted to survive in Modern Spanish after the adjustment of [ð], producing modern [xuθɣár]; in the rest of the examples given, the segment brought into syllable-final position was spirantized (if it was not already fricative) and then vocalized.[32] In **cobdo** (→ **codo**), vocalization of the –b– produced the diphthong [ow], regularly reduced to [o] (see page 83).

The stage **cabdi(e)llo, debda, cobdo, bebdo**, etc., is found documented from the earliest manifestations of written Spanish, but it seems certain that this stage of syncope was the latest. Such forms were unstable, and vocalization soon begins to show through even the orthography of conservative scribes: **caudillo,**

beudo already appear in the early fourteenth century, and, although the consonant still survived a while longer, it was considered archaic by the sixteenth century.

What is more, unsyncopated forms (which otherwise show a completely popular development) such as **tridigo** (< TRITICU, M. Sp. **trigo** 'wheat') are also found documented (see Menéndez Pidal 1972:163); dialects other than Castilian show different results in some forms: thus Berceo (writing in La Rioja in the thirteenth century) uses **vendegar** for Castilian **vengar**; Castilian has **trébedes** 'trivet' (< TRIPEDES), while Aragonese had **estreudes** and Astur-Leonese **estreldes** (Corominas and Pascual 1980–, s.v. pie).

Cases such as these, which tend to fall outside the general consideration of syncope because of their apparent 'irregularity', surely indicate how syncope, by this time virtually moribund, was losing its generality of application.

The extensive effects produced by this process in Spanish are probably not limited to what we know traditionally as syncope. It is more than likely that the apocope which took place in Old Spanish and which we discussed in chapter 3 (see pages 45–6) was merely another aspect of the general loss of internal unstressed vowels which we refer to as syncope.[33] Neither apocope nor syncope are rules of contemporary Spanish: forms introduced into the language since the Middle Ages show no tendency to lose unstressed vowels; indeed, the enormous amount of foreign words (taken especially from the classical languages) absorbed by Spanish since the Renaissance period has led to the notable presence of proparoxytonic forms in Spanish today.

So what has the study of syncope in the history of Spanish shown us? It has shown:

(a) that syncope began as a (possibly variable) rule in Latin, restricted to a small number of forms with a specific SD, very closely linked to surface-structure constraints;

(b) that it spread to more and more forms in a gradual fashion, and that these expansions can best be understood and analysed by reference to surface structure and phonetic parameters;

(c) that the successive contexts in which syncope applied were not necessarily simple rule extensions of their predecessors, nor easily collapsible with them, despite the fact that, thanks to the generality of the final contexts, all the processes of syncope in the history of Spanish could perhaps be expressed as one rule;

(d) if this one rule were formulated, it would not only cause problems by excluding the possibility of 'interdigitation' with other rules (particularly the voicing of intervocalic obstruents), but also considerably cloud over our understanding of the historical process involved. This is of no consequence for generativists in a synchronic analysis perhaps, but we maintain that it is an essential feature of historical study. It certainly does not offer any support for a concept of historical change which pays no attention to surface structure and phonetic relationships; to the delicate balance between the momentum of a well-established ongoing change and the resistance of surface-structure constraints; or to the reality of empirical evidence as opposed to the requirements of a neat formalism.

Notes

1. For a detailed description of an essentially similar model of change, see Labov, Yaeger, and Steiner (1972).
2. Straka (1951) had worked upon the same principle, though he dealt with change as isolated in time; i.e., as if one change could not begin until another had 'finished', thus producing a minutely detailed, though totally misleading, chronology.
3. Despite the impression given by some of the manuals; for instance: 'In Vulgar Latin, pretonic internal vowels (except **a**) disappeared in most cases . . . .All posttonic interior vowels regularly fell (with the exception of a few words with a posttonic **a**)' (Lathrop 1980:71–2).
4. For a rather more detailed treatment of the spread of syncope, see Harris-Northall (forthcoming).
5. *Appendix Probi* is the convenient name usually given to a list of words, one of a number of texts found attached to a manuscript of a work by Valerius Probus. The list, now believed to have been composed in the seventh century AD, seems to have been made out in an attempt to correct common scribal errors. All the words are shown in two forms, one 'correct' and the other 'wrong': hence the enormous value of the *Appendix Probi* for the history of the Romance languages. For further details, see Díaz y Díaz (1962: 46–53) and Robson (1963).
6. Menéndez Pidal (1972:263) adduces considerable evidence in favour of the survival of two outcomes of FRIGIDU in the Peninsula, as do Corominas and Pascual (1980–, s.v. frío). For the complex interaction between syncope and loss of –D– in forms ending in -IDU, see especially Dworkin (1978), and Malkiel (1986:177, note 31).
7. Hoenigswald (1978:179) is of a rather different opinion, and believes that 'any attempt to explain why syncope occurred . . . in some sequences but not in others . . . is doomed', though his conclusions are somewhat sweeping bearing in mind that he does not consider the chronological spread of syncope from one context to another.

For a similar opinion, see Pensado Ruiz (1984, chapters VI–XII *passim*, particularly pages 226-30).
8. For the subsequent development of –C'L–, –G'L– preceded by a vowel to [ĺ] and the later delateralization to [ž], see pages 79–81 above. As may be seen, the groups of nasal plus –C'L–, –G'L– produced different palatals. It is unclear why this should have been so. SINGULOS also gave **sendos**, which is the Modern Spanish form, having completely supplanted the older **seños**; the development of these groups, particularly –NG'L–, has not been convincingly explained.
9. Note in comparison such forms as MACRU → **magro** 'lean', and ECLESIA → **iglesia** 'church'.
10. Note that the Latin form ALTUS 'high' itself corresponds to an earlier form ALITUS.
11. We thus cannot agree with Eckert (1980:206) that front vowels should be 'consistently assigned a greater height (and thus weakness) value than back vowels', at least on a universal basis.
12. For the series of rules 23, 24, 25, 26 see pages 73–80. Certain rules not crucial to the discussion (for example, the spirantization rule 1, page 12 above) are omitted from the derivations in this chapter.
13: Throughout this chapter, the term 'Italian' is to be understood as referring to the Tuscan-based standard.
14. The Italian forms corresponding to Spanish **delgado** and **jamelgo** are **delicato** and **famelico**; but they tell us little, since they are likely to have been taken into Italian at a later date directly from Latin. See Cortelazzo and Zolli (1979–, s.v. delicato, fame).
15. *Pace* Lathrop (1980:82), who surprisingly uses **abrir** as an example to illustrate how voicing must have taken place before the action of syncope!
16. Italian also has **edera** (parallel to Spanish **hiedra**), though in some sources it is labelled as 'learned', presumably merely on the basis of its preservation of the posttonic vowel.
17. It is not our intention to impose any sort of absolute chronology on the linguistic dismembering of the Empire; such attempts can only be made by assuming certain methodological premises which are not concordant with our view of change; i.e., the categorical nature of all change, the idea that change is 'completed' in a given time-span, etc. See, for example, Straka (1951, 1956).
18. Although only [k], [t], [b], and [g] are represented in the examples, we have generalized the preceding segment to [–son, –cont], since forms with the other stops are scarce and present certain problems. The case of Spanish **almendra** 'almond' < *AMY(N)DULA, Class. AMYGDALA (originally from Greek) is clearly a special one which cannot be considered here, though it also shows syncope. The labial in contact with the liquid produced a whole variety of results: see note 46 to chapter 4 and Harris-Northall (forthcoming).
19. If we accept Guile's (1972) proposals for syncope rules, the loss of the vowel in these forms must still have been later than in –CUL–,

-GUL-, since here the segments brought together by syncope are both [+obstruent].
20. In such compounds, Classical Latin stress was shifted onto the prefix, hence the weakening of the (now posttonic) radical vowel; the popular tendency was, however, to re-form such verbs with the stress on the root. See Elcock (1960:41), Pensado Ruiz (1984:235), and especially Janson (1979:46–59).
21. The unusual Spanish variant **áncora** is probably a borrowing. There are exceptions in Italian to the generalization made here; for example, LEPORE → **lepre** 'hare' (Sp. **liebre**). But even in this case many variants, including **lievore**, and perhaps most importantly, **lepere**, still existed in the fourteenth century. See Cortelazzo and Zolli (1979–, s.v. lepre).
22. For further evidence of this gradualness, see Harris-Northall (forthcoming).
23. It has already been pointed out that the relative lateness of this type of syncope is reflected in the voicing of the stop in the relevant Spanish forms (see page 100 above).
24. At the time syncope took place in this form, the cluster would not have been [ks'n], but rather [js'n]. See rules 23 and 24, pages 73 and 78 above.
25. Note that these syncope rules could not be conflated under Picard's (1980) scheme either, since they do not satisfy his requirements for complement rules. In his sense, therefore, although we are dealing in each case with rules of syncope, they cannot be 'collapsed into one process' (1980:11).
26. For a similar concept within the realm of syntax, see Naro and Lemle (1976). Cp. also Bailey's use of heavy and light environments (for example, Bailey 1973).
27. The situation in Portuguese, where intervocalic -L- and -N- were regularly lost, also demonstrates quite clearly that the relative chronology suggested here is correct; even, perhaps, rather simplified. See Harris-Northall (forthcoming).
28. Despite the powerful action of syncope in this period, it still did not take place where the restoration of a surface canonical structure was not viable. Thus it is difficult to admit Corominas and Pascual's (1980–) derivation of **columbrar** from CULMINARE via the syncopated form *culmbrar ('casi impronunciable' in their own words; given Spanish surface phonotactics, the word 'casi' ought to be omitted!) and anaptyxis, especially when we find parallel forms like **carmenar** < CARMINARE.
29. Another indication of the operative time-limits of this process is evident in the development of personal names such as FRIDENANDU → **Frednando, Fernando**; RADIMIRU → **Radmiro, Ramiro** (Menéndez Pidal 1972:312), imported with the Germanic invasions of the Peninsula.
30. Forms such as **semedeiro** can hardly be explained by appealing to Latinizing influence on the part of scribes, given that the voiced

stop, the development of **-eiro** < –ARIU and the pretonic –e– (Latin –I–) itself all betray their popular nature.
31. For other sporadic cases, see Harris-Northall (forthcoming).
32. Further examples are given on pages 82–3 above.
33. This hypothesis is advanced and justified in detail by Hooper (1976:107–9).

Chapter six
Conclusion

In the foregoing chapters, we have tried to demonstrate that fundamental aspects of the standard generative theory of sound change contain certain flaws which can be brought to light in the study of a reasonably well-documented language such as Spanish. Generativists have to a large extent been involved in the search for a proper linguistic theory which may form the basis of the analysis of synchronic grammars: a search of eminent importance which has produced great advances in our knowledge of language. It has generally been supposed that such a theory could then be applied to diachronic analyses with few (if any) adjustments, though it has never been made clear why this should be so.[1] Kiparsky (1982:57) has said: 'Historical investigations in the framework of generative grammar have generally aimed at developing a theory of change which could hook up to the existing synchronic theory, so as to correctly characterize the possible forms of linguistic change.'

Some of the basic tenets of generative orthodoxy, when transferred to the diachronic sphere, do not seem to make much sense; or at least, the viability of their application is highly questionable. To take one obvious example, how is it possible to interpret, in diachronic terms, the well-known need (imposed by the theory's formalism) that the grammar described is that of 'an ideal speaker-listener, in a completely homogeneous speech-community' (Chomsky 1965:3), when it is precisely the dynamics and variable nature of a heterogeneous speech-community that reflect change (Labov, Yaeger, and Steiner 1972; Bailey 1973: 1–20; see also Kanngiesser (1972:39–45) for the homogeneity problem in synchronic and diachronic linguistics)? How are we to abstract an 'ideal speaker-listener' over several generations, unless we make *a priori* judgements concerning the particular modern dialect whose development we wish to trace and then sieve historical information for only those data which will fit into the scheme of things we have designed?² And if generative grammar is a model of competence, can we claim that simply by noting change in competence we are observing change in language, when we have to disregard anything other than purely internal change (see Romaine (1982b) and Cravens (forthoming))? Such an analysis can only be considered partial.

Unfortunately, in our opinion, many generativists have often neglected empirical data, or perhaps used them too selectively, to allow a true reflection of their importance on the theory. It thus seemed appropriate to take a look at a relatively large selection of data taken from a language whose history is comparatively accessible, in order to see how far standard generative theory could cope with a sequence of sound changes affecting a geographically limited set of dialects over a long period of time.

What we believe to be the failure of generative theory in this respect is, perhaps, due in part to different approaches to the question of sound change in general; in other words, discrepancies regarding the status of historical rules, what they represent, and what they should represent, what change is, and what the relationship is between rules and change. King (1969:80), in commenting on the implantation of a historical rule, makes the following remarks:

> We can, if we like, speculate on **why** this rule was added . . . .
> Such speculation is interesting but outside our immediate
> major concern, which is to give an account in our grammar of a
> change in speech habits. The simplest way to do this is to
> assume that our speaker has added [the rule **hw → w**] to his
> grammar.

This relegation of the motivation of change seems unjustified if the goal of diachronic linguistics is that of searching for insights into language and linguistic behaviour in general. Of course, the generativists will say that is precisely what they are doing, but that since change takes place in the grammar, it is the grammar that has to be studied. But this involves ignoring a large body of research, championed particularly by Labov (see especially Labov, Yaeger, and Steiner 1972), which suggests that change essentially starts as a function of performance³ and spreads gradually through the community according to a series of variable constraints, and in some cases, perhaps gradually through the lexicon too (Wang 1969, 1977; Chen and Hsieh 1971; Chen and Wang 1975; Labov 1981).

First of all, though, let us take a look at the requirement that change should only be expressed as a rule in the grammar. In a way, this takes us back to the problem we mentioned earlier: what does this grammar represent? Presumably, generativists would wish to describe diachrony as a sequence of synchronic grammars in which rule change(s) may be demonstrated from one to another throughout the sequence. But this does nothing other than demonstrate that certain changes have taken place: it in no way reflects the ongoing entity which we know language to be.[4]

From the data we have presented here, we can see a number of other problems. In the first place, the typical categorical rules of generative phonology, apart from being unable (and/or unwilling) to take into account the inherent heterogeneity of the speech-community – a heterogeneity of great importance for the question of change – are also unable to give adequate descriptions of the following phenomena whose existence we have illustrated:

(a) chain shifts typified in the history of Spanish especially by the development of the Latin stops: d → ð (→ ∅); t → d → ð; tt → t (see chapter 2). Such shifts are obviously related from a functional viewpoint, but this relationship cannot be captured formally by generative rules (cf. Eckert 1980).

(b) Developments which, without falling into the category of chain shifts, nevertheless clearly share many characteristics showing a relationship of a different kind: the path taken by (word- and syllable-)final consonants cannot satisfyingly be analysed without studying it from a global viewpoint (as we have tried to do in chapters 3 and 4). This is not to say that all these consonants share the same developments, which would be manifestly untrue, but it is no less untrue to suggest, for example, that the palatalization of syllable-initial [t] after [k] is an isolated idiosyncrasy when in fact it forms part of the much wider issue of the weakening of syllable-final consonants (see chapter 3); this sort of dissociation is typical of the restrictions which are inherent in generative formalism.

(c) Innovations, which are certainly not all as sweeping as generative theory would have us believe (see, for example, Lass 1981). Presumably, rule addition or rule loss (two of the types of innovation recognized by the generativists: see King 1969) in the grammar will mean that, with the exception of relatively insignificant amounts of lexical restructuring, the innovation must be absolute. There may be types of sound change which are virtually absolute: the voicing of intervocalic voiceless stops described in chapter 2 has all the signs of being one;[5] but this is by no means always the case: morphological interference may often be a factor involved in halting change (see pages 40–1, 46), and we have shown at various points how an ongoing change may be truncated or overruled by constraints which essentially refer to surface structure (for instance, pages 46–7, 64–5, 68–9, 78, 99, 101). This is a question we shall return to later.

Generative rules can, of course, capture the results of change in a particular way, but then other aspects of the formalism choke the expression of other facets of historical processes. Explicitly, a categorical rule (always supposing that the exceptions to it, if they exist, can be convincingly accounted for) can often summarize the **result** of a completed historical change.[6] This would presumably satisfy those generativists for whom change is reflected only in the grammar, as part of the speaker's competence, and is therefore uninteresting in so far as it may have had its origins in performance phenomena. This seems to us to be an unambitious target for historical descriptions, since the result of a change is only one of its facets, and perhaps one of the least helpful in gaining insight into how language changes.

Rules, according to standard generative theory, should be able to capture information in linguistically significant generalizations;[7] no-one would deny that the result of change has its significance, but it is not the only significant fact available to us in most cases. We believe that the mechanism of change, what sparks it off, and its implementation are also significant in a theory of historical linguistics, and these aspects, we feel, are lost in the formalism of the standard theory.[8]

Categorical rules are, as we have already suggested, by nature static and therefore imply that what they represent is also static. Again, for synchronic analysis it may be useful to consider a grammar as a series of static generalizations; but it is difficult to conceive of a diachronic description so expressed (cf. Longmire 1976:179). It also begs the question of whether we can even describe a change as completed. There undoubtedly are some historical rules which have run their course and are no longer present in a synchronic grammar of Spanish (one is the rule suppressing [n] before [f], as discussed on pages 57–8 above), but there are many others whose application is still necessary, such as the following one:

33   $\emptyset \rightarrow e \: / \: \# \_\_\_ sC$

which has been part of the grammar since Latin times (Pensado 1985:314):

STARE	→	estar	**to be**
SCRIBO	→	escribo	**write (1st sg. pres.)**
SCHOLA	→	escuela	**school**

and is still exceptionless today, for example, in foreign words taken into the modern language:

English	**stand**	→	[están]
	slogan	→	[ezlóɣan]
	stop	→	[estó(p)]

(whether or not the e- is actually reflected in the orthography). Is no distinction to be made between these rules in a diachronic description? There is no mechanism in generative rules for indicating that one rule is ongoing while another has no application after a certain period, unless they are implicationally linked and weighted in a Baileyan-type description (which of course makes assumptions that fall outside what is permissible in generative theory).

It is our opinion that many sound changes in a given language or family of languages are related to each other in the sense of being extensions of changes previously undergone; that is to say, that rules generalize as they spread through time and space (cf. Bailey's (1973) wave theory). We tried to bring this out most forcefully in our treatment of syncope in Spanish, but it also applies to many other processes we have seen, such as weakening in final consonants and palatalization (see, for example, pages 76–82). Now this idea is in no way original; but it means that if we wish to reflect faithfully the phonetic motivation for these changes, our description must consist not of one process, but of a series of graduated changes, such as we showed in the case of syncope. Again we return to the problem of what rules represent: if all we consider relevant is the result of these changes, one rule is sufficient; indeed, if the process is part of a synchronic grammar, such a rule may be desirable to eliminate unnecessary reference to the historical aspect. But as the expression of the historical process it would be false and misleading. Standard generative practice, in these cases, as one would expect in a coherent theory, is to require that such rules should be telescoped.

We have seen, however, various clear-cut cases in which such a requirement cannot be upheld, not simply because it might be counter-intuitive (which it often is), but also because it actually produces the wrong results. Thus the chain-shift of intervocalic consonants described in chapter 2 has been deformed by Walsh (1979) in order to telescope what are really three separate (though functionally related) rules (d → ð, t → d, tt → t) into one (rule 6, page 13). As we pointed out, the rule thus produced, apart from being a suspicious manipulation of Greek-letter variables, neither gives all the correct results nor shows any convincing motivation for the monstrous upheaval in the consonant system it seems to reflect. Many generativists would probably recoil at the thought of going to these extremes, but it is a good example of the way formalism has come to play a seemingly greater role than data.[9]

And this is not the only instance we have seen of telescoping being impossible from the empirical point of view. In the case discussed on pages 76–8 we found that the rules palatalizing [t], [s] to [č], [š] under the influence of a preceding palatal glide, attracting the glide into postnuclear position, and reducing intervocalic geminates, all interacted in such a way as to make it impossible to formulate a single rule in each case applicable once as part of an ordered series. Telescoping will obviously destroy the true chronological implementation of change, which, as in this case, may be of crucial importance in the sense that certain processes will continue to form part of the speaker's grammar while other innovations are made. Similar problems brought about by this rejection of chronologically ordered rules were encountered in the discussion on pages 79–82 concerning the palatalization of sonorants as distinct from that of obstruents, and perhaps the most outstanding and clear-cut case is that of syncope, acting over a period of centuries and crossing other rules, such as that voicing the intervocalic obstruents (see chapter 5).

The other question regarding the telescoping of historical rules is the way in which it is related to rule loss (or, perhaps more accurately in this case, adjustments in surface structure constraints). We have seen (pages 57–8) how in Old Spanish the ancient rule suppressing [n] before [s] seems to have been extended, though perhaps only variably, to have effect before [f] too. Such an obvious rule extension means that the two rules must be collapsed in the standard theory. But we find later that [n] before [f] was largely restored (placenames being the exception), while [n] before [s] was not, and it still remains as a variable rule in Modern Spanish.

How is this to be interpreted? For King (1969) it would supposedly be a clear case of rule loss. But is it feasible for part of a rule to be lost, in the sense of the environment having to be complicated by the addition of more features to restrict the segments affected?[10] Are we to suppose that rules which are collapsed are in some way still independent in their behaviour in the grammar? If indeed we are, what exactly is the significance to be attached to the formalism of uniting them, beyond a mere reduction in the number of rules and/or features?

This is, of course, not by any means the first time the formal requirements of the theory have led to contradictions of this kind, unavoidably embarrassing for generativists. Selkirk (1972, discussed in Love 1981), in her analysis of French, collapses into one the rules of truncation and final consonant deletion,[11] even though, as Love (1981:55) points out, her own analysis suggests they really function quite separately: she in fact says, 'This shows that two rules so collapsed may have some "independent" existence in spite of their tight connection.' Love (1981: 55) comments:

> If, as Selkirk suggests, there are two rules with an independent existence, then we may inquire what was the basis for supposing that they had a 'tight connection' in the first place. Selkirk offers no answer to this. All she says is that they 'can be collapsed'. But if her own arguments for saying that they have an independent existence are taken seriously, then it is precisely because of those arguments that they cannot be collapsed.[12]

Much the same holds true for the case dealt with here (on pages 57–8); the collapsing of the rule deleting [n] before [f] with that deleting [n] before [s] can only have one possible interpretation, judging by the following remarks made by Kiparsky:

> of the two descriptively equivalent grammars, one of which contains the two rules [of vowel shortening] as separate processes, and the other as a single process combined into [one rule] by factoring out their common part . . . it is the latter which is the pychologically correct one. (1968:346)

> we should expect the formal grouping of rules to result in entities whose unity is reflected in common changes – [they] should be reordered or generalized in the same way. (1972:193)

> Do blocks of rules collapsed by braces form units of a kind which can undergo systematic change? . . . .if not, we will have *prima facie* evidence that it is a spurious notation. (1968:346)

The evidence seems perfectly straightforward. Not only is the loss of the rule n → ∅ / ___f **not** a simplification of the grammar if it is collapsed with its partner, since the part of the rule left behind will need to be specified with an extra feature, but according to Kiparsky's explanations, it may not even be collapsed in the first place.

We would suggest that such collapsing is misleadingly spurious. It not only destroys in many cases the phonetic explicability of the change, which in itself is of no interest in the standard theory, but also makes changes in the grammar such as rule loss difficult to accommodate convincingly, which is of more importance to those who follow the theories of King and other generativists. As well as the question of the mechanism of rule loss, it has implications for other aspects of the standard generative theory. The loss of the rule suppressing the nasal before [f], as we have already mentioned, results in a complication in the standard sense: more features are needed to specify [s] alone than the natural class of voiceless fricatives [s f]. Such a complication is a counterexample to the hypothesis that 'the transmission of a grammar, whether through time or geographic space, is in general accompanied by equal or increased simplicity, and not by complication (reduction in generality)', as maintained by King (1969:65) and other generativists working within the standard theory as applied to historical linguistics.[13]

Finally, the use of categorical rules and other formalisms of standard generative theory, as well as specific statements by its advocates (King 1969:106–19) reject the notion of gradualness in sound change as being untenable. Instrumental evidence adduced by Labov and his followers (see, for example, Labov, Yaeger, and Steiner 1972) suggests, on the other hand, that one of the characteristics of certain sound changes in progress is allophonic drift.[14] This does not mean that it 'requires us to regard such variation as **causing** sound change' as King (1969:111, emphasis in the original) says, but it seems undeniable that it is an aspect **of** change.[15] As well as the question of change by 'infinitesimal' phonetic steps, there is also the issue of gradualness in spread, generally referred to as lexical diffusion. More and more evidence is coming to light for this, particularly in the work of scholars of Chinese (for example, Wang 1977).[16] Neither of these aspects of change can be successfully captured by generative formalism; though perhaps the first is less crucial from this point of view than the second, given the generativists' conception of change as only existing once it has broken into the grammar itself.

The second, however, is more interesting. We have not specifically concerned ourselves in this study with searching for cases of lexical diffusion, which would have required a different approach from ours. Nevertheless, there do seem to be cases where forms are 'left behind', ignored by what has elsewhere been taken to be a categorical rule. This is the case of many examples which present conflicting pictures of the result of rule 5 (pages 7–12 above): there is a considerable residue of forms which did not undergo this rule, while the other rules involved in the shift are virtually categorical.

We can suggest various theoretical conclusions: first, that such a lack of vigour may be typical of the end of chain-shifts; Eckert (1980:202) points out that 'only once the first shift becomes categorical does the following shift begin'[17] – in other words, the ongoing part of the shift is variable to a greater or lesser extent and may peter out leaving residue behind. Second, if certain scholars are right in that at least part of the chain-shift started in more westerly dialects than Castilian (see pages 11–12 above), this may well be a counterexample to the claim that rules generalize as they spread (King 1969:92).[18] However, the argument would at this point be circular, as the claim is largely based on evidence of decreasing generality.

Whatever the case may be, the isolation of one supposedly homogeneous dialect for historical analysis is in itself based on a dangerously artificial assumption which can only be aggravated by the use of generative formalism. We have already pointed out how 'ideal speaker-listener' and 'homogeneous speech-community' make little sense in diachronic terms; it is also apparent that in a discussion of sound change, we cannot isolate one dialect from all others[19] and hope to give an account of its historical development, bearing in mind the existence of phenomena such as the spread of innovations from one community to another and sociolinguistic variation. Despite its apparent theoretical necessity, many generativists seem only to have paid minimal lip-service to the principle of describing dialects in isolation. Love (1981:62) takes Schane (1968) to task for seeking 'to base an analysis of one dialect on arbitrarily selected facts from another': specifically, for trying to justify an underlying final schwa in a number of forms in standard (northern) French on the grounds that the schwa appears phonetically in southern dialects in precisely the forms in question.

Another clear example of the misuse of categorical rules is the expansion of the syncope rule, as described here in chapter 5. We have tried to demonstrate that a single syncope rule[20] not only lacks any indication of how the process was implemented, but also misrepresents the change as being completely categorical, when, as we have seen, even if we exclude borrowings which do not undergo it (by marking them in the lexicon as [–popular] or some other similarly meaningless device) and forms left unsyncopated to maintain morphological paradigms, we still have to account for the variability of the rule in its final stages; and even then there is no indication of why the vowel [a] should have been exceptionally (as it would seem) preserved.

Up to now, our comments have largely been negative ones, in the sense that we have found serious difficulties and some deficiencies in the application of the standard generative theory to the historical development of languages. What positive suggestions can be made? First, it seems that surface-structure constraints play an active part in historical change; specifically, those that function with reference to syllable structure. The syllable, largely ignored as a linguistic unit by Chomsky and Halle (1968), has, in the last decade or so, begun to win a place for itself in linguistic theory, thanks to evidence presented in Hooper (1972, 1976), Anderson and Jones (1974), Bell and Hooper (1978), and others. In the present study we have noted both how the syllable boundary functions in the context of a change (pages 31–2), and how it may even be indispensable for the correct expression of that concept (page 72).

Reference to surface structure is necessary if we want to explain why otherwise very general processes do not operate in certain contexts (for example pages 64–5, 74, 99, 101), why adjustments have to be made obligatorily to the results of certain rules (for example, after apocope, MILLE → **mil** 'thousand', not *[miĺ]; see note 3 to chapter 3), or why a particular process has specific characteristics (pages 103–5). In order to be able to do this in standard generative notation we should need to include in the contexts of the rules features with a tenuous phonetic basis with the sole purpose of excluding certain forms, as well as a complex machinery of marking. And it would still not explain why apparently 'unnatural' series of phonetic segments can seem to work together, as we showed on page 106.

The most satisfying way of doing this would be to set up syllable-structure constraints. In chapter 3 we discussed the acceptable word-final segments in standard Modern Castilian, indicating the direction of the processes necessary to make underlying segments phonotactically admissible in this context, and also the direction in which historically more advanced dialects are moving. As we should expect, the situation of internal syllable-final consonants is much the same, with one important difference: in the status of the fricatives. We have shown elsewhere (pages 84–5) that in Modern Spanish voiced fricatives are comparatively common in internal syllable-final position; indeed, any underlying stops in this position will automatically undergo a spirantization rule. What does not exist in this position is the devoicing rule that we suggested was optional for fricatives in absolute final position (pages 49–51). The resistance of the fricatives in internal syllable-final position – indeed their very presence as voiced fricatives – indicates that syllable-final position in the interior of the word is stronger than absolute final position, a point we shall return to later. It is not true to say that **no** devoicing affects syllable-final fricatives, but as we have pointed out (page 85), this is not a weakening process, but rather a strengthening process which takes place in formal speech under certain sociolinguistic conditions.

Accurate descriptions of possible syllable structures, such as those given by Hooper for Spanish (1976, chapters 10 and 11)[21] will have the power to block ongoing changes which would otherwise violate them, as we have commented with reference to processes of palatalization which would potentially have left [č] in a cluster or final (pages 64–5), and of syncope, which was disallowed where inadmissible clusters would have resulted (pages 99 and 101); thus avoiding clumsy and counter intuitive methods of excepting forms from otherwise very general processes.

One way of expressing these constraints is by referring them to hierarchies of phonetic 'strength', much in the way that Hooper does. A major preoccupation of this book has been to show the essentially phonetic explicability of many historical changes. This does not mean that we subscribe to such vague notions as 'ease of articulation',[22] but it seems from our studies undeniable that the phonetic configuration of segments is of great importance in considering their behaviour. We have tried to show how segments sharing phonetic characteristics can be seen to behave with a similarity relative to their degree of phonetic identity. Such constructs as hierarchies based on **phonetic** parameters therefore seem to be of some significance in understanding historical developments and the directions they take. We find little evidence, however, that using such hierarchies on more abstract levels, in the manner Foley (1977) does, as pseudo-universal theorems, gives any but the grossest indication of relationships. Such hierarchies do not seem to be universal, except in interactions of the widest categories.[23]

It has also become clear that such parameters as strength hierarchies are not absolute: the behaviour of a segment depends not only on its intrinsic properties, as reflected on a hierarchy, but also on more circumstantial aspects, such as its phonetic surroundings in a particular environment (cf. Escure 1975:21–5). In this sense too, reference to such constructs as the syllable and other notions, such as phrase boundaries, is essential. We showed the importance of phrase boundaries in the weakening of intervocalic obstruents (pages 30–1), and we have already illustrated the indispensability of the syllable as a phonological unit in historical descriptions.

It appears that a simple hierarchy of sonority is not enough; we have already cast doubts on the idea that [voice] functions in the same way as articulation features on such a hierarchy (page 48), and in fact we may need a series of inter-related hierarchies in order to account correctly for certain developments. One of these hierarchies should reflect the relative strength of the environments in which a segment is permitted to appear by the syllable structure constraints (page 48). We have seen on various occasions that the weakest position for consonants in Spanish is word-final, followed by internal syllable-final; while the strongest is word- (or rather phrase-)initial, followed by internal syllable-initial.[24] (Other syllable-internal positions for consonants in Spanish have little theoretical importance, since in initial clusters, the second element must be [l] or [r], and syllable-final clusters are limited to a few groups, such as –rs$, –ns$, and –ks$ in a few learned forms, in which the [r], [n], or [k] is weakened or lost in spontaneous speech.[25])

Only such an interaction of hierarchies can explain the fact that, for example, processes designated as 'weakenings' may follow different paths in different contexts. Thus, we defined voicing as a weakening process for intervocalic voiceless stops (that is, in internal syllable-initial position), while the weakening of word-final stops included devoicing, at least in Old Spanish. This will cease to be a paradox when we realize that 'weakening' in many cases (and particularly in the incipient phase), is characterized by the tendency of a segment to undergo assimilation to (one of) its neighbours; this will normally involve voicing in an intervocalic position, while before a phrase boundary, that is, followed by a lack of phonetic activity, what we expect is precisely a process of **de**voicing (pages 47–8).

This does not mean, of course, that surface phonetic constraints are not tightened, relaxed, or lost altogether in the course of time. We have seen instances of Spanish accepting, as a result of historical change, combinations of segments which constraints had previously disallowed (for example, pages 108–9), and even, on an apparently temporary basis, admitting elements in word-final position only to return subsequently to its earlier practice of rejecting them (page 46).[26]

The role of surface structure is so important in historical developments that it may even be possible to conceive of diachronic phonology as the development of a series of admissibility conditions on surface-structure output rather than as a mere inventory of rules. Not all sound change, of course, would involve adjustments to the admissibility conditions, but a change in these conditions would probably be a much closer approximation to the 'psychological reality' of the speaker than the abstract juggling of generative historical rules, judging from what we have seen; since one of the few native-speaker intuitions we can depend on to some extent is that of the well-formedness of surface structures (see Vincent 1978:417). The investigation and possible development of this notion lies outside the scope of this book, but it seems to be an area in which future research could find some reward.

At this point, it may be appreciated that our argument is running a serious risk of being reduced to absurdity. On the one hand we are claiming that surface-structure constraints must be introduced into the formal resources of historical linguistics in order to demonstrate that the fact that rules function in a certain manner or have certain exceptions may be perfectly natural; and that such constraints will have the power to override the expected action of historical rules. On the other hand, we are arguing that surface constraints may not only alter their configuration over the course of time, but that they may actually be **broken** by historical rules. How can these claims be reconciled?

We believe, in fact, that this reconciliation is not only feasible, but will also help us to understand the implementation of many historical changes among those we have discussed. It seems that many sound changes begin as variable phenomena (Labov, Yaeger, and Steiner 1972; Bailey 1973) within the restrictions imposed by surface structure constraints; that is to say, they break in, as it were, where they are least noticeable (cf. Naro and Lemle's (1976) 'scale of phonetic salience'). Once established in a particular environment, the change may spread to others, and this is partly where the fundamental importance of the hierarchy lies; the spread will proceed along two parameters: first, one governing the position of the environment (that is, for example, a weakening process will spread from absolute final position to internal syllable-final position, or a strengthening process from word-initial to internal syllable-initial position); and second, one governing the segment (or those surrounding, as in the case of syncope) itself. Thus a change may spread through various environments and affect a variety of segments; exceptions may occur as we have suggested, through the action of surface-structure constraints. There may come a point, however, where the impetus of the change is such that it may break certain of those constraints; that is to say, that until a change has become established in contexts where it does not interfere with surface structure, and only then as long as it still continues fully active, will it begin to 'break through' and be found in situations where constraints would previously have disallowed it.

In this study, we have looked at several clear examples of historical processes which seem to be best interpreted in this way. There is evidence that the loss of word-final consonants was already underway in Latin, and it is doubtful that the Latin of Spain maintained more than the liquids, a nasal, [s], and possibly a dental as a morphological marker.[27] On the other hand, the loss of internal syllable-final consonants (the natural next step) was later and/or slower: we have seen how the fricative reflexes of syllable-final stops were still to be heard in some varieties of Spanish after the Moorish invasions of the eighth century (page 73).

The apocope of final [-e] was also introduced on a gradual but constantly expanding scale, until the twelfth century (page 45); but it is important to note that the first cases localized by Menéndez Pidal (1972:186–92) involve forms in which the consonant left behind was [s], [r], [n], and [l]; for example, **leonés** < LEGIONENSE 'Leonese', **sen** < SINE 'without', **tal** < TALE 'such', etc., that is, precisely those we should expect, from their greater sonority or the fact that they already existed in final position. That apocope, at its height, should have produced such forms as **noch, princep, siet**, etc. (page 46), thereby leaving final consonants previously unknown, only later to revert to **noche, príncipe, siete**, and so on, indicates that the process had reached a point of maximum activity, which may or may not have been due to the powerful cultural influence exerted by French (Lapesa 1975, 1981:169, 200–1). (French had, by that time, lost final [-e] in all cases: only after clusters was it preserved in a weakened form as a schwa (Ewert 1966:34-35).)

Finally, syncope provides us with the clearest case of spread carried out in this fashion, as we demonstrated throughout chapter 5, where we saw how the interaction of phonetic parameters and surface-structure constraints accounted naturally for the development of the process. In fact, throughout all of this book, we have tried to show that change is not erratic, but follows clearly definable paths in its progression; for example, the palatalization of internal syllable-initial consonants (page 76).

The problem for future research, as we see it, is a much more thorough study of historical processes which are sufficiently documented and of ongoing change, in order to establish with greater accuracy the point at which a rule will gain sufficient footing and impulse to break through constraints; why some rules do while others do not; in other words, why some are more active than others. Some of these questions may be answered by sociolinguistics; the influence of both social and geographical dialects is clearly of paramount importance in understanding diachronic change (see Romaine 1982a).

On the whole, we agree with Spence (1978) that change often depends – either for its advancement or its truncation – on considerations of existing surface structure, though we cannot share his apparent optimism (1978:323) that (standard) generative phonology will be able, or even want, to incorporate such considerations into its formal resources, given the type of theory we understand it to be. Indeed, since the ontological status of generative rules is the subject of no clear consensus, even among generativists themselves, and this is even more disturbingly apparent in diachronic analyses,[28] there seems little point in continuing to apply the theory to descriptions of historical phonology until such theoretical questions are examined with the seriousness they deserve. One of Love's (1981) principal criticisms of the generative approach to French phonology is the seeming unwillingness of its practitioners to investigate the validity of the theoretical underpinning of their analyses (see especially his conclusion). As we have already said, it is questionable whether the generative formalism can be used to describe any language diachronically, even though the regular recourse to diachronic evidence (more or less camouflaged according to the theoretical orientation of the writer) in synchronic generative analyses made the transfer of the machinery from synchrony to diachrony a step whose validity was originally questioned by few.

In recent years, however, more and more linguists have reached the conclusion that generative theory will not give us the correct results when applied on a large scale (that is, to the phenomena of a language as a whole, rather than selected slices of data) even in synchronic analyses (see Love (1981) for the case of Modern French). We hope to have shown here that historical phonology is even more resistant to being reduced to the formalism of the standard theory.

Perhaps it is worthwhile making one further aspect of our position clear: we have tried in this study to make a contribution to the understanding of how historical change works; in other words, of its implementation and spread. What we do not claim is that any of the techniques we have used will have predictive power. Like Lass (1980:13, 33–5, 69, 109–14) we do not believe any theory of language change will have such power to any significant extent; the function of variable elements is too random, at least for our present understanding. Unlike Lass, however, we are convinced that explanation can (and indeed should) exist without prediction (cf. Bailey 1982:39). This of course largely reduces historical linguistics to *post hoc* elucidation (just like other historical disciplines within the social sciences), but there is nothing so terrible about that if it provides us with the insights we are searching for, even if we are limited to expressing these insights in statistical (i.e., probabilistic) models (cf. Harris 1982, Romaine 1984). We have already observed that to expect synchronic analysis to provide us with the theoretical foundations for doing historical linguistics is mistaken: there is no more reason to expect explanation in historical linguistics to provide us with a crystal ball.

We believe that theories of diachronic change can bring us insights into the way linguistic developments are implemented and spread, and that this knowledge is a proper concern of linguistics (cf. Bailey 1980, 1981). What is more, we have tried to demonstrate that the standard generative theory has relinquished any attempt to gain this knowledge, by imposing on historical data a theory which is neither interested in, nor capable of, capturing this type of insight.

Notes

1. This also applies in diachronic studies of syntax. Lightfoot seems to believe that a properly constructed synchronic theory, by marking the restrictions necessary to limit possible grammars, will also indicate how 'different' two successive stages of a language can be. Since the generativist view of history is a series of successive stages, the theory would thereby obviate the need for any specifically diachronic principles. See Lightfoot (1979:16).
2. Nor is it possible, of course, to rely on the solipsistic argument of intuitions regarding one's own dialect.
3. Whether or not Labov can be taken to be working within generative theory (as he himself has maintained; see Sankoff and Labov (1979) in response to Kay and McDaniel (1979)) is questionable; cf. Dressler (1978), who skirts the issue somewhat by claiming that the

'purely linguistic Chomskyan notion of competence must be extended to the notion of sociolinguistic competence' (page 151). For the status of Labov's findings *vis-à-vis* generative theory, see Romaine (1981).
4. Cf. Romaine's (1983b:479) criticism of Lightfoot. This is, of course, also true the other way around; i.e., the use of diachronic information by generativists in establishing a synchronic analysis. As Love (1981:155–6) says, 'the idea . . . that the diachronic "adjacency" of two different synchronic systems is relevant to determining their grammars, is fundamentally incoherent . . . the notion "synchronic grammar" involves an idealization of reality that is bought at the price of forcing its proponent into a conceptual framework in which there is no place for a notion of linguistic change at all.'
5. At least within the geographical limits of Castile: some Pyrenean valleys of Aragón resisted intervocalic voicing (Elcock 1960:50–1). Again, compare the situation in Italian varieties of Romance, as seen by Wanner and Cravens (1980), and Lass's statement that 'when you get the appearance of a genuinely categorical change . . . it is almost invariably the case that this is an illusion' (1981:539). We are, of course, playing with arbitrarily established linguistic 'borders'.
6. On the need to distinguish 'process' from 'result', see Vincent (1978) and Lass (1981). As Corbett says, 'The principal value of traditional diachronic research, as opposed to purely synchronic analysis, has always stemmed from its attempts – whether successful or not – to grapple with the HOW and the WHY of linguistic change' (1970:275).
7. That is, as long as we can agree upon what a 'linguistically significant generalization' is; up to now, it has largely been a question of the linguist's intuition, or, with intolerable circularity, what the notation can interpret as such. See Hurford (1977) and Love (1981:192–6).
8. See, for example, the article by Milroy and Milroy (1985), in which they discuss linguistic change and its spread in the community, making a clear distinction between **innovators** of change and those who **spread** it through community networks.
9. Presumably, analyses like Walsh's reflect the unease felt by advocates of the standard theory at being unable to show the relationship between changes involved in a chain-shift of this kind. But Walsh's rule presents more problems than it solves: what about the second shift (rules 4 and 5, page 12 above), which is clearly related to the first – so clearly that the results of rules 1 and 4 are in principle identical? How is this relationship to be shown? Are both shifts to be telescoped into one super-rule, thus necessitating a double application? The theoretical problems are evidently numerous, and lead us further and further away from the true nature of the changes involved.
10. Studies in language death may provide us with further insight into

rule disintegration and loss. Cf. Romaine (1983a:274).
11. The reason being, presumably, that both rules involve loss of a final consonant.
12. For the arbitrary character of rule collapsing, see also Romaine (1982a:218–24).
13. The notion of the nature of transmission is generally rather simplified by the generativists. Cf. the description of the wave model in Bailey (1973).
14. This was basically Hockett's (1965) view. See also Lass (1978:255–9).
15. The quote from King again illustrates the confusion, prevalent among generativists, regarding the result of change and its cause, motivation, and implementation. Cf. note 8.
16. Labov himself has recently tried to align what he sees as these two notions of change, namely that either **sounds** change or **words** change, in Labov (1981).
17. Note that this does not necessarily contradict Bailey's principle 16 that 'all the environments of a rule become variable before the oldest becomes categorical' (Bailey 1973:74), since we are talking about chain-shifts, not a single rule.
18. There seems to be no evidence for morphological or any other type of inhibition being imposed on the rule which could otherwise explain its incomplete nature. On the other hand, of course, this fits in well with the claims of the wave model theory that the further away the 'wave' is from its origin, the longer it will take to become categorical, and is therefore more likely to be truncated or to die out (Bailey 1973:73–4).
19. What is generally understood by 'one dialect' will never form a satisfactory basis for the study of the speech either of an individual or of a community anyway, since an average speaker's competence will include comprehension, if not active use, of more than one mode of speech. It is therefore often very difficult to appreciate where interference might have taken place. For the arbitrariness involved in 'geographical regularity', specifically in Romance, see Wright (1982:6–8).
20. Or even a rule divided into two parts, such as those formulated by Otero (1971:294, 310) and Eastlack (1976:101, 111–12).
21. It should be borne in mind that Hooper is describing a dialect of American Spanish (though this is not always made absolutely clear), and for this reason her description differs in certain aspects from ours. The most important of these differences is her rejection of the voiced fricatives in syllable-final position (see her discussion on pages 215–17). We have already noted that the pronunciation of these fricatives is quite frequent in the Castilian norm.
22. For interesting recent discussions of 'ease of articulation' as a supposed motivation for sound change, though from different viewpoints, see Guitart (1982) and Westbury and Keating (1986). For Lass, of course, none of these concepts are 'explanations',

because (among other reasons) he gives no theoretical content to (phonetic) 'naturalness' (Lass 1980:15–17, 25, 143), which, he observes, is merely probabilistic. But probabilistic claims do have some relevance in historical linguistics. See page 131.
23. Coates (1982:168) suggests a way of incorporating hierarchies into standard generative theory as part of a no-ordering stratagem.
24. Just as we have seen the polarity of language at work in syllable-final position, where weakening (specifically, voicing and spirantization) processes may be optionally counterbalanced in slow speech styles by others with an opposite effect (pages 84–5), it may be seen at work in, for example, word-initial position, where the expected strengthening processes (see Lozano 1979) are counterbalanced by sandhi phenomena spirantizing initial stops (if these stops are really underlying; see above, note 34 to chapter 2).
25. Witness the common pronunciations of **constar** [kostár] 'to exist, be evident', **perspectiva** [pespeɣtíβa] 'perspective', and **exponer** [esponér] 'to expose'. For further details, see Hooper (1976:211–12, 219–20). We are excluding the glides, because of their recognized semivocalic properties.
26. Such profound changes in surface-structure admissibility may be due to external pressure; that is, in contact situations with other languages. In the case of apocope, French influence has sometimes been suggested (cf. Bailey's 'abnatural' developments (Bailey 1982:10–11, 66, 69)).
27. See pages 39–41. The morphological function of certain segments will, of course, often mean that they offer greater resistance to weakening and loss: we insist on the point that no account of historical change will be completely predictive. The question of the preservation of morphological markers is naturally in consonance with the point of view expressed here: that change will take place first where it is least noticeable.
28. See our comments above on the status of historical rules and the general lack of distinction made between motivation, implementation, result, and other aspects of phonological change.

References

Ahlqvist, A. (ed.) 1982: *Papers from the Fifth International Conference on Historical Linguistics* (Current Issues in Linguistic Theory, vol. 21). Amsterdam: John Benjamins
Alarcos Llorach, E. 1951: 'Esbozo de una fonología diacrónica del español', *Estudios dedicados a R. Menéndez Pidal* 2.9–39. Madrid: Consejo Superior de Investigaciones Científicas
—— 1971: *Fonología española*. 4th edn, reprint. Madrid: Gredos
Allen, J.H.D., Jr. 1977: 'Apocope in Old Spanish', *Estudios ofrecidos a Emilio Alarcos Llorach* 1.15–30. Oviedo: Universidad de Oviedo
Allen, W.S. 1978: *Vox Latina*. 2nd edn. Cambridge: Cambridge University Press
Alonso, A. 1969: *De la pronunciación medieval a la moderna en español*, vol. 2. Madrid: Gredos
—— 1976: *De la pronunciación medieval a la moderna en español*, vol. 1, 2nd edn, 1st reprint. Madrid: Gredos
—— and Lida, R. 1945: 'Geografía fonética: '-l' y '-r' implosivas en español', *Revista de Filología Hispánica* 7.313–45
Alvar, M. 1953: *El dialecto aragonés*. Madrid: Gredos
Amastae, J. and Elías-Olivares, L. (eds) 1982: *Spanish in the US: Sociolinguistic Aspects*. Cambridge: Cambridge University Press
Anderson, J.M. 1965: 'A study of syncope in Vulgar Latin', *Word* 21.70-85
—— and Jones, C. 1974: 'Three theses concerning phonological representations', *Journal of Linguistics* 10.1–26
Anwar, M.S. 1974: 'Consonant devoicing at word boundary and assimilation', *Language Sciences* 32.6–12
Bach, E. and Harms, R. (eds) 1968: *Universals in Linguistic Theory*. New York: Holt
Badía Margarit, A.M. 1972: 'Por una revisión del concepto de "cultismo" en fonética histórica', in *Studia Hispanica in Honorem R. Lapesa*, 1.137–52
Bailey, C.-J.N. 1973: *Variation and Linguistic Theory*. Arlington (Virginia): Center for Applied Linguistics
—— 1980: 'Yroëthian linguistics and the marvelous mirage of minilectal methodology', in Ureland 1980:39-50

—— 1981: 'What can rightly be required of a decent theory of language', *Language Sciences* 3.19-26
—— 1982: *On the Yin and Yang Nature of Language*. Ann Arbor: Karoma
Basbøll, H. 1981: 'On the function of boundaries in phonological rules', in Goyvaerts 1981b:245–69
Bauer, L. 1988: 'What is lenition?', *Journal of Linguistics* 24.381–92
Bell, A. and Hooper, J.B. (eds) 1978: *Syllables and Segments*. Amsterdam: North Holland
Bergquist, M.F. 1981: *Ibero-Romance: Comparative Phonology and Morphology*. Washington, DC: University Press of America
Bjarkman, P.C. 1978: 'Theoretically relevant issues in Cuban Spanish phonology', *Chicago Linguistic Society Regional Meeting* 14.13–27
Bley-Vroman, R. 1975: 'Opacity and interrupted rule schemata', *Chicago Linguistic Society Regional Meeting* 11.73–80
Botha, R. 1973: *The Justification of Linguistic Hypotheses*. The Hague: Mouton
Brüch, J. 1930: 'L'évolution de l'l devant les consonnes en espagnol', *Revista de Filología Española* 17.1–17
Bruck, A., Fox, R.A., and LaGaly, M.W. (eds) 1974: *Papers from the Parasession on Natural Phonology*. Chicago: Chicago Linguistic Society
Canfield, D.L. and Davis, J.C. 1975: *An Introduction to Romance Linguistics*. Illinois: Southern Illinois University Press
Catalán Menéndez-Pidal, D. 1968: 'La pronunciación [ihante] por /iffante/ en La Rioja del siglo XI', *Romance Philology* 21.410–35
Chen, M.Y. 1973a: 'Predictive power in phonological description', *Lingua* 32.173-91
—— 1973b: 'On the formal expression of natural rules in phonology', *Journal of Linguistics* 9.223-49
—— 1974a: 'Natural phonology from the diachronic viewpoint', in Bruck *et al.* 1974:43–80
—— 1974b: 'Metarules and universal constraints in phonological theory', in Heilmann 1974:909–24
—— and Hsieh, H.-I. 1971: 'The time variable in phonological change', *Journal of Linguistics* 7.1–13
—— and Wang, W.S.-Y. 1975: 'Sound change: actuation and implementation', *Language* 51.255–81
Chomsky, N. 1965: *Aspects of the Theory of Syntax*. Cambridge (Mass.): MIT Press
—— and Halle, M. 1968: *The Sound Pattern of English*. New York: Harper & Row
Coates, R. 1982: 'Why Hungarian isn't as extrinsic as Vago thinks', *Journal of Linguistics* 18.167–72
Cohen, V. 1971: 'Foleyology', *Chicago Linguistic Society Regional Meeting* 7.316–22
Cooley, M. 1978: 'Phonological constraints and sound changes', *Glossa* 12.125–36

Corbett, N. 1970: 'Reconstructing the diachronic phonology of Romance', *Romance Philology* 24.273–90

Corominas, J. and Pascual, J.A. 1980–: *Diccionario crítico etimológico castellano e hispánico*. Vol. 1: A-Ca, 1980; 2: Ce-F, 1980; 3: G-Ma, 1980; 4: Me-Re, 1981; 5: Ri-X, 1983. Madrid: Gredos

Cortelazzo, M. and Zolli, P. 1979–: *Dizionario etimologico della lingua italiana*. Vol. 1: A-C, 1979; 2: D-H, 1980; 3: I-N, 1983; 4:O-R, 1985. Bologna: Zanichelli

Cravens, T.D. 1984: 'Implicational phonology: Martinet, Foley and beyond', in Manning *et al.* 1984:141–8

—— (forthcoming): 'Problems and solutions in diachronic phonology: historical correspondences and phonological evolution', to appear in P.M. Bertinetto and M. Loporcaro (eds): *Certamen Phonologicum. Papers from the 1987 Cortona Phonology Meeting*

Cressey, W.W. 1974: 'Homorganic in generative phonology', *Papers in Linguistics* 7.69–82

Dekeyser, X. 1978: 'Some considerations on voicing with special reference to spirants in English and Dutch: a diachronic-contrastive approach', in Fisiak 1978:99–121

Díaz y Díaz, M.C. 1962: *Antología del latín vulgar*. 2nd edn. Madrid: Gredos

Dinnsen, D.A. 1977: 'A functional explanation of dialect difference', *Language Sciences* 46.1–7

—— (ed.) 1979: *Current Approaches to Phonological Theory*. Bloomington: Indiana University Press

Dressler, W. 1978: 'How much does performance contribute to phonological change?', in Fisiak 1978:145–58

Dworkin, S.N. 1978: 'Derivational transparency and sound change: the two-pronged growth of –IDU in Hispano-Romance', *Romance Philology* 31.605–17

Eastlack, C.L. 1976: 'The phonology of twelfth century Castilian and its relation to the phonology of Proto-Romance', *Papers in Linguistics* 9.89–126

—— 1977: 'Iberochange: a program to simulate systemic sound change in Ibero-Romance', *Computers and the Humanities* 11.81–8

Eckert, P. 1980: 'The structure of a long-term phonological process: the back vowel chain shift in Soulatan Gascon', in Labov 1980:179–219

Elcock, W.D. 1960: *The Romance Languages*. London: Faber

Entwistle, W. 1936: *The Spanish Language*. London: Faber

Escure, G. 1975: 'Weakening and deletion processes in language change', doctoral dissertation, Indiana University. Ann Arbor: University Microfilms

—— 1977: 'Hierarchies and phonological weakening', *Lingua* 43.55–64

Ewert, A. 1966: *The French Language*. 3rd edn. London: Faber

Felix, S.W. 1979: 'Anatomy of a sound change in Canarian Spanish', *Zeitschrift für Romanische Philologie* 95.358–81

Fisiak, J. (ed.) 1978: *Recent Developments in Historical Phonology*. The Hague: Mouton

Foley, J. 1970: 'Phonological distinctive features', *Folia Linguistica* 4.87–92
—— 1971: 'Phonological change by rule repetition', *Chicago Linguistic Society Regional Meeting* 7.376–84
—— 1972: 'Rule precursors and phonological change by metarule', in Stockwell and Macaulay 1972:96–100
—— 1975: 'Latin origin of Romance rules', in Saltarelli and Wanner 1975:37–54
—— 1977: *Foundations of Theoretical Phonology*. Cambridge: Cambridge University Press
Frengle, D.P. 1975: 'A generative phonology of thirteenth-century Castilian', doctoral dissertation, University of Michigan. Ann Arbor: University Microfilms
Gaeng, P.A. 1968: *An Inquiry into Local Variations in Vulgar Latin* (University of North Carolina Studies in the Romance Languages and Literatures, number 77). Chapel Hill: University of North Carolina Press
Galmés de Fuentes, A. 1983: *Dialectología mozárabe*. Madrid: Gredos
García de Diego, V. 1955: *Diccionario etimológico español e hispánico*. Madrid: Saeta
Gimson, A.C. 1970: *Introduction to the Pronunciation of English*. 2nd edn. London: Edward Arnold
Goyvaerts, D.L. 1975: *Present-day Historical and Comparative Linguistics*. Ghent/Antwerp: E. Story-Scientia
—— 1981a: 'Introduction' to Goyvaerts 1981b:1–26
—— (ed.) 1981b: *Phonology in the 1980s*. Ghent: E. Story-Scientia
Grandgent, C.H. 1908: *An Introduction to Vulgar Latin*. Boston: Heath
Guile, T. 1972: 'A generalization about epenthesis and syncope', *Chicago Linguistic Society Regional Meeting* 8.463–9
—— 1973: 'Glide-obstruentization and the syllable "coda" hierarchy', *Chicago Linguistic Society Regional Meeting* 9.139–56
Guitart, J.M. 1982: 'On Caribbean Spanish phonology and the motivation for language change', in Lantolf and Stone 1982:63–70
Haadsma, R.A. and Nuchelmans, J. 1963: *Précis du latin vulgaire*. Groningen: J.B. Wolters
Hall, R.A., Jr. 1976: *Comparative Romance Grammar, Vol. 2: Proto-Romance Phonology*. New York: Elsevier
Hammond, R.M. 1980: 'Weakening chains and relative syllable strength positions in Caribbean Spanish', in Nuessel 1980:97–107
Harris, J.W. 1969: *Spanish Phonology*. Cambridge (Mass.): MIT Press
—— 1970: 'Distinctive feature theory and nasal assimilation in Spanish', *Linguistics* 58.30–7
—— 1980: 'Palatal/Ø alternations in Spanish', in Nuessel 1980:108–30
—— 1982: 'On explaining language change', in Ahlqvist 1982:1–14
Harris-Northall, R. (forthcoming): 'The spread of sound change: another look at syncope in Spanish', to appear in *Romance Philology*
Hartman, S.L. 1974: 'An outline of Spanish historical phonology',

Papers in Linguistics 7.123-91
—— 1980: 'La etimología de DULCE: ¿realmente una excepción?', *Nueva Revista de Filología Hispánica* 29.115-27
Heilmann, L. (ed.) 1974: *Proceedings of the Eleventh International Congress of Linguists*. Bologna: Mulino
Hock, H.H. 1986: *Principles of Historical Linguistics* (Trends in Linguistics, Studies and Monographs 34). Berlin: Mouton de Gruyter
Hockett, C.F. 1965: 'Sound change', *Language* 41.185-204
Hoenigswald, H.M. 1978: 'Secondary split, typology, and universals', in Fisiak 1978:173-81
Hooper, J.B. 1972: 'The syllable in phonological theory', *Language* 48.525-40
—— 1976: *An Introduction to Natural Generative Phonology*. New York: Academic Press
—— 1979: 'Child morphology and morphophonemic change', *Linguistics* 17.21-50
Houlihan, K. 1979: 'On assimilatory and non-assimilatory phonological rules', *Glossa* 13.13-23
Hurford, J.R. 1977: 'The significance of linguistic generalizations', *Language* 53.574-620
Hyman, L. 1975: *Phonology: Theory and Analysis*. New York: Holt Rinehart & Winston
Hyman, R. 1956: 'ŋ as an allophone denoting open juncture in several Spanish American dialects', *Hispania* 39.293-9
Janson, T. 1979: *Mechanisms of Language Change in Latin*. Stockholm: Alqvist & Wiksell
Jungemann, F. 1955: *La teoría del sustrato y los dialectos hispano-romances y gascones*. Madrid: Gredos
Kanngiesser, S. 1972: *Aspekte der synchronen und diachronen Linguistik*. Tübingen: Niemeyer
Kay, P. and McDaniel, C.K. 1979: 'On the logic of variable rules', *Language in Society* 8.151-87
Keiler, A.R. (ed.) 1972: *A Reader in Historical and Comparative Linguistics*. New York: Holt Rinehart & Winston
Kenstowicz, M.J. and Kisseberth, C.W. (eds) 1973: *Issues in Phonological Theory*. The Hague: Mouton
Kent, R.G. 1945: *The Sounds of Latin*. 3rd edn, revised. Baltimore: Linguistic Society of America
King, R.D. 1969: *Historical Linguistics and Generative Grammar*. Englewood Cliffs (NJ): Prentice-Hall
—— 1974: 'Can rules be added in the middle of grammars?'. Bloomington: Indiana University Linguistics Club
Kiparsky, P. 1968: 'Linguistic universals and linguistic change', in Keiler 1972:338-67. Originally in Bach and Harms 1968:170-202
—— 1972: 'Explanation in phonology', in Peters 1972:189-227
—— 1973: 'Productivity in phonology', in Kenstowicz and Kisseberth 1973:169-76
—— 1982: *Explanation in Phonology*. Dordrecht: Foris

Kisseberth, C. 1970: 'On the functional unity of phonological rules', *Linguistic Inquiry* 1.291–306
Koutsoudas, A. (ed.) 1976: *The Application and Ordering of Grammatical Rules*. The Hague: Mouton
Labov, W. (ed.) 1980: *Locating Language in Time and Space*. New York: Academic Press
—— 1981: 'Resolving the Neogrammarian controversy', *Language* 57.267–308
——, Yaeger, M., and Steiner, R. 1972: *A Quantitative Study of Sound Change in Progress*. 2 vols. Philadelphia: US Regional Survey, University of Pennsylvania
Lantolf, J.P. and Stone, G.B. (eds) 1982: 'Current Research in Romance Languages'. Bloomington: Indiana University Linguistics Club
Lapesa, R. 1975: 'De nuevo sobre la apócope vocálica en castellano medieval', *Nueva Revista de Filología Hispánica* 24.13–23
—— 1981: *Historia de la lengua española*. 9th edn. Madrid: Gredos
Lass, R. 1971: 'Boundaries as obstruents: Old English voicing assimilation and universal strength hierarchies', *Journal of Linguistics* 7.15–30
—— 1976: 'On generative taxonomy, and whether formalizations "explain"', *Studia Linguistica* 30.139–54
—— 1978: 'Mapping constraints in phonological reconstruction: on climbing down trees without falling out of them', in Fisiak 1978:245–86
—— 1980: *On Explaining Language Change*. Cambridge: Cambridge University Press
—— 1981: 'Undigested history and synchronic "structure"', in Goyvaerts 1981b:525–44
—— 1984: *Phonology: An Introduction to Basic Concepts*. Cambridge: Cambridge University Press
Lathrop, T.A. 1980: *The Evolution of Spanish*. Newark (Delaware): Juan de la Cuesta Monographs, University of Delaware
Lehmann, W.P. and Malkiel, Y. (eds) 1968: *Directions for Historical Linguistics*. Austin: University of Texas Press
Lightfoot, D.W. 1979: *Principles of Diachronic Syntax*. Cambridge: Cambridge University Press
Lightner, T.M. 1981: 'New explorations into derivational morphology', in Goyvaerts 1981b:93–9
Lipski, J.M. 1983: 'La norma culta y la norma radiofónica: /s/ y /n/ en español', *Language Problems and Language Planning* 7.239–62
Lloyd, P.M. 1979: 'On the definition of "Vulgar Latin"', *Neuphilologische Mitteilungen* 80.110–22
Lodge, K. 1986: 'Allegro rules in colloquial Thai: some thoughts on process phonology', *Journal of Linguistics* 22.331–54
Longmire, B.J. 1976: 'The relationship of variables in Venezuelan Spanish to historical sound changes in Latin and the Romance languages', doctoral dissertation, Georgetown University. Ann Arbor: University Microfilms

Love, N. 1981: *Generative Phonology: A Case-Study from French*. Amsterdam: John Benjamins

Lozano, M.C. 1979: 'Stop and spirant alternations: fortition and spirantization processes in Spanish phonology'. Bloomington: Indiana University Linguistics Club

Luján, M. and Hensey, F. (eds) 1976: *Current Studies in Romance Linguistics*. Washington: Georgetown University Press

Lyons, C.G. 1978: 'A look into the Spanish future', *Lingua* 46.225–44

Macpherson, I.R. 1975: *Spanish Phonology: Descriptive and Historical*. Manchester: Manchester University Press

Malkiel, Y. 1960a: 'Paradigmatic resistance to sound change; the Old Spanish preterite forms **vide**, **vido** against the background of the recession of primary –d–', *Language* 36.281–346

—— 1960b: 'Fuentes indígenas y exóticas de los sustantivos y adjetivos verbales en –e (continuación)', *Revue de Linguistique Romane* 24.201–53

—— 1967: 'Multiple vs. simple causation in linguistic change', in *To Honor Roman Jakobson: Essays on the Occasion of his Seventieth Birthday* 2.1228–46. The Hague: Mouton

—— 1968: 'The inflectional paradigm as an occasional determinant of sound change', in Lehmann and Malkiel 1968:21–64

—— 1973: 'Etiological studies in Romance diachronic phonology', *Acta Linguistica Hafniensia* 14.201–42

—— 1975: 'En torno al cultismo medieval: los descendientes hispánicos de DULCIS', *Nueva Revista de Filología Hispánica* 24.24–45

—— 1976: 'In search of "penultimate" causes of language change: studies in the avoidance of /ž/ in Proto-Spanish', in Luján and Hensey 1976:27–36

—— 1978: 'The classification of Romance languages', *Romance Philology* 31.467–500

—— 1981: 'Drift, slope and slant: background of, and variations upon, a Sapirian theme', *Language* 57.535–70

—— 1984: 'Old Spanish resistance to diphthongization, or previous vowel lengthening?', *Language* 60.70–114

—— 1986: 'Diachronic phonology as a clue to the transmission of etyma (exemplified with Old Portuguese verbs)', *General Linguistics* 26.149–81

Manning, A., Martin, P., and McCalla, K. (eds) 1984: *Tenth LACUS Forum*. Columbia: Hornbeam Press

Martinet, A. 1970: *Économie des changements phonétiques*. 3rd edn. Berne: A. Francke

—— 1982: 'A new generation of phonemes: the French intervocalic voiced stops', in Lantolf and Stone 1982:1–12

Menéndez Pidal, R. 1958: *Manual de gramática histórica española*. 10th edn. Madrid: Espasa-Calpe

—— 1972: *Orígenes del español: estado lingüístico de la Península Ibérica hasta el siglo XI*. 7th edn. Madrid: Espasa-Calpe

Milroy, J. and Milroy, L. 1985: 'Linguistic change, social network and speaker innovation', *Journal of Linguistics* 21.339–84

Moliner, M. 1971: *Diccionario del uso del español*. 2 vols. Madrid: Gredos

Naro, A.J. and Lemle, M. 1976: 'Syntactic diffusion', in Steever *et al*. 1976:221–40

Navarro Tomás, T. 1977: *Manual de pronunciación española*. 19th edn. Madrid: Consejo Superior de Investigaciones Científicas

Newton, B. 1971: 'Ordering paradoxes in phonology', *Journal of Linguistics* 7.31–53

—— 1972: 'Interdigitation in French phonology', *Language Sciences* 19.41–3

Niedermann, M. 1953: *Précis de phonétique historique du latin*. 3rd edn. revised. Paris: Klincksieck

Nuessel, F.H. (ed.) 1980: 'Contemporary studies in Romance languages'. Bloomington: Indiana University Linguistics Club

Núñez Cedeño, R. 1980: 'Procesos finales en el español de Santo Domingo', *Nueva Revista de Filología Hispánica* 29.128–38

Otero, C.P. 1971: *Evolución y revolución en romance I*. Barcelona: Seix Barral

—— 1976: *Evolución y revolución en romance II*. Barcelona: Seix Barral

Pensado, C. 1985: 'On the interpretation of the non-existent: non-occurring syllable types in Spanish phonology', *Folia Linguistica* 19.313–20

Pensado Ruiz, C. 1984: *Cronología relativa del castellano*. Salamanca: Ediciones Universidad

Peters, S. (ed.) 1972: *Goals of Linguistic Theory*. Englewood Cliffs (NJ): Prentice-Hall

Picard, M. 1980: 'A constraint on rule complementation'. Bloomington: Indiana University Linguistics Club

Poplack, S. 1980a: 'The notion of the plural in Puerto Rican Spanish: competing constraints on (s) deletion', in Labov 1980:55–67

—— 1980b: 'Deletion and disambiguation in Puerto Rican Spanish', *Language* 56.371–85

Posner, R.R. 1974: 'Ordering of historical phonological rules in Romance', *Transactions of the Philological Society* 98–127

Robson, C.A. 1963: 'L'*Appendix Probi* et la philologie latine', *Le Moyen Age* 69.37–54

Romaine, S. 1981: 'The status of variable rules in sociolinguistic theory', *Journal of Linguistics* 17.93–119

—— 1982a: *Socio-Historical Linguistics: Its Status and Methodology*. Cambridge: Cambridge University Press

—— 1982b: 'Contributions from sociolinguistics to historical linguistics'. Unpublished paper

—— 1983a: Review of *Language Death. The Life Cycle of a Scottish Gaelic Dialect*, by N.C. Dorian. *Journal of Linguistics* 19.272–7

—— 1983b: Review of *Complementation in Middle English Syntax and the Methodology of Historical Syntax*, by A. Warner. *Journal of Linguistics* 19.478–80

—— 1984: 'The status of sociological models and categories in explaining language variation', *Linguistische Berichte* 90.25–38
Saltarelli, M. and Wanner, D. (eds) 1975: *Diachronic Studies in Romance Linguistics*. The Hague: Mouton
Sampson, R. (ed.) 1980: *Early Romance Texts: An Anthology*. Cambridge: Cambridge University Press
Sanders, G.A. 1976: 'On the exclusion of extrinsic ordering constraints', in Koutsoudas 1976:203–58
Sankoff, D. and Labov, W. 1979: 'On the uses of variable rules', *Language in Society* 8.189–222
Schane, S.A. 1968: *French Phonology and Morphology*. Cambridge (Mass.): MIT Press
Schiffman, H.F. 1982: Review of *Language and Linguistic Area: Essays*, by M.B. Emeneau. *Language* 58.185–93
Selkirk, E.O. 1972: 'The phrase phonology of English and French', doctoral dissertation, MIT
Sommerstein, A.H. 1977: *Modern Phonology*. London: Edward Arnold
Spence, N.C.W. 1978: 'Phonetic change and phonotactic rules in proto-French', *Revue de Linguistique Romane* 42.307–23
Stahl, F.A. and Scavnicky, G.E.A. 1973: *A Reverse Dictionary of the Spanish Language*. Urbana: University of Illinois
Steever, S.B., Walker, C.A., and Mufwene, S.S. (eds) 1976: *Papers from the Parasession on Diachronic Syntax*. Chicago: Chicago Linguistic Society
Stockwell, R.P. and Macaulay, R.K.S. (eds) 1972: *Linguistic Change and Generative Theory*. Bloomington: Indiana University Press
Straka, G. 1951: 'Observations sur la chronologie et les dates de quelques modifications phonétiques en roman et en français prélittéraire', *Revue des Langues Romanes* 71.247–307
—— 1956: 'La dislocation linguistique de la Romania et la formation des langues romanes à la lumière de la chronologie relative des changements phonétiques', *Revue de Linguistique Romane* 20.249–67
Strang, B.M.H. 1970: *A History of English*. London: Methuen
Sturtevant, E.H. 1940: *The Pronunciation of Greek and Latin*. 2nd edn. Philadelphia: University of Pennsylvania
Suñer, M. (ed.) 1978: *Contemporary Studies in Romance Linguistics*. Washington: Georgetown University Press
Tekavčić, P. 1972: *Grammatica storica dell'italiano; volume I: Fonematica*. Bologna: Mulino
Terrell, T.D. 1982: 'Current trends in the investigation of Cuban and Puerto Rican phonology', in Amastae and Elías-Olivares 1982:47–70
Tiersma, P.M. 1980: 'The lexicon in phonological theory'. Bloomington: Indiana University Linguistics Club
Traugott, E.C., Labrum, R., and Shepherd, S. (eds) 1980: *Papers from the Fourth International Conference on Historical Linguistics*. Amsterdam: John Benjamins
Ureland, P.S. (ed.) 1980: *Sprachvariation und Sprachwandel: Probleme der Inter- und Intralinguistik; Akten des 3. Symposions über*

Sprachkontakt in Europa, Mannheim 1979 (Linguistische Arbeiten, nr. 92). Tübingen: Niemeyer
Väänänen, V. 1963: *Introduction au latin vulgaire*. Paris: Klincksieck
Vidos, B.E. 1977: *Manual de lingüística románica*. 2nd edn, 2nd reprint. Translated from the 1959 Italian edition by F. de B. Moll. Madrid: Aguilar
Vincent, N. 1978: 'Is sound change teleological?', in Fisiak 1978:409–30
Walsh, T.J. 1979: 'On the characterization of certain sound changes in Romance'. Bloomington: Indiana University Linguistics Club
Wang, W.S.-Y. 1968: 'Vowel features, paired variables and the English vowel shift', *Language* 44.695–708
—— 1969: 'Competing changes as a cause of residue', *Language* 45.9–25
—— (ed.) 1977: *The Lexicon in Phonological Change*. The Hague: Mouton
Wanner, D. and Cravens, T.D. 1980: 'Early intervocalic voicing in Tuscan', in Traugott *et al.* 1980:339–47
Ward, R.L. 1944: 'Afterthoughts on g as ŋ in Latin and Greek', *Language* 20.73–7
Westbury, J.R. and Keating, P.A. 1986: 'On the naturalness of stop consonant voicing', *Journal of Linguistics* 22.145–66
Whitley, S. 1978: 'Rule reordering in the phonological history of Spanish (o sea, ¿tiene el idioma un espíritu?)', in Suñer 1978:378–402
Wright, R. 1982: *Late Latin and Early Romance in Spain and Carolingian France* (ARCA Classical and Medieval Texts, Papers and Monographs, 8). Liverpool: Francis Cairns
—— 1983: 'Unity and diversity among the Romance languages', *Transactions of the Philological Society* 1–22
Yavas, M. 1982: 'Natural phonology and borrowing assimilations', *Linguistics* 20.123–32
Zauner, A. 1929: 'Esp. **pujar** y **soso**', *Revista de Filología Española* 16.154–60
—— 1930: 'Encore une fois l devant consonne', *Revista de Filología Española* 17.286–90

Subject Index

abstractness 2, 52
affrication 17, 68. v. also palatalization
apocope 23, 36 n.30, 40, 45–8, 51, 52 n.3, 54 n.15, 56, 65, 89 n.22, 111, 125, 129, 134 n.26
Appendix Probi 79, 94–5, 96, 97, 98, 102, 105, 112 n.5
Arabic 40, 47, 55 n.20, n.25, 89 n.15
Aragonese 10, 11, 25, 33 n.5, 64, 90 n.31, 111, 132 n.5
assibilation 22, 26
assimilation 19, 22, 23, 35 n.22, 41–2, 44, 47, 48, 51, 56, 57, 59, 61, 65, 67, 68, 69, 71–2, 78, 79, 80–1, 83, 85, 86, 87, 87 n.2, 90 n.29, 127
Asturian 43, 53 n.7, 89 n.19. v. also Astur-Leonese
Astur-Leonese 90 n.31, 111. v. also Asturian, Leonese

-b-, loss of 9, 24–6, 33 n.6

Catalan 10, 11, 40, 48, 53 n.7, 60, 62, 73, 77–8, 89 n.16, n.17, 90 n.31, 91 n.44, 99, 105
categorical rules 1–2, 5 n.2, n.5, n.6, 11, 24, 26, 32, 87, 91 n.40, 93, 94, 96, 99, 113 n.17, 118, 119, 123, 124–5, 132 n.5, 133 n.17
chain shift 6–9, 12–15, 16–7, 29–31, 32 n.1, 34 n.11, 51, 54 n.17, 83, 118, 120–1, 124, 132 n.9, 133 n.17, n.18
competence 1, 117, 119, 131–2 n.3, 133 n.19
conspiracies 56, 87, 103
constraints, v. surface structure

-d, final, loss of 38, 45, 49–50, 85
-d-, intervocalic, loss of 7–12, 13, 15, 17–8, 22, 27, 29, 31, 33 n.9, 33–4 n.10, n.11, 112 n.6, 123–4
delateralization 80, 81, 113 n.8
dentals, syllable-final 83–4, 92 n.50, 129
depalatalization 52 n.3, 125
devoicing 13–14, 16, 17, 47–51, 55 n.20, n.21, n.26, 70, 84, 85, 126, 127

ease of articulation 126, 133 n.22
epenthesis 108, 109
exceptions 11, 26, 65, 74, 94, 99, 101, 111, 118–19, 124–5, 126, 128, 129
explanation 94, 123, 126, 133–4 n.22

-f, syllable-final 70
French 20–1, 25, 36 n.28, 38, 40, 41, 46, 62, 73, 94, 96, 98, 122, 124, 129, 130, 134 n.26

-g-, intervocalic, loss of 8–10, 12, 13, 15, 18, 21–2, 23, 27, 28–9, 31, 33 n.8, 36 n.29, 124

145

Subject Index

-g, syllable-final 71, 78–82, 95, 97, 113 n.8
Galician 64, 89 n.20, 90 n.31
geminates 6–7, 12, 13–14, 16, 18, 22–3, 34 n.12, 35 n.22, 35–6 n.27, 69, 71–2, 77, 78, 86, 88 n.5, 97, 108, 121
Germanic 9, 15, 48, 88 n.7, 89 n.15, 114 n.29
glide formation 17, 20, 31, 39, 59–60, 63–4, 67–8, 73, 75, 79, 81–3, 85–6, 89 n.20
gradualness 2, 45, 83, 89 n.17 104, 111, 117, 123. v. also lexical diffusion
Greek-letter variables 13, 120–1

heterogeneity 11, 116–17, 118
homogeneity 1, 5 n.2, 11, 116–17, 124

idealization 116–17, 132 n.4. v. also homogeneity
implementation of change 4, 11–12, 20–1, 24, 25–6, 32, 37, 67, 76, 81–2, 86–7, 89 n.17, 93, 94, 97–8, 101–8, 111, 112 n.4, n.7, 119, 120–1, 123, 124–5, 128–9, 131, 132 n.8, 133 n.15, 134 n.28
interdigitation 29, 75–8, 79–81, 82, 86–7, 93–4, 95, 111–12, 121
Italian 33 n.5, 40, 41, 71, 98–9, 100, 101–2, 103–4, 105–6, 108, 113 n.13, n.14, n.16, 114 n.21, 132 n.5

[k], final, loss of 38–9
[k], syllable-final 71, 72–8, 79–82, 89–90 n.23, 95–7, 113 n.8

-l, final 40, 47, 48, 54 n.13, 56, 129
-l, syllable-final 59–62, 63–5, 67, 69, 74, 80, 81, 88 n.9, n.10, n.14, 89 n.16, 90 n.23, 97–8
labials, syllable-final 65–6, 70–1, 72, 82–3, 85–6, 110–11. v. also -m, final

Leonese 25, 33–4 n.10, 91 n.38. v. also Astur-Leonese
lexical diffusion 32, 33 n.5, 60, 63, 117, 123–4
loanwords 7, 12, 43, 47, 50, 54 n.11, 55 n.20, n.26, 69, 77–8, 85–6, 89 n.15, 114 n.21, 120, 124–5

-m, final, loss of 33 n.2, 38, 43–4, 53 n.9
metathesis 18, 24, 25, 35 n.19, 35–6 n.27, 40, 70, 76–7, 91 n.42, 92 n.51, 108
monophthongization 31, 61–3, 70, 74–5, 76, 78, 83, 88 n.13, 89 n.17, 91 n.41, 99, 110
morpheme structure v. surface structure
Mozarabic 25, 33 n.5, 73, 90 n.31, 99

-n, final, loss of 43–4
nasals, final 39–40, 42–4, 47, 48, 52 n.4, 53 n.9, 53–4 n.10, 56, 129
nasals, syllable-final 57–9, 60, 65–7, 69, 71, 78, 88 n.6, n.7, 108–9, 119, 121–3
naturalness 2, 3, 13–14, 20, 26, 29, 34 n.15, 47, 48, 50, 51, 69, 70, 76, 80–1, 87, 102–3, 104, 106, 107, 125, 128
neogrammarianism 3, 7
neutralization 52

Occitan 40, 62, 77

palatalization 17–26, 28–9, 32, 34 n.17, 35 n.19, n.22, 37, 54 n.11, 59–60, 62–8, 69, 73–8, 79, 80–2, 86–7, 89 n.20, 91 n.42, 92 n.53, 108, 118, 120–1, 126, 130
performance 1–2, 117, 119
phonetic parameters 20, 42, 44, 93, 97, 105, 107, 111, 126–7, 129. v. also strength hierarchies
Portuguese 10, 25, 52 n.2, 60, 62, 64, 73, 76, 88 n.13, 89 n.20, 90

n.31, 96, 99, 105, 114 n.27
predictability 32, 107, 131, 134 n.27
proto-Romance 4
psychological reality 2, 122, 128

-r, final 40, 46–7, 48, 54 n.13, 56, 129
-r, syllable-final 57, 58, 60, 65, 69, 90 n.25
reconstruction 2, 3–4
relative chronology 3, 12, 21–2, 27–9, 36 n.36, 50–1, 62–3, 76–8, 79, 80–1, 82, 86, 91 n.45, 97–8, 100, 105, 108–10, 112 n.2, 114 n.27, n.29
Rhaeto-Romance 20
rule collapsing 2, 13–14, 19–20, 21–2, 24, 26, 27–9, 34 n.14, 64, 75, 80, 82, 87 n.2, 92 n.47, 93, 94, 104–5, 106, 111, 114 n.25, 120–3, 132 n.9, 133 n.12
rule ordering 2, 20–1, 22, 51, 72, 75–7, 93, 121, 122
Rumanian 9, 33 n.7, 40, 41, 62, 89 n.17, 98

-s, final 39, 40, 41–2, 44–5, 46–7, 48, 49, 52 n.4, 53 n.9, 54 n.12, 56, 129
-s, syllable final 68–70, 90 n.30
Sardinian 19, 20
semi-learned forms 25, 58, 88 n.14, 96
simplicity 2, 5 n.6, 13–14, 24, 26, 29, 80, 122
simplification (of rules) 19–20, 87, 93, 103, 104–5, 121–3
spirantization 6–9, 12, 13–14, 15, 20, 27, 31, 36 n.34, 42, 47, 50–1, 54 n.17, 55 n.25, 73, 79–80, 81, 83–5, 86, 92 n.52, 110, 126, 134 n.24
spread of change v. implementation
strength hierarchies 14–15, 29, 31–2, 37, 41, 42, 44, 47–8, 51, 54 n.11, n.12, 55 n.22, n.23, n.26, 67, 71, 87, 92 n.48, 93, 94, 110, 113 n.11, 126–9, 134 n.23. v. also phonetic parameters
structuralism 3, 6, 32 n.1
substrate influence 12
surface structure 31, 42, 43, 46–7, 52, 56, 64–5, 68–9, 74, 76, 77, 84–6, 87, 93, 94, 96, 98, 99, 101, 102–3, 106–7, 108, 109, 110, 111–12, 114 n.28, 119, 121, 125–8, 129–30, 134 n.26
syllable boundary 31, 36 n.33, 68–9, 72, 79, 82, 96, 125
syllable structure v. surface structure
syncope 27–9, 36 n.29, n.36, 61–2, 65, 70, 71, 74, 78, 79, 81, 83–4, 89 n.15, 91 n.46, 93–115, 120, 121, 124–5, 126, 129

telescoping v. rule collapsing

variable rules 11, 12, 45–6, 50, 51–2, 53 n.5, 58, 65, 85, 95, 96, 111, 117, 121, 124, 128
variation 1, 4, 11, 60, 124
velarization 43–4, 53–4 n.10, 60–2, 63, 65, 67, 90 n.24
[voice] 48, 55 n.23, 86, 107, 127
voicing 6, 11–12, 16, 21, 27, 29–31, 33 n.5, 34 n.16, 36 n.32, 42, 47, 57, 62–3, 69–70, 71, 75–6, 80, 83, 85, 87, 91 n.40, 96–7, 99, 100, 102, 110, 112, 113 n.15, 114 n.23, 118, 121, 127, 132 n.5, 134 n.24
vowels, loss of v. apocope, syncope
Vulgar Latin 4, 33 n.2

wave theory 11, 82, 133 n.13, n.18
Western Romance 7, 12, 14, 27, 35 n.23, 41, 63, 69, 71, 73, 80, 82, 90 n.33, 96, 98, 101

[x], final 45, 47, 48–9, 56

Index of Forms

AB 38
abad 13
abatir 13
ABBATE 13
ABBATTUERE 13
abeja 79, 96, 98
ábrego 30, 99
abrigar 30
abrir 100, 103, 113
açada 68
acero 18
ACIARIU 18
actor 85
actriz 49
ACUTIARE 17
AD 38
ADDUCERE 13
adquirir 85
*AD-ROTULARE 79
aducir 13
advertir 85
aer(e) 77
AERE 77
AESTIVU 68
AETATE 45
AFFLARE 70
AFRICU 30, 99
agosto 7, 10, 68
agua 34
aguzar 17
aipo (Pt.) 35
aire 77
alabanza 66
ALBINIANA 88
álbum 43

alcahuete 55
alcaide 55
alcayaz 55
algo 39, 97
ALIQUOD 38, 39, 97
ALITUS 113
alma 108
almendra 113
ALTERIU 60, 74, 91
ALTERU 60, 100, 103
alto 61, 88
altro (It.) 100, 103
ALTU(S) 61, 88, 113
alzar 88
ama 39
amades 34
amado 34
amáis 34
amar 55
AMARE 55
AMAT 38, 39
AMATIS 34
AMATU 34
AMAVIT 61
amó 61
amou (Pt.) 62
AMYGDALA 113
*AMYNDULA 113
ancla 100, 104
ANCORA 100, 104
áncora 114
àncora (It.) 100, 104
andad 49
ANG(U)LUS 95
ANIMA 108

Index of Forms   149

anima (It.) 108
ANSA 57
ANUCLA 95
ANUS 95
apaciguar 70
APERIRE 100, 103
APICULA 79, 96, 98
apio 35
APIU 35
APPECTORARE 74
apretar 74
APRICARE 30
aprire (It.) 100, 103
apto 85
APUD 38
APUT 38
AQUA 34
árbol 101
ARBORE 101
arco 30, 97
ARCU 30, 97
ardid 49, 50
arrojar 79
arrope 55
ARTIC(U)LUS 95
asa 57
*ASCIATA 68
asear 72
asino (It.) 106
ASINU 68, 106
asno 68, 106
(A)SPARAGU 101
*ASSED(I)ARE 72
atestiguar 70
atmósfera 85
atril 74, 78
AUDIRE 8
AUGUSTU 7, 10, 68
aur (Oc., Rm.) 62
AURICULA 61, 89
AURIS 95
AURU 61, 62, 83
AUSARE 16, 76
A(U)SCULTARE 63
AUT 38, 39
avestruz 49
avispa 68
AXE 39, 72

azada 68
azúcar 40
azul 40, 45

baby 7
baço 34
BACULUS 95
baden (G.) 9
BADIU 34
bailar 77
bajar 75, 76, 77, 78, 91
bajo 91
BALBU 60
BALNEARE 61
BALNEOLOS 61
BA(L)NEU 61
banco 66
baño 61
BAPLO 95
bas (Fr.) 91
BASIU 31, 35, 75, 76, 77
*BASSIARE 75, 76, 77
*BASSIU 91
basso (It.) 91
BASSU 91
bas(s)ura 57
bebdo 110
beben (G.) 9
beber 7, 8
beodo 110
beso 31, 35, 75, 77
beudo 111
bevra 16, 27
BIBERE 7
BIBITU 110
bide (Dn.) 9
BIFERA 16, 27
bobo 60
boca 6
bochorno 63
boj 45, 49
Boñar 61
BONU 31
Boñuelos 61
BRACCHIU 18
braço 18
breva 16, 27
BUCCA 6

150 *Index of Forms*

bueno 31, 36
buitre 63, 64, 65
BUXU 49

cabalgar 97, 105
CABALLICARE 97, 99, 105
caballo 7, 8,
CABALLU 7, 9
cabdal 70, 82, 83
cabdi(e)llo 70, 82, 83, 110
cabo 39
cabra 30, 100
caçar 71
cadeira (Pt., Gl.) 31
cadera 31
CADERE 8
caer 8
cage (Fr.) 25
caixa (Ct.) 77
caja 77, 78
cajilla 78
cal (Rm.) 9
calcar 88
CALCE 61
calce 88
calçe 62
caldo 97
CALICE 61, 83, 99
CAL(I)DA 95, 97, 98, 105
CALIDU 97
calzar 88
calze 62, 99
cambiar 66
campo 30
CAMPU 30, 62
caña 78
CANNA 78
cantan 45
CANTARE 62
CAPIAT 18
CAPIO 103
CAPITALE 70, 82
CAPITELLU 70, 82, 109, 110
CAPITULUM, -CLUM 95
CAPRA 30, 100
CAPSA 77, 78, 91
capsa 91
*CAPSEU 78

cápsula 85
CAPTARE 71
*CAPTIARE 71
CAPUT 38, 39
carcaj 47, 49
cárcel 101
CARCERE 101
cargar 99, 105
caricare (It.) 99, 105
carmenar 114
CARMINARE 114
carregar (Pt., Ct.) 99, 105
CARRICARE 99, 105
CASA 16
casa 16
CASEU 35, 75, 77
*CASSEU 78
catar 71
CATHEDRA 31
CATTU 36
cauce 61, 83, 99
caudal 70, 82
caudillo 70, 82, 109, 110
CAULE 62
*CAUP- 62
CAUSA 16, 34, 61, 62, 76, 83
CAUTU 34, 62
cauze 62
cavalcare (It.) 99, 105
CAVEA 24, 25
cazar 71
cebolla 7
cepo 6, 37
CEPULLA 7
CERA 37
cera 37
champ (Fr.) 62
chanter (Fr.) 62
chanza 68
chose (Fr.) 62
chou (Fr.) 62
chupón 69
cibdat, -d(e) 50, 70, 83
Cid 49
CIPPU 6, 37
ciudad, -t 45, 47, 70, 83
CIVITATE 70, 83
club 50

COAGULARE 96
COAGULU 79
co(b)dicia 82, 83
cobdo 83, 110
cócedra 60
codo 83, 110
cofonder 58
coger 21
COGITARE 8
COGNATU 30
cogorza 58
cohechar 58
Cohiño 58
cohonder 58
coitelo (Gl.) 64
COIUGI 58
cojo 72
COLARE 62
colgar 100, 105
COLLIGERE 21
COLLOCARE 100, 105
Colloto 88
*COLOBRA 31
COLORE 62
columbrar 114
comde 65
COMEDERE 8, 28
comer 8, 27, 28, 45
COMITE 46, 65
COMMUNICARE 109
COMPARARE 101
*COMPERARE 101
comprar 101
comulgar 109
con 53
coñac 50
conce(p)to 86
concertar 66
concha 66, 67, 96
CONC(H)ULA 96
conde 46, 65
*CONFECTARE 58
CONFICIO 103
CONFINIU 58
CONFORTIARE 58
CONFUNDERE 58
CONLIGO 103
constar 134

CONSUERE 57, 87
CONSUTURA 102
CONTINEO 103
cop- 62
copa 6
COPHINU 16
coricare (It.) 100, 105
correa 18, 23
corred 49
correggia (It.) 35
CORRIGIA 18, 23, 24, 35
corteza 18
*CORTICEA 18
cosa 16, 34, 61, 76, 83
coser 57
cos(s)o 57
costura (Sp., It.) 102
COSUL 57
coto 34, 62
couler (Fr.) 62
couleur (Fr.) 62
COVENTIO 58
COXU 72
coz 61
CRASSU 16
crecer 68
creçer 68, 84
CREDO 8
creo 8
CRESCERE 68, 84
cru (Pt., Ct.) 10
CRUCE 46
CRUDA 9
crudă (Rm.) 9
CRUDELE 8, 10, 46
crudo 10, 11
CRUDU 10
cruel (Sp., Pt., Ct.) 8, 10, 45, 46
crúo 11
cruz 45, 46, 49
cuajaleche 73
cuajar 96
cuajo 79
cuan 53
cuando 66
CUBITU 83, 110
cuchillo 63
cuen(d)(e) 46, 65

152 *Index of Forms*

cuévano 16
cuidar 8
cuitelo (Gl.) 64
cuitre 63
CULCITA 60
culebra 31
CULMEN 38
CULMINARE 114
CULMINE 38, 60
CULTELLU 63
CULTRU 63
CUM 38, 53
cumbre 60, 65
cuñado 30
cup- 62
*CUPIDITIA 82
CUPPA 6
CURSU 57

dar 31, 36
DARE 31
debda 82, 83, 110
DEBITA 82, 110
decho 91
decir 31
dedo 8, 10
delgado 97, 98, 99, 113
delicato (It.) 113
DELICATU 97, 98
DENS 38
denso 66
DENTE 27
deschanzado 68
deschuponar 68
desde 69
desdén 54
desdeñar 54
desleal 106
desmentir 106
desnaturalizar 106
desnudo 11
desnúo 11
deuda 82, 110
di 39
DIC 38, 39
DICERE 31
dices 91
dicho 91

DICIT 46
DICTU 91
diente 27
DIGITU 8, 10
di(g)no 86
digo 91
dije 91
dijiste 91
DILIGO 103
dix 46
DIXI 46
diz 46
doblar 30
DOMINU(M) 38
don 54
duen(de) 54
dueño 54
DULCE 60
dulce 60, 65, 88
DUPLARE 30
DURACINU 28
durazno 28
duz 60

ECLESIA 113
edad 45, 54
edera (It.) 113
eix (Ct.) 77
eje 39, 72
ELEEMOSINA 106
elemosina (It.) 106
ELIGO 103
ell 52
empujar 59
eñadir 13
encía 37
enebro 100, 103
enseñar 87
enteiro (Pt., Gl.) 31
entero 31
entre 40
eres 45
ERICIU 18, 23
erizo 18, 23
es 39
esbozo 69
escaño 108
escas(s)o 57

Index of Forms   153

escoplo 61
escribo 119
escrito 71
escuchar 63
escuela 119
(e)scuitare 64
ese 71
(e)snob 50
espárrago 101
espeso 16
esposo 57
EST 38, 39
estar 119
estiércol 101
estío 68
estrecho 72
estreldes 111
estreudes 111
ex 46
EXCAR(P)SU 57
exe 39
EXIT 46
exponer 134

FABRICA 90
FABULARE 96
faç(e) 68
FACERE 23, 31, 35
FACIO 103
FACIS 38, 39
FACLA 95
FACTU 72, 74
FAGEA 18
fait (Fr.) 73
FALCE 60
famelico (It.) 113
FAMELICU 97
FASCE 68
FASTIDIU 18, 24
FAX 95
fazer 23, 31
fazes 39
fecho 91
feito (Pt.) 73
FEL 38, 40
fel (Oc., Ct.) 40
*FELE 40
FEMINA 108

FENUCULU 79
feo 8, 11
Fernando 114
fet (Ct.) 73
FICTU 74
fiel (Fr.) 40
fiele (It.) 40
fiere (Rm.) 40
fijo 80
FILIA 17
FILIU 80
FOCU 31
FOEDU 8
FOLLICARE 97
Fontefrida 11
FONTICULA 96
FORTE 30, 46
FOVEA 18, 24
*FRABICA 90
*FRABICATU 83
frac 50
fragua 90
fraile 77
frassino (It.) 106
fraucato 83
frauga 90
FRAXINU 68, 78, 106
Frednando 114
freír 21
fresno 68, 78, 106
FRICDA 95
FRICTU 24, 74, 75
FRIDENANDU 114
frido 11
FRIDUM 21
FRIGERE 21
FRIGIDA 95
FRIGIDU(M) 8, 21, 112
frío 8, 11, 21
frito 24, 74, 75
fuego 31
fuert(e) 30, 46
FUGIO 18
FUMIGARE 10
fútbol 85

gag 50
gaiva (Pt.) 25

galgo 97, 100
galigos 100
Gállego 100
GALLICU 97
gato 36
GAUDIU 31
gavia 24, 25
genero (It.) 108
GENERU 108
gente 36
GERMANU 37
ginepro (It.) 100, 103
GINGIVA 37
gota 6, 31, 36
gozo 31
grado 10, 11
GRADU 10
graso 16
grau (Pt., Ct.) 10
GREGE 21, 22
grey 21
groggy 7
GUTTA 6, 31
GYPSU 71

HABEAM 18
HABEAS 18
HABEAT 24
haber 8
HABERE 8
hablar 96
HABUI 46
haç(e) 68
haces 39
hallar 70
hastío 18, 24
haya (n.) 18
haya (v.) 18, 24, 26
hayas 18
haz (n.) 68
haz (v.) 55
hecho 72, 73
(H)EDERA 28, 100
hedo 11
hembra 108
hermano 37
HIBERNU 58
hiedra 27, 28, 100, 113

hiel 40
hijo 80
HINC 38
hinojo 79
hito 74
HOC 38
HODIE 18, 35
holgar 97
hombre 36, 108
hombro 108
HOMINE 108
HOSTE 46
hoy 18
hoya 18, 24
hoz 49, 60
hube 46
huérfano 27, 58, 101
hueso 53
huest(e) 46
humear 10
HUMERU 108
humildad 46
HUMILITATE 46
humilt, -de 46, 47
huyo 18

IACUI 63
IAM 38, 53
ifante 57
IFERI 58
ifierno 58
iglesia 113
ignorante 85
IINIPERU 100, 103
ILLINC 38
impluvio 25
IMPULSARE 59, 60
*IMPULSIARE 59
INFANTE 57
infante 57
infarto 58
inferir 58
INFERNU 57
infierno 57, 58
inflamar 58
informe 58
ingle 40
INGUEN 38

*INGUINE 38, 40
*IN(N)ADDERE 13
INOPS 39
INSIGNARE 87
INSULA 57, 106
INSULSU 59, 60
INTEGRU 31
INTER 38, 40
invierno 58
IOVIS 38, 39
IPSE 71, 77
isla 57, 106
isola (It.) 106
iubi (Rm.) 33
IUDEX 38
IUDICARE 83, 110
IUG(U)LUS 95
IUNCU 27
IUNIPERU 100, 103

jamelgo 97, 113
jubgar 92
judgar 83, 84, 110
jueves 39
jugdar 92
junco 27
juventud 49
juzgar 83, 84, 110

kadedras 36
kage (Dn.) 9
købe (Dn.) 9

labio 24, 25
LABIU 24
LABORARE 100
labrar 100
labro 25
*LACTARIA 73
LACTE 46, 72, 74, 75, 76, 77, 79, 81
LACTUCA 72
lait (Fr.) 73
LAQ(U)EU 18
latril 74
LAUDARE 8
laXtájra (Mz.) 73
lazo 18

lê (Pt.) 33
leal 8, 10
lech(e) 46, 53, 65, 72, 73, 75, 77, 78, 81, 89
lechuga 72
LECTORILE 74
lee 8, 33
leer 21
lega (Rm.) 9
LEGALE 8, 10
LEGERE 21, 22
LEGIONENSE 129
LEGIT 8
LEGO 103
legumbre 10, 33
legume (Pt.) 33
LEGUMEN 10
*LEGUMINE 10
leite (Pt.) 73, 76
léjte (Mz.) 73
leña 78, 81
lenteja 79
LENTICULA 79
leonés 129
lepere (It.) 114
LEPORE 27, 114
lepre (It.) 114
leudo 70
*LEVITU 70
LIBERARE 36, 100
libertad 45, 49
librar 36, 100
lid 49
lidiar 10
l(i)ebdo 70
liebre 27, 114
lievore (It.) 114
LIGARE 9
LIGNA 78, 79, 81
limde 65, 109
LIMITE 65, 109
limosna 106
LIMPIDU 8
limpio 8
linde 65, 109
LITIGARE 10
ljubiti (Sl.) 33
llaga 7, 10

llet (Ct.) 53, 73
llobo (As.) 53
lloco (As.) 53
lluna (Ct.) 53
lluvia 24, 25
loar 8
Lob 47
lobezno 29
lobo 7, 53
lóbrego 99
loco 53
Lope 47
LUBRICU 99
luen 54
lueñe 54
luna 53
LUPICINU 29
LUPU 7

macchia (It.) 98
macho 98
MACRU 30, 113
maestro 8
MAGISTRU 8
magro 30, 113
majšéīa (Mz.) 73
maleza 17
MALITIA 17
ma(n)çana 18, 23, 69, 84, 92
mancha 96, 98
*MA(N)CULA 96
mandar 66
manga 27, 28, 109
mangual 53
MANICA 27, 28, 109
manojo 79
MANUALE 53
MANUCULU 79
mar 45
MARE 45
mármol 101
MARMORE 101
masa 16
maschio (It.) 98
MASC(U)LUS 95
MASSA 16
MATTIANA 18, 23, 69, 84

MAXILLA 72
maXšéīa (Mz.) 73
mecer 68
meçer 68
mejilla 72
MEL 38, 40
mel (Oc., Ct.) 40
*MELE 40
menguar 53
MENS 38
MENSE 45, 57
MENSURA 57
merced 45, 54
MERCEDE 45
mermar 108
mes 45, 57
MESSE 45
mesura 57
meter 6
miel (Sp., Fr.) 40
miele (It.) 40
miere (Rm.) 40
mies 45
mil 52, 125
mill 52
MILLE 52, 125
mimbre 108
MINIMARE 108
MINUARE 53
MINUS 38
MISCERE 68
mismo 69
MITTERE 6
MONS 38
Montoto 88
mosca 68
much(o) 52, 63, 64, 65, 89
mugir 33
MUGIRE 33
muito (Pt., Sp.) 64
MULTU 63, 64, 91
MUSCA 68
muy 63, 64, 65

navear 10
navegar 10
NAVIGARE 10
NAVIGIU 18, 24

navío 18, 24
nebbia (It.) 98, 102
NEBULA 27, 96, 102
NEC 38, 39
negar (Sp., Pt.) 10, 33
NEGARE 10
NEPTICLA 95
NEPTIS 95
ni 39
nido 7, 11
NIDU 7, 8, 11
niebla 27, 96, 98, 102
ninfa 58, 66
niño 66
nío 8, 11
no 40
nó (Pt.) 10
noch(e) 46, 65, 72, 89, 129
NOCTE 46, 72
NODU 10
noivo (Pt.) 25
nójte (Mz.) 73
NON 40
non 40
NOSTRU 68
nou (Ct.) 10
NOVE 46
novio 25
*NOVIU 25
nóXte (Mz.) 73
nudo 10, 11
NUDU 11
nuef 46, 47, 50
nuestro 68
nueve 46, 50

o 39
objeto 85, 86
obtener 85
occhio (It.) 98, 102
ocho 72
OCTO 72
OC(U)LU(S) 79, 81, 95, 98, 102
of 46, 47
oggi (It.) 35
oír 8
ojo 79, 81, 98, 102
olmo 60

omero (It.) 108
omre 109
once 109, 110
ongle (Fr.) 96
Ontígola 96
orecchia (It.) 98
oreja 61, 89, 98
ORIC(U)LA 89, 95
oro 61, 83
ORPHANU 27, 58, 101
osar 16, 76
os(s)o 57
OSTIU 68
otero 60, 74
oto 88
otro 60, 100, 103
ouro (Pt.) 62
ova 60
ove 46
oveja 96
OVICULA 96
Oviñana 88

PACIFICARE 70
padre 30
pájaro 101
pan 30, 45
PANE 30
PANNU 78
paño 66, 67, 78
PARTE 46
part(e) 46
paso 16
PASSARE, -ERE 101
PASSU 16
PATRE 30
PAUCU 34, 62
PAUPERE 89
PAUSARE 76, 88
peç(e) 68
pecho(s) 72, 78
PECTINE 109
PECTORALE 74, 100
PECTUS 72
PEDES 38, 39
pedregoso 99
peine 109
PELLE 52

158 *Index of Forms*

pelo 30
PERCIPIO 103
pereza 17, 31
PERFICIO 103
PERFIDIA 18, 30, 58
PERSICA, -U 102
perspectiva 134
PERTINEO 103
pesca (It.) 102
pescar 68
petral 74, 78, 100
PETRICOSU 99
pez 45, 46, 49, 68
piel 52
pies 39, 45
PIGRITIA 17, 31
pija 91
PILU 30
PISCARE 68
PISCE 46, 68
*PISSIARE 91
pixar (Ct.) 91
PLACITU 84
PLACUI 63
PLAGA 7
plaz(d)o 84
PLEBS 39
plogue 63
PLUVIA 24
pluvial 25
pluvioso 25
pobre 89
poco 34, 62
PODIU 17, 23, 35
poggio (It.) 35
POLLICARE 97
pon 46, 55
PONIT 46
PONTE 46
pop 50
por 40
PORCU 30, 97
porfía 18, 30, 58
PORTA 30
portadgo 27, 83, 84
PORTATICU 27, 83
portazgo 27, 83, 84
posar 76, 88

POSITU 102
poso 88
POST 38, 39
posto (It.) 102
POSUI 17
POTUI 63
poyo 17, 23
pozo 17, 23
prado 7, 34
PRATU 7
pretal 74, 100
príncep 46, 129
PRINCIPE 46
príncipe 46, 129
prisco 102
PROFECTU 15, 72
provecho 15, 72
pub 50
pude 63
puent(e) 46
PUER 38
puerco 30, 97
puerta 30
pues 39
puesto 102
PUGNU 78
pujar 59
pulce (It.) 99, 105
pulga 97, 98, 99, 105
pulgar 97, 100
*PULICA 97, 98, 105
pulicar 100
PULICE 97, 99, 105
pulice (It.) 99, 105
pulsar 60
PULSARE 59
PULSU 88
puño 78
PUTEU 17, 23

qâ'id (Ar.) 55
qawwad (Ar.) 55
QUAM 38, 53
QUEM 53
quepa 18
queso 35, 75, 77
QUID 38
quien 53

Index of Forms

quiero 36
quijada 78
QUIT 38

rábano 101
*RABIA 24, 25
rabia 24, 25
RABIES 24
RADIARE 17
RADICE 8
RADIMIRU 114
Radmiro 114
rage (Fr.) 25
rainha (Pt.) 33
raiva (Pt.) 25
raíz 8
Ramiro 114
RAPHANU 101
RAPIDU 110
RATIONE 17
raudo 110
rayar 17
razón 17
real 10
REBUCINARE 29
rebujo 34
rebuznar 29
recepción 85
RECIPIO 103
RECITARE 84, 110
recobrar 100
RECUPERARE 100
re(d) 46, 49
REGALE 10
REGE 21
REGINA 8
REGULA 79, 81, 96
reina 8, 33
reja 79, 81, 96
reloj 45, 47, 49
REPUDIU 34
resollar 70
restañar 78, 79, 81
RETE 46
*RETINA 109
REX 38
rey 21
rezar 84, 110

rezno 28, 109
RICINU 28, 109
RIDEO 18, 24
rienda 109
río (n.) 33
río (v.) 18, 24
RIVU 33
roble 36, 100, 104
robre 36
ROBORE 36, 100, 104
RODERE 11
rodié 11
Rodric, -go 47, 50
roer 11
ROGANT 38, 39
rogar 10
ROGARE 10
ROGITUS 21
ROITUS 21
rojo 78
ROSA 16
rosa 16
roto 71
rovere (It.) 100, 104
royo 18, 24, 25
rubb (Ar.) 55
RUBEU 18, 24
rubio 25
ruegan 39
rugir 33, 36
RUGIRE 33
RUGITU 8
ruido 8, 33
ruído (Pt.) 33
ruivo (Pt.) 25
rumiar 10
RUMIGARE 10
RUPTU 71
RUSSEU 78

SABANA 27
sábana 27
SABUCU 33
sache (Fr.) 25
sacudir 72
saeta 8, 23
Safagun(d) 58
sagen (G.) 9

160 *Index of Forms*

SAGITTA 8, 23
Sahagún 58
Sahelices 58
sal (n.) 40, 45, 52
sal (v.) 46, 55
salce 88, 99
SAL(E) 40, 52
SALICE 61, 83, 99, 105
salice (It.) 99, 105
šal(i)ch(o) (Mz.) 99
SALIT 46
SALSA 59
salto 88, 97
SALTU 60, 88, 97
salze 62, 99
SAN(CTI) FACUNDI 58
SAN(CTI) FELICIS 58
SANCTIFICARE 70
santiguar 70
SAPIAT 18, 25
SARTAGINE 8, 10, 28, 45
sartén 8, 10, 28, 45
SATIONE 17
sauce 61, 83, 99, 105
saúco 33
*SAUP- 62
sauze 62
sazón 17
SCALPRU 61
SCAMNU 108
scanno (It.) 108
SCHOLA 119
SCRIBO 9, 119
SCRIPTU 71
scriu (Rm.) 9
sea 18
SECARE 7, 31
seco 6, 31
se(c)ta 86
SECUNDU 64
SECURU 7
SED 38
se(d) 49
SEDEAT 18
sedmana 109
segar 7, 31
Segovia 25
Segoyuela 25

según 64
seguro 7
seis 39
selva 63
semana 109
sembrar 108
semda 65
semdero 109
semedeiro 109, 114
SEMINARE 108
SEMITA 27, 65, 109
SEMPER 38, 40
sen 129
seña 78
senda 27, 65, 109
sendos 96, 113
seños 96, 113
SENSU 57
sepa 18
SEPTE 46, 71
SEPTIMANA 109
sesma 78
seso 57
SET 38
SEX 38, 39
*SEXIMA 78
sí 39
SIC 38, 39
SICCU 6, 31
siempre 40
siet(e) 46, 71, 129
SIGNA 78
signo 85
SILVA 63
SIMIA 25
SINE 129
singe (Fr.) 25
SINGULOS 96, 113
sleale (It.) 106
slogan 120
smentire (It.) 106
snaturare (It.) 106
sobrar 100
sobre 40
SOCRA 30
SOL 38
soldar 61
SOLIDARE 61

SOLIDU 61, 97
SOMNU 108
son 39
sonno (It.) 108
sop- 62
SORS 38
Sosa, La 59
soso 59, 60
soto 60, 88, 97
SPEC(U)LUM 95
SPISSU 16
SPONSU 57
SPOSUS 57
STAB(U)LUM 95
STAGNARE 78, 79, 81
stand 120
STARE 119
STERCORE 101
stop 120
STRICTU 72
suar (Sp., Pt., Ct.) 8, 10
SUB 38
SUCCUTERE 72
sudar 7, 10
SUDARE 7, 8, 10
sudoare (Rm.) 9
sudor 11
SUDORE 9, 11
suegra 30
sueldo 61, 89, 97
sueño 108
SUFFLARE 70
sulco 30, 60
SULCU 30, 60
SUNT 38, 39
suor 11
sup- 62
SUPER 38, 40
SUPERARE 100
surco 30, 60, 65

TAB(U)LA 95
tal 129
TALE 129
TAM 53
tan 53
taur (Oc., Rm.) 62
TAURU 61, 62

TAXU 72, 75, 76, 77
techo 72
técnico 85
TECTU 72
TEGULA 79, 96
teixo (Pt) 76
teja 79, 96
tejo 72, 75
temblar 108
TEMPORANU 100
temprano 100
TEMPUS 38
ten 55
TENEO 103
tenero (It.) 108
TENERU 30, 108
TERRA 30
*TESTIFICARE 70
tez 49
tierno 30, 108
tierra 30
TITIONE 17
tizón 17
toro 61
torpe 30
touro (Pt.) 62
trébedes 111
trece 109, 110
TREDECIM 109
tredze 110
tremolare (It.) 108
TREMULARE 108
Treviño 15
TRIB(U)LA 95
tridigo 111
TRIFINIU 15
trigo 111
TRIPEDES 111
tristeza 17
TRISTITIA 17
TRITICU 111
triunfo 66
trucha 72
TRUCTA 72
TURPE 30

uço 68
ULMU 60

Index of Forms

ultimátum 43
ULVA 60
uña 96, 98, 102
UNDECIM 109
unghia (It.) 98, 102
UNGULA 96, 102
unha (Pt.) 96
URBS 39
ureche (Rm.) 89
URSU 57
USTIU 68
uzo 68

vacío 33
VACIVU 33
VACLUS 95
*VADEAT 26
vado 11
VADU 11
VAGINA 8, 21
vaina 8, 21
val 52
VALLE 52
valle 52
VAPULO 95
vaya 26
vayáis 26
ve 8
vecchio (It.) 98, 102
VECLUS 79, 95, 102
vedette 7
velho (Pt.) 96
vendegar 111
vengar 109, 110, 111
veo 18, 24
verda(d), -t 47, 49
verde 97

VERECUNDIA 105
vergogna (It.) 105
vergüeña 105
vermut 50
VERNAC(U)LUS 95
*VERSURA 57
VESPA 68
VETULU(S) 79, 95, 102
VICLUS 95
vida 7
VIDEO 18, 24
VIDET 8
vidrio 30
vieil (Fr.) 96
viejo 79, 96, 98, 102
vigilar 36
Villota 88
*VIMINE 108
VINDICARE 109
VIRIDE 97
VIR(I)DIS 95, 97, 98, 105
virtud 49
VITA 7
VITREU 30
VITULUS 95
VULPECULA 30
vulpeja 30
VULTURE 63
VULTURNU 63

ya 53
yedra 100
yerno 108
yeso 71
yogue 63

zigzag 50